*The rich folklore
of Hawaii*

is embodied in these exotic
tales by a master teller

Other books by W.D. Westervelt

Hawaiian Legends of Volcanoes

Legends of Old Honolulu

Hawaiian Legends of Ghosts and Ghost Gods

Hawaiian Historical Legends

MYTHS AND LEGENDS OF HAWAII

Myths and Legends of Hawai'i

by W. D. Westervelt

Selected and Edited by
A. Grove Day

MUTUAL PUBLISHING

ISBN 1-56647-706-9

Library of Congress Catalog Card Number:

Cover design by Emily Lee

First Printing, February 2005
1 2 3 4 5 6 7 8 9

Mutual Publishing
1215 Center Street, Suite 210
Honolulu, Hawaii 96816
Ph: (808) 732-1709
Fax: (808) 734-4094
email: mutual@mutualpublishing.com
www.mutualpublishing.com

Printed in Australia

FOREWORD: *Hawaii, Islands of Folklore*

"THE ANCIENT Hawaiians were not inventive," wrote W.D. Westervelt in 1913. "They did not study new methods of housebuilding or farming. They did not seek new tools or new weapons. They could live comfortably as their ancestors lived. But they were imaginative, and therefore told many a wonderful tale of gods and goblins and men. Some of these stories were centuries old, and were closely akin to legends told in Tahiti, Samoa, Fiji, New Zealand, and many other islands of the Pacific Ocean. Most of them were, of course, limited to the locality from which they came."

Dr. Westervelt knew whereof he spoke. The most prolific and popular of the retellers of Hawaiian folktales, he published five volumes and dozens of articles on the subject, and read widely in the lore of a number of other Pacific islands.

Among tribal people, all science and religion begin with the attempt to explain their surroundings to each other. Usually, this effort assumes little distinction between humankind and the rest of visible nature. The religion of the premissionary days in the Hawaiian Islands was founded on an animistic reverence for the manifestations of nature, and ceremonies were performed to set up and preserve proper relations between humanity and the surrounding powers. Although a Supreme Being was supposed to rule over the universe, there were many other gods that symbolized the manifold objects and aspects of nature, which had to be invoked or placated.

The island pantheon was, in fact, somewhat over-crowded; one chant speaks of "the four hundred thousand gods." The four Polynesian gods most fervently worshipped in Hawaii were Kane, father of living creatures and identified with sunlight, fresh water, and the forests; Ku, fierce god of war, to whom human sacrifices were made; Kaneloa, ruler of the land of departed spirits; and Lono, god of growing things, rain, harvest, sports, and peace, during whose autumn makahiki festival a truce from war was joyously celebrated. Pele, goddess of the volcanoes that form a brooding profile on the Hawaiian skyline, was respected and feared, especially in the southernmost islands. Certain deities were patrons of particular activities: Hina presided over kapa beating and other women's work; Laka was goddess of the hula schools; and Kuula was the god of fishermen. The gods were considered the ancestors of men, and long genealogies traced descent back to a deity or demi-god. There were also many legendary heroes, ghosts, and elves, as well as familiar demons belonging to a particular kahuna or sorcerer. Trees, rocks, plants, animals, heavenly bodies, and other natural objects might also be deified, even the rainbow.

Each family had an ancestral guardian spirit, a ghost or totemic creature called an aumakua, worshipped at the family altar and invoked when help was needed. The main public worship, however, was conducted on the enclosed temple platform called the heiau, decorated by large carved images of the gods, where rites were performed on certain days of each month. The sites of at least five hundred of these temples are known in the islands. In addition, every activity of Hawaiian life, from the felling of a tree to the planning of a military campaign, would be inaugurated by prayer or a religious ritual.

Two main ideas stand out in Hawaiian religion: "mana" and "kapu." Mana is the supernormal power that might be possessed by a person or an object. A man endowed with mana might perform superhuman feats of courage, skill, or magic. He could obtain it by descent from sacred beings, or by observing tabus, offering sacrifices, or uttering prayers and rituals. It was believed that contact between objects or persons possessing different

iv

amounts of this spiritual power could be dangerous to the weaker one.

To regulate the handling of such power in the Hawaiian community, a network of prohibitions, called the kapu system, grew up. The word is a variant of the Polynesian "tabu," and not only connoted a simple warning of trespass but extended to every phase of Hawaiian life. Superficially, the systems seems invented to assure autocratic domination of the society by the favored ruling caste, which was presumably descended from the gods; but fundamentally, the idea grew out of a dualistic view of nature. Penalties for violating a kapu were severe, death being a common punishment. Ignorance of the kapu was no excuse—a person could violate it unknowingly, but he nevertheless must suffer the penalty.

The alliance of chiefs and priests finally came to use the kapu system as a main method of government. Its abuse led to the abolition of the widespread, often oppressive, code a few months after the death of Kamehameha I in 1819.

As will be shown, certain recurring patterns, plots, and types of characters may be characteristic of Hawaiian myths and legends. In some stories the hero has to overcome cruel brothers or half-brothers on his path to success. Sometimes the antagonist, either human or supernatural, has powers that seem to render him invincible. The hero, however, is usually possessed of an almost godlike skill in some one or more accomplishments—spear throwing, bone breaking, weightlifting, surfriding, or riddling and disputing. Often the hero is the secret son of a chief, who has left with the mother some token by which the son later proves his royal blood.

Many of the heroes are kupua, people possessed of supernatural powers. Some kupua can change from human form to animal form at will—there are dog men, rat men, bird men, shark men, and hog men. A kupua may be born in a non-human form, either as an animal or as some such inanimate object as a rope. This infant freak may be tossed on a rubbish heap by the mother, but is saved and brought up by some other relative, who recognizes its latent human characteristics.

In addition to tales of gods and goddesses, heroes and heroines, the stories that follow often deal with ghosts and aumakuas or ghost-gods. A frequent theme is the reviving of a person dead to all appearances. Sharks and shark gods are prominent, as well as the legendary giant lizards or dragons called "mo-o." Many are the stories of the prowess and cleverness of the menehune clan, elflike engineers who perform stupendous feats in a single night. A rock by the seashore may be the vestige of a transformed giant. Occasional tales deal with cannibals or cannibal creatures, but cannibalism was not a custom among the ancient Hawaiians or, for that matter, the ancient Americans. These are among the themes of Hawaiian myths and legends, which are often shared with those of tribal peoples not only in the Pacific but in other oceans of the globe.

The material in these retellings drawn from the prose and poetry of the ancient Hawaiians — a literature handed down orally for a multitude of generations — have been termed "myths" and "legends." Strictly speaking, a myth is a story of the doings of godlike beings, whereas a legend deals with heroes or other human beings. Maui, the pervasive trickster-hero of broad Polynesia, is usually called a demi-god. In this anthology, the terms myth and legend are used interchangeably, principally because the many collectors and translators of the tales often failed to make the strict distinction themselves.

The material that William Drake Westervelt (1849-1939) wrote and published on Hawaiian legends during the first quarter of the twentieth century surpasses, in quantity at least, the output of any other reteller of tales. Between 1900 and 1925, more than one hundred articles by him appeared in Honolulu periodicals and annuals, and many were later reprinted in other publications.

From these, Westervelt selected and edited enough material for half a dozen books, totalling more than a thousand pages, printed between 1910 and 1923.

Westervelt was born in Oberlin, Ohio, on Boxing Day —December 26, 1849. He received both a B.A. and a B.D. degree at Oberlin College, and in 1926 an honorary D.D. degree. An ordained minister, after serving as a pastor of various churches on the mainland he came to Hawaii in 1889 to spend two years studying the work of missionaries. He returned in 1899 to make Hawaii his permanent home. By daily study with a native Hawaiian and diligent research, he made himself an authority on the ancient customs, beliefs, history, and legends of the islands. He formed an extensive collection of Hawaiiana, which is now housed in the Hamilton Library of the University of Hawaii. He was also a pioneer stamp collector. In 1905 he married Caroline Dickinson Castle of the missionary family, and their Diamond Head home was a popular gathering spot for decades.

Westervelt classified the legends to some extent in his books; that is to say, a single book usually contains legends related to one another in type, leading character, or locale. His first book, *Legends of Ma-ui* (1910), contains tales of the demi-god Maui and Hina, his feminine counterpart. The stories are not all Hawaiian in origin: some come from Samoa, New Zealand, the Ellice group, Manihiki, and the Herveys.

His second and smallest book is *Around the Poi Bowl, and Legends of Paao* (1913), reprinted from plates used by *Cram's Magazine* in 1899. It contains an account of Paao and his voyages, as well as a group of brief legends drawn from Abraham Fornander's *Polynesian Researches.* No selections have been here taken from this early and sketchy volume.

Westervelt published two books in 1915: *Legends of Old Honolulu* and *Legends of Gods and Ghosts.* The former contains stories connected with places in Honolulu or elsewhere on Oahu. The latter contains a rich collection of folklore of ghosts and ghost-gods, as well as a few miscellaneous stories about sharks and kupunas.

Hawaiian Legends of Volcanoes (1916) celebrates the epic tale of the goddess Pele and her faithful sister Hiiaka, as well as the glorious troupes of maidens emanating both from the snowy heights of Mauna Kea and the sturdy surf of the ocean beaches.

A much later retelling, *Hawaiian Historical Legends* (1923), with a seemingly contradictory title, has not been drawn upon for the present collection; where a documentary source of a topic is available, it is seldom necessary to consult folk accounts. Westervelt also wrote a life of Kamehameha I, which appeared serially in *Paradise of the Pacific* between 1911 and 1914, and translated two books into Hawaiian.

A scholarly objection that might be brought against Westervelt is his frequent failure to indicate by footnotes the exact sources of his materials. In general, his sources were three: oral accounts from Hawaiian friends; published accounts in English; and, perhaps most important, published accounts in Hawaiian to be translated. He does acknowledge valuable versions in Hawaiian newspapers. English sources include not only Fornander but also Jules Remy, William Ellis, A.O. Forbes, Thomas G. Thrum, and the collection published by King Kalakaua and edited by R.M. Daggett, former United States minister to the kingdom.

In general, Westervelt's attitude is that of collector, interpreter, and popularizer rather than that of literal translator. He did the same thing for Hawaiian mythology that Thomas Bulfinch did for the Greek. Sometimes he breaks the spell of the narrative, in fact, by referring to a Hawaiian hero as a Greek counterpart. In one "historical legend," a ruler of Oahu is a Polynesian King Arthur. At other times he interpolates remarks about the locale which immediately bring the reader back to the twentieth century.

Although Westervelt's legends are abbreviated, and

although the translator intrudes perhaps too frequently, many passages possess great stylistic merit. The following prose passage, presumably a translation of a Hawaiian chant, conveys a great deal of the modes, content, and graphic imagery of this type of Hawaiian literature:

"Then she called for the kite-flying winds when the birds sport in the heavens and the surf lies quiet on incoming waves, and then she sang of the winds kolonahe, softly blowing; and the winds hunahuna, breaking into fragments; and the winds which carry the mist, the sprinkling shower, the falling rain, and the severe storm; the winds which touch the mountaintops, and those which creep along the edge of the precipice, holding on by their fingers, and those which dash over the plains and along the sea beach, blowing the waves into mist. Then she chanted how the caves in the seacoast were opened and the guardians of the winds lifted their calabashes and let loose evil winds, angry and destructive, to sweep over the homes of the people and tear in pieces their fruit trees and houses."

"The best of Westervelt," a broadly inclusive selection from his folklore now completely edited and reset for the reader of today, is here offered for the enjoyment of all students of mythology wherever they may be found. Many of the tales embody the ethos of the Hawaiian race that is still sought by the thousands of descendants of the original tellers — the Hawaiians and part-Hawaiians who will remember Maui and Pele even in the twenty-first century.*

A. GROVE DAY
University of Hawaii

*See also *Hawaiian Legends in English: An Annotated Bibliography* by Amos P. Leib and A. Grove Day, second edition, 1979, Honolulu: University Press of Hawaii.

Contents

I. Maui and Hina

Maui the Fisherman

Oh, the great fishhook of Maui!
Manai-i-ka-lani (made fast to the heavens) its name;
An earth-twisted cord ties the hook.
Engulfed from the lofty Kauiki,
Its bait the red-billed alae,
The bird made sacred to Hina.
It sinks far down to Hawaii,
Struggling and painfully dying.
Caught is the land under the water,
Floated up, up to the surface.
But Hina hid a wing of the bird
And broke the land under the water.
Below was the bait snatched away
And eaten at once by the fishes,
The ulua of the deep, muddy places.

ONE OF Maui's homes was near Kauiki, a place well known throughout the Hawaiian Islands because of its strategic importance. For many years it was the site of a fort around which fierce battles were fought by the natives of the island of Maui, repelling the invasions of their neighbors from Hawaii.

Haleakala (The House of the Sun), the mountain from which Maui the demi-god snared the sun, looks down ten thousand feet upon the Kauiki headland. Across the channel from Haleakala rises Mauna Kea (The White Mountain or The Snowcapped), which almost all the year round rears its white head in majesty among the clouds.

In the snowy breakers of the surf which washes the beach below these mountains are broken coral reefs — the fishing grounds of the Hawaiians. Here near Kauiki, according to some Hawaiian legends, Maui's mother Hina had her grass house and made and dried her kapa

3

cloth. Even to the present day it is one of the few places in the islands where the kapa is still pounded into sheets from the bark of the hibiscus and kindred trees.

Here is a small bay partially reef-protected, over which year after year the moist clouds float and by day and by night crown the waters with rainbows — the legendary sign of the home of the deified ones. Here when the tide is out the natives wade and swim, as they have done for centuries, from coral block to coral block, shunning the deep resting places of their dread enemy, the shark, sometimes esteemed divine. Out on the edge of the outermost reef they seek the shellfish which cling to the coral, or spear the large fish which have been left in the beautiful little lakes of the reef. Coral land is a region of the seacoast abounding in miniature lakes and rugged valleys and steep mountains. Clear waters with every motion of the tide surge in and out through the sheltered caves and submarine tunnels, according to an ancient Hawaiian song:

Never quiet, never failing, never sleeping,
Never very noisy is the sea of the sacred caves.

Sea mosses of many hues are the forests which drape the hillsides of coral land and reflect the colored rays of light which pierce the ceaselessly moving waves. Down in the beautiful little lakes, under overhanging coral cliffs, darting in and out through the fringes of seaweed, the purple mullet and royal red fish flash before the eyes of the fisherman. Sometimes the many-tinted, glorious fish of paradise reveal their beauties, and then again a school of black and gold citizens of the reef follow the tidal waves around projecting crags and through the hidden tunnels from lake to lake, while above the fisherman follows, spearing or snaring as best he can.

Maui's brothers were better fishermen than he. They sought the deep sea beyond the reef and larger fish. They made hooks of bone or of mother-of-pearl, with a straight, slender, sharp-pointed piece leaning backward at a sharp angle. This was usually a consecrated bit of

4

bone or mother-of-pearl, and was supposed to have peculiar power to hold fast any fish which had taken the bait.

These bones were usually taken from the body of someone who while living had been noted for great power or high rank. This sharp piece was tightly tied to the larger bone or shell, which formed the shank of the hook. The sacred barb of Maui's hook was a part of the magic bone he had secured from his ancestors in the underworld—the bone with which he struck the sun whole, lassooing him and compelling him to move more slowly through the heavens.

"Earth-twisted" fibers of vine, twisted while growing, was the cord used by Maui in tying the parts of his magic hook together.

Long and strong were the fish lines made from the olona fiber, holding the great fish caught from the depths of the ocean. The fibers of the olona vine were among the longest and strongest found in the Hawaiian Islands.

Such a hook could easily be cast loose by the struggling fish, if the least opportunity were given. Therefore it was absolutely necessary to keep the line taut, and pull strongly and steadily, to land the fish in the canoe.

Maui did not use his magic hook for a long time. He seemed to understand that it would not answer ordinary needs. Possibly the idea of making the supernatural hook did not occur to him until he had exhausted his lower wit and magic upon his brothers.

It is said that Maui was not a very good fisherman. Sometimes his end of the canoe contained fish which his brothers had thought were on their hooks until they were landed in the canoe.

Many times they laughed at him for his poor success, and he retaliated with his mischievous tricks.

"E!" he would cry, when one of his brothers began to pull in, while the other brothers swiftly paddled the canoe forward. "E!" See, we both have caught a great fish

5

at the same moment. Be careful now! Your line is loose. Look out! Look out!"

All this time he would be pulling his own line in as rapidly as possible. Onward rushed the canoe, each fisherman shouting to encourage the others. Soon the lines by the tricky manipulation of Maui would be crossed. Then, as the great fish was brought near the side of the boat, Maui, the little, the mischievous one, would slip his hook toward the head of the fish and flip it over into the canoe, causing his brother's line to slacken for a moment. Then his mournful cry rang out: "Oh, my brother, your fish is gone. Why did you not pull more steadily? It was a fine fish and now it is down deep in the waters." Then Maui held up his splendid catch (from his brother's hook) and received somewhat suspicious congratulations. But what could they do? Maui was the smart one of the family.

Their father and mother were both members of the household of the gods. The father was "the supporter of the heavens" and the mother was "the guardian of the way to the invisible world"; but pitifully small and very few were the gifts bestowed upon their children. Maui's brothers knew nothing beyond the average home life of the ordinary Hawaiian, and Maui alone was endowed with the power to work miracles. Nevertheless, the student of Polynesian legends learns that Maui is more widely known than almost all the demi-gods of all nations as a discoverer of benefits for his fellows, and these physical rather than spiritual.

After many fishing excursions, Maui's brothers seemed to have wit enough to understand his tricks, and thenceforth they refused to take him in their canoe when they paddled out to the deep-sea fishing grounds. Then those who depended upon Maui to supply their daily needs murmured against his poor success. His mother scolded him and his brothers ridiculed him.

The ex-Queen Liliuokalani, in a translation of what is called "the family chant," says that Maui's mother sent him to his father for a hook with which to supply his need.

Go hence to your father,
'Tis there you find line and hook.
This is the hook, "Made Fast to the Heavens";
"Manaia-ka-lani" 'tis called.
When the hook catches land
It brings the old seas together.
Bring hither the large alae,
The bird of Hina.

When Maui had obtained his hook, he tried to go fishing with his brothers. He leaped on the end of their canoe as they pushed out into deep water. They were angry and cried out: "This boat is too small for another Maui!" They threw him off and made him swim back to the beach.

When they returned from their day's work, they brought back only a shark. Maui told them if he had been with them, better fish wuld have been upon their hooks — the ulua, for instance, or possibly the pimoe, the king of fish. At last they let him go far out, outside the harbor of Kipahula to a place opposite Ka-iwi-o-Pele (The Bone of Pele), a peculiar piece of lava lying near the beach at Hana on the eastern side of the island of Maui. There they fished, but only sharks were caught. The brothers ridiculed Maui, saying: "Where are the ulua, and where is pimoe?"

Then Maui threw his magic hook into the sea, baited with one of the alae birds, sacred to his mother and Hina. He used the incantation: "When I let go my hook with divine power, then I get the great ulua."

The bottom of the sea began to move. Great waves arose, trying to carry the canoe away. The fish pulled the canoe two days, drawing the line to its fullest extent. When the slack began to come in the line, because of the tired fish, Maui called for the brothers to pull hard against the coming fish. Soon land rose out of the water. Maui told them not to look back or the fish would be lost.

7

One brother did look back. The line slacked, snapped, and broke, and the land lay behind them in islands.

Maui evidently had no scruples against using anything which would help him carry out his schemes. He indiscriminately robbed his friends and the gods alike.

Down in the deep sea sank the hook with its struggling bait, until it was seized by "the land under the water." But Hina the mother saw the struggle of her sacred bird and hastened to the rescue. She caught a wing of the bird, but could not pull the alae from the sacred hook. The wing was torn off. Then the fish gathered around the bait and tore it in pieces. If the bait could have been kept entire, then the land would have come up in a continent rather than as an island. Then the Hawaiian group would have been unbroken. But the bait broke—and the islands came as fragments from the underworld.

Maui Lifting the Sky

MAUI'S home was for a long time enveloped by darkness. The heavens had fallen down, or, rather, had not been separated from the earth. According to some legends, the skies pressed so closely and so heavily upon the earth that when the plants began to grow, all the leaves were necessarily flat. According to other legends, the plants had to push up the clouds a little, and thus the leaves were caused to flatten out into larger surfaces, so that they could better drive the skies back and hold them in place. Thus the leaves became flat at first, and have so remained through all the days of mankind. The plants lifted the sky inch by inch until men were able to crawl about between the heavens and the earth, and thus pass from place to place and visit one another.

After a long time, according to the Hawaiian legends,

a man, supposed to be Maui, came to a woman and said: "Give me a drink from your gourd calabash, and I will push the heavens higher." The woman handed the gourd to him. When he had taken a deep draft, he braced himself against the clouds and lifted them to the height of the trees.

Again he hoisted the sky and carried it to the tops of the mountains; then, with great exertion, he thrust it upwards once more, and pressed it to the place it now occupies. Nevertheless, dark clouds many times hang low along the eastern slope of Maui's great mountain — Haleakala — and descend in heavy rains upon the hill Kauwiki; but they dare not stay, lest Maui the strong come and hurl them so far away that they cannot come back again.

A man who had been watching the process of lifting the sky ridiculed Maui for attempting such a difficult task. When the clouds rested on the tops of the mountains, Maui turned to punish his critic. The man had fled to the other side of the island. Maui rapidly pursued and finally caught him on the seacoast, not many miles north of the town now known as Lahaina. After a brief struggle, the man was changed, according to the story, into a great black rock, which can be seen by any traveler who desires to localize the legends of Hawaii.

Maui Snares the Sun

THE MOON, pale and dead in appearance, moved slowly; while the sun, full of life and strength, moved quickly. Thus days were very short and nights were very long. Mankind suffered from the fierceness of the heat of the sun and also from its prolonged absence. Day and night were alike a burden to men. The darkness was so great and lasted so long that fruits would not ripen.

After Maui had succeeded in throwing the heavens into their place, and fastening them so that they could not fall, he learned that he had opened a way for the sun god to come up from the lower world and rapidly run across the blue vault. This made two troubles for men — the heat of the sun was very great and the journey too quickly over. Maui planned to capture the sun and punish him for thinking so little about the welfare of mankind.

Maui's mother was troubled very much by the heedless haste of the sun. She had many kapa cloths to make, for this was the only kind of clothing known in Hawaii, except sometimes a woven mat or a long grass fringe worn as a skirt. This native cloth was made by pounding the fine bark of certain trees with wooden mallets until the fibers were beaten and ground into a wood pulp. Then she pounded the pulp into thin sheets from which the best sleeping mats and clothes could be fashioned. These kapa cloths had to be thoroughly dried, but the days were so short that, by the time she had spread out the kapa, the sun had heedlessly rushed across the sky and gone down into the underworld, and all the cloth had to be gathered up again and cared for until another day should come. There were other troubles. "The food could not be prepared and cooked in one day. Even an incantation to the gods could not be chanted through, ere they were overtaken by darkness."

These ills were very discouraging and caused great suffering, as well as unnecessary trouble and labor. Many complaints were made against the thoughtless sun.

Maui pitied his mother and determined to make the sun go slower, so that the days might be long enough to satisfy the needs of men. Therefore, he went over to the northwest of the island on which he lived. This was Mount Iao, an extinct volcano, in which lies one of the most beautiful and picturesque valleys of the Hawaiian Islands. He climbed the ridges until he could see the course of the sun as it passed over the island. He saw that the sun came up the eastern side of Mount Hale-akala.

He crossed over the plain between the two mountains and climbed to the top of Haleakala. There he watched the burning sun as it came up from Koolau and passed directly over the top of the mountain. The summit of Haleakala is a great extinct crater nearly twenty miles in circumference, and nearly twenty-five-hundred feet in depth. There are two tremendous gaps or chasms in the side of the crater wall, through which in days gone by the massive bowl poured forth its flowing lava. One of these was the koolau, or eastern, gap, in which Maui probably planned to catch the sun.

The Hawaiian legends says Maui was taunted by a man who ridiculed the idea that he could snare the sun, saying, "You will never catch the sun. You are only an idle nobody."

Maui replied: "When I conquer my enemy and my desire is attained, I will be your death."

After studying the path of the sun, Maui returned to his mother and told her that he would go and cut off the legs of the sun, so that he could no run so fast.

His mother said: "Are you strong enough for the work?" He said, "Yes." Then she gave him fifteen strands of well-twisted fiber and told him to go to his grandmother, who lived in the great crater of Haleakala, for the rest of the things needed for his conflict with the sun. She said: "You must climb the mountain to the place where a large wiliwili tree is standing. There you will find the place where the sun stops to eat cooked bananas prepared by your grandmother. Stay there until a rooster crows three times; then watch your grandmother go out to make a fire and put on food. You had better take away her bananas. She will look for them and find you and ask who you are. Tell her you belong to Hina."

When she had taught him all these things, he went up the mountain to Kaupo, to the place Hina had directed.

11

There was a large wiliwili tree. Here he waited for the rooster to crow. The name of that rooster was Kalauhelemoa. When the rooster had crowed three times, the grandmother came out with a bunch of bananas to cook for the sun. She took off the upper part of the bunch and laid it down. Maui immediately snatched it away.

In a moment she turned to pick it up, but could not find it. She was angry and cried out: "Where are the bananas of the sun?" Then she took off another part of the bunch, and Maui stole that. Thus he did until all the bunch had been taken away. She was almost blind and could not detect him by sight. She sniffed all around her until she detected the smell of a man. She asked: "Who are you? To whom do you belong?"

Maui replied: "I belong to Hina."

"Why have you come?"

Maui told her: "I have come to kill the sun. He goes so fast that he never dries the kapa Hina has beaten out."

The old woman gave him a magic stone for a battleax and one more rope. She taught him how to catch the sun, saying: "Make a place to hide here by this large wiliwili tree. When the first leg of the sun comes up, catch it with your first rope, and so on until you have used all your ropes. Fasten them to the tree; then take the stone ax to strike the body of the sun."

Maui dug a hole among the roots of the tree and concealed himself. Soon the first ray of light—the first leg of the sun—came up along the mountainside. Maui threw his rope and caught it. One by one the legs of the sun came over the edge of the crater's rim and were caught. Only one long leg was still hanging down the side of the mountain. It was hard for the sun to move that leg. It shook and trembled and tried hard to come up. At last it crept over the edge and was caught by Maui with the rope given by his grandmother.

When the sun saw that his sixteen long legs were held fast by the ropes, he began to go back down the mountainside into the sea. Then Maui tied the ropes fast to the tree and pulled until the body of the sun came up again. Brave Maui caught his magic stone club or ax, and began to strike and wound the sun until he cried: "Give me my life!"

Maui said: "If you live, you may be a traitor. Perhaps I had better kill you." But the sun begged for life. After they had conversed a while, they agreed that there should be a regular motion in the journey of the sun. There should be longer days, and yet half the time he might go quickly as in the wintertime, but the other half he must move slowly as in summer. Thus men dwelling on the earth should be blessed.

Maui returned from his conflict with the sun and sought for Moemoe, the man who had ridiculed him. Maui chased this man around the island from one side to the other until they had passed through Lahaina. There on the seashore near the large black rock of the legend of Maui lifting the sky, he found Moemoe. Then they left the seashore and the contest raged up hill and down, until Maui slew the man and "changed the body into a long rock, which is there to this day, by the side of the road going past Black Rock."

Maui Finds Fire

HINA, Maui's mother, wanted fish. One morning early, Maui saw that the great storm waves of the sea had died down and the fishing grounds could be easily reached. He awakened his brothers and with them hastened to the beach. This was at Kaupo on the island of Maui. Out into the gray shadows of the dawn they paddled. When they were far from the shore, they began to fish. But Maui, looking landward, saw a fire on the mountainside.

"Behold!" he cried. "There is a fire burning. Whose can this fire be?"

13

"Whose, indeed?" his brothers replied.

"Let us hasten to the shore and cook our food," said one.

They decided that they had better catch some fish to cook before they returned. Thus, in the morning, before the hot sun drove the fish deep down to the dark recesses of the sea, they fished until a bountiful supply lay in the bottom of the canoe.

When they came to land, Maui leaped out and ran up the mountainside to get the fire. For a long, long time they had been without fire. The great volcano Haleakala above them had become extinct — and they had lost the coals they had tried to keep alive. They had eaten fruits and uncooked roots and the shellfish broken from the reef, and sometimes the great raw fish from the far-out ocean. But now they hoped to gain living fire and cooked food.

But when Maui rushed up toward the cloud pillar of smoke, he saw a family of birds scratching the fire out. Their work was finished and they flew away just as he reached the place.

Maui and his brothers watched for fire day after day, but the birds, the curly-tailed alae, or mud hens, made no fire. Finally the brothers went fishing once more. When they looked toward the mountain, again they saw flames and smoke. Thus it happened to them again and again.

Maui proposed to his brothers that they go fishing, leaving him to watch the birds. But the alae counted the fishermen, and refused to build a fire for the hidden one who was watching them. The said among themselves, "Three are in the boat and we know not where the other one is. We will make no fire today."

Thus the experiment failed again and again. If one or two remained, or if all waited on the land, there would be no fire — but the dawn that saw the four brothers in the boat saw also the fire on the land.

Finally, Maui rolled some kapa cloth together and

stuck it up in one end of the canoe so that it would look like a man. He then concealed himself near the haunt of the mud hens, while his brothers went out fishing. The birds counted the figures in the boat and then started to build a heap of wood for the fire.

Maui was impatient. Just as the old alae began to select sticks with which to make the flames, he leaped swiftly out and caught her and held her prisoner. He forgot for a moment that he wanted the secret of firemaking. In his anger against the wise bird, his first impulse was to taunt her and then kill her for hiding the secret of fire.

The alae cried out: "If you are the death of me, my secret will perish also, and you cannot have fire."

Maui then promised to spare her life if she would tell him what to do.

Then came the contest of wits. The bird told the demi-god to rub the stalks of water plants together. He guarded the bird and tried the plants. Water instead of fire ran out of the twisted stems. Then she told him to rub reeds together—but they bent and broke and could make no fire. He twisted her neck until she was half dead. Then she cried out: "I have hidden the fire in a green stick!"

Maui worked hard, but not a spark of fire appeared. Again he caught his prisoner by the head and wrung her neck, and she named a kind of dry wood. Maui rubbed the sticks together, but they only became warm. The neck-twisting process was resumed, and repeated again and again, until the mud hen was almost dead, and Maui had tried tree after tree.

At last Maui found fire. Then as the flames rose he said: "There is one more thing to rub." He took a fire stick and rubbed the top of the head of his prisoner until the feathers fell off and the raw flesh appeared. Thus the Hawaiian mud hen and her descendants have ever since had bald heads, and the Hawaiians have had the secret of fire making.

Maui and Peapea the Eight-eyed

MAUI had been fishing and had caught a great fish upon which he was feasting. He looked inland and saw his wife, Kumulama, seized and carried away by Peapea-maka-walu (Peapea the Eight-eyed).

Maui pursued Peapea, but could not catch him. He carried Maui's wife over the sea to a faraway island.

Maui was greatly troubled, but his grandmother sent him inland to find an old man who would tell him what to do. Maui went inland and looking down toward Waipahu saw this man, Kuolokele. He was humpbacked. Maui threw a large stone and, hitting "the hill on the back," knocked it off and made the back straight. The old man lifted up the stone and threw it to Waipahu, where it lies to this day.

Then he and Maui talked together. He told Maui to go and catch birds and gather ti leaves and fibers of the ieie vine, and fill his house. These things Maui secured and brought to him. He told Maui to go home and return after three days.

Kuolokele took the ti leaves and the ieie threads and made the body of a great bird, which he covered with bird feathers. He fastened all together with the ieie. This was done on the first day. The second day he placed food inside and tried his bird, and it flew out all right. "Thus," as the Hawaiians say, "the first flying ship was made in the time of Maui."

On the third day, Maui came and saw the wonderful bird-body thoroughly prepared for his journey. Maui went inside. Kuolokele said: "When you reach that land, look for a village. If the people are not there, look to the beach. If there are many people, your wife and Peapea the Eight-eyed will be there. Do not go near, but fly out over the sea. The people will say, 'Oh, the strange bird!',

16

but Peapea will say, 'This is my bird. It is kapu.' You can then come to the people."

Maui pulled the ieie ropes fastened to the wings and made them move. Thus he flew away into the sky. Two days were his journey before he came to that strange island, Moana-liha-i-ka-waokele. It was a beautiful land. He flew inland to a village, but there were no people. According to the ancient chant:

> The houses of Limaloa stand,
> But there are no people;
> They are at Mana.

The people were by the sea. Maui flew over them. He saw his wife, but he passed on, flying out over the sea, skimming like a sea bird down to the water and rising gracefully up to the sky. Peapea called out, "This is my bird. It is kapu!"

Maui heard and came to the beach. He was caught and placed in a kapu box. The servants carried him up to the village and put him in the chief's sleeping house, when Peapea and his people returned to their homes.

In the night, Peapea and Maui's wife lay down to sleep. Maui watched Peapea, hoping he would soon sleep. Then he would kill him. Maui waited. One eye was closed, seven eyes were open. Then four eyes closed, leaving three. The night was almost past and dawn was near. Then Maui called to Hina with his spirit voice: "O Hina, keep it dark!" Hina made the gray dawn dark in the three eyes, and two slept. The last eye was weary, and it also slept.

Then Maui went out of the bird body and cut off the head of Peapea and put it inside the bird. He broke the roof of the house, until a large opening was made. He took his wife, Kumulama, and flew away to the island of Oahu. The winds blew hard against the flying bird. Rain fell in torrents around it, but those inside had no trouble.

"Thus Maui returned with his wife to his home in Oahu. The story is pau (finished)."

17

Maui Invents Kite Flying

THE Hawaiian myths are perhaps the only ones of the Pacific Ocean that give to any of the gods the pleasure and excitement of kite flying. Maui, after repeated experiments, made a large kite for himself. It was much larger than any house of his time or generation. He twisted a long line from the strong fibers of the native plant known as the olona. He endowed both kite and string with marvelous powers and launched the kite up toward the clouds. It rose very slowly. The winds were not lifting it up into the sky.

Maui remembered that an old priest lived in Waipio Valley, the largest and finest valley of the large island of Hawaii, on which he made his home.

This priest had a covered calabash in which he compelled the winds to hide when he did not wish them to play on land and sea. The priest's name was Kaleiioku, and his calabash was known as Ipu-makani-a-ka-maumau (The Calabash of the Perpetual Winds). Maui called for the priest who had charge of the winds to open his calabash and let them come up to Hilo and blow along the Wailuku River.

The natives say that the place where Maui stood was marked by the pressure of his feet in the lava rocks of the river bank as he braced himself to hold the kite against the increasing force of the winds that pushed it towards the sky. Then the enthusiasm of kite flying filled his youthful soul and he cried aloud, screaming his challenge along the coast of the sea toward Waipio:

O winds, winds of Waipio,
In the calabash of Kaleiioku,
Come from the ipu-makani!
O wind, the wind of Hilo,
Come quickly, come with power!

Then the priest lifted the cover of the calabash of the winds and let the strong winds of Hilo escape. Along the seacoast they rushed until as they entered Hilo Bay they heard the voice of Maui calling:

O winds, winds of Hilo,
Hasten and come to me!

With a tumultuous rush, the strong winds turned toward the mountains. They forced their way along the gorges and palisades of the Wailuku River. They leaped into the heavens, making a fierce attack upon the monster which Maui had sent into the sky. The kite struggled as it was pushed upward by the hands of the fierce winds, but Maui rejoiced. His heart was uplifted by the joy of the conflict in which his strength to hold was pitted against the power of the winds to tear away. And again he shouted toward the sea:

O winds, the winds of Hilo,
Come to the mountains, come!

The winds which had been stirring up storms on the face of the waters came inland. They dashed against Maui. They climbed the heights of the skies until they fell with full violence against their mighty foe hanging in the heavens.

The kite had been made of the strongest kapa cloth that Maui's mother could prepare. It was not torn, although it was bent backward to its utmost limit. Then the strain came on the strong cord of olona fiber. The line was stretched and strained as the kite was pushed back. Then Maui called again and again for stronger winds to come. The cord was drawn out until the kite was far above the mountains. At last it broke, and the kite was tossed over the craters of the volcanoes to the land of the district of Ka-u on the other side of the island.

Then Maui was angry, and hastily leaped over the mountains, which are nearly fourteen thousand feet high. In half a dozen strides he had crossed the fifty or sixty miles from his home to the place where the kite lay. He could pass over many miles with a single step.

His name was "Maui Mama" (Maui the Swift). When Maui returned with his kite, he was more careful in calling the winds to aid him in his sport.

The people watched their wise neighbor and soon learned that the kite could be a great blessing to them. When it was soaring in the sky, there was always dry and pleasant weather. It was a day for great rejoicing. They could spread out their kapa cloth to dry as long as the kite was in the sky. They could carry out their necessary work without fear of the rain. Therefore, when anyone saw the kite beginning to float along the mountainside he would call out joyfully: "E! Maui's kite is in the heavens!" Maui would send his kite into the blue sky and then tie the line to the great black stones in the bed of the Wailuku River.

Maui soon learned the power of his kite when blown upon by a fierce wind. With his accustomed skill he planned to make use of his strong servant, and therefore took the kite with him on his journeys to the other islands, using it to aid in making swift voyages. With the wind in the right direction, the kite could pull his double canoe very easily and quickly to its destination.

Time passed, and even the demi-god died. The fish-hook with which he drew the Hawaiian Islands up from the depths of the sea was allowed to lie on the lava by the Wailuku River until it became a part of the stone. The double canoe was carried far inland and then permitted to petrify by the riverside. The two stones which represent the double canoe now bear the name of Waa Kauhi; and the kite has fallen from the sky far up on the mountainside, where it still rests, a flat plot of rich land between Mauna Kea and Mauna Loa.

Hina and the Wailuku River

THERE are two rivers of rushing, tumbling rapids and waterfalls in the Hawaiian Islands, both bearing the name of Wailuku. One is on the island of Maui, flowing out of a deep gorge in the side of the extinct volcano Iao. Precipices surround this majestically walled crater. The name Iao means "asking for clouds." The head of the crater-valley is almost always covered with great masses of heavy rain clouds. Out of the crater the massed waters rush in a swift-flowing stream of only four or five miles, emptying into Kahului Harbor.

The other Wailuku River is on the island of Hawaii. The snows melt on the summits of the two great mountains, Mauna Kea and Mauna Loa. The water seeps through the porous lava from the eastern slope of Mauna Loa and the southern slope of Mauna Kea, meeting where the lava flows of centuries from each mountain have piled up against each other. Through the fragments of these volcanic battles, the waters creep down the mountainside toward the sea.

At one place, a number of miles above the city of Hilo, the waters were heard gurgling and splashing far below the surface. Water was needed for the sugar plantations, which modern energy has established all along the eastern coast of the large island. A tunnel was cut into the lava, the underground stream was tapped, and an abundant supply of water was secured and sluiced down to the large plantations below. The headwaters of the Wailuku River gathered from the melting snow of the mountains found these channels, which centered at last in the bed of a very ancient and very interesting lava flow. Sometimes breaking forth in a large, turbulent flood, the stream forces its way over and around the huge blocks of lava that mark the course of the eruption of long ago. Sometimes it courses in a tunnel left by the

21

flowing lava and comes up from below in a series of boiling pools. Then again it falls in majestic sheets over high walls of worn precipices. Several large falls and some very picturesque smaller cascades interspersed with rapids and natural bridges give to this river a beauty peculiarly its own.

The most weird of all the rough places through which the Wailuku River flows is that known as the basin of Rainbow Falls near Hilo. Here Hina, the moon goddess of the Polynesians, lived in a great open cave, over which the falls hung their misty, rainbow-tinted veil. Here Maui, the mighty demi-god of Polynesia, had extensive lands along the northern bank of the river. Here among his cultivated fields he had his home, from which he went forth to accomplish the wonders attributed to him in the legends of the Hawaiians.

Below the cave in which Hina dwelt, the river fought its way through a narrow gorge and then, in a series of many small falls, descended to the little bay, where its waters mingled with the surf of the salt sea. Far above the cave, in the bed of the river, dwelt Kuna, a dragon. The district through which that portion of the river runs bears to this day the name Waikuna (Kuna's River).

The Hawaiians told of the annoyances which Hina endured from Kuna while he lived above her home in the Wailuku. He would stop up the river and fill it with dirt, as when the freshets brought down the debris of the storms from the mountainsides. He would throw logs and rolling stones into the stream, that they might be carried over the falls and drive Hina from her cave. He had sought Hina in many ways and had been repulsed again and again, until at last hatred took the place of all more kindly feelings and he determined to destroy the goddess.

Hina was frequently left with but little protection, and yet from her home in the cave feared nothing that Kuna could do. Precipices guarded the cave on either side, and any approach of an enemy through the falling water could be easily thwarted. So her chants rang out through the river valley even while floods swirled around her, and Kuna's missiles were falling over the rocky bed of the stream toward her.

Kuna became very angry and, uttering great curses and calling upon all his magic forces to aid him, caught a great stone and at night hurled it into the gorge of the river below Hina's home, filling the river bed from bank to bank.

"Now, Hina! Now is the danger, for the river rises. The water cannot flow away. Awake! Awake!"

Hina was now aware of this evil that was so near. The water rose and rose, higher and higher. "Auwe! Auwe! Alas, alas, Hina must perish!" The water entered the opening of the cave and began to creep along the floor. Hina could not fly, except into the very arms of her great enemy, who was waiting to destroy her.

Then Hina called for Maui. Again and again her voice went out from the cave. It pierced through the storms and the clouds that attended Kuna's attack upon her. It swept along the side of the great mountain. It crossed the channel between the islands of Hawaii and Maui. Its anguish smote the side of the great mountain of Haleakala, where Maui had been throwing his lassoes around the sun and compelling him to go more slowly. When Maui heard Hina's cry for help echoing from cliff to cliff and through the ravines, he leaped at once to rush to her assistance.

Down the mountain he leaped to his magic canoe. Pushing it into the sea with two mighty strokes of his paddle, he crossed the sea to the mouth of the Wailuku River. Here even to the present day lies a long, double rock, surrounded by the waters of the bay, that the natives call Ka-waa-o-Maui (The Canoe of Maui). It represents to Hawaiian thought the magic canoe with which Maui always sailed over the ocean more swiftly than any winds could carry him.

Leaving his canoe, Maui seized the magic club with

which he had conquered the sun after lassoing him, and rushed along the dry bed of the river to the place of danger. Swinging the club swiftly around his head, he struck the dam holding back the water of the rapidly rising water.

"Ah! Nothing can withstand the magic club. The bank around one end of the dam gives way. The imprisoned waters leap into the new channel. Safe is Hina the goddess!"

Kuna heard the crash of the club against the stones of the river bank and fled up the river to his home in the hidden caves by the pool in the riverbed. Maui rushed up the river to punish Kunamoo for the trouble he had caused Hina. When he came to the place where the dragon was hidden under deep waters, he took his magic spear and thrust it through the dirt and lava rocks along one side of the river, making a long hole through which the waters rushed, revealing Kunamoo's hiding place. This place of the spear thrust is known among the Hawaiians as Ka-puka-a-Maui (The Door Made by Maui). It is also known as "the natural bridge of the Wailuku River."

Kunamoo fled to his different hiding places, but Maui broke up the riverbed and drove the dragon out from every one, following him from place to place as he fled down the river. Apparently this is a legendary account of earthquakes. At last Kunamoo found what seemed to be a safe hiding place in a series of deep pools, but Maui poured a lava flow into the river. He threw red-hot burning stones into the water until the pools were boiling and the steam was rising in clouds.

Kuna uttered incantation after incantation, but the water scalded and burned him. Dragon as he was, his hard, tough skin was of no avail. The pain was becoming unbearable. With cries to his gods, he leaped from the pools and fled down the river. The waters of the pool were no longer scalding, but they have never lost the tumbling, foaming, boiling swirl that Maui gave to them when he threw into them the red-hot stones with which he hoped to destroy Kuna, and they are known today as "The Boiling Pots."

Maui chased the dragon, striking him again and again with his consecrated weapons, following Kuna down from falls to falls until he came to the place where Hina dwelt. Then, feeling that there was little use in flight, Kuna battled with Maui. His struggles were of no avail. He was forced over the falls into the stream below.

Hina and her women encouraged Maui by their chants, and strengthened him by the most powerful incantations with which they were acquainted. Great was their joy when they beheld Kuna's ponderous body hurled over the falls. Eagerly they watched the dragon as the swift waters swept him against the dam with which he had hoped to destroy Hina. And when the whirling waves caught him and dashed him through the new channel made by Maui's magic club, they rejoiced and sang the praise of the mighty warrior who had saved them.

Ghosts of the Hilo Hills

THE LEGENDS about Hina and her famous son Maui, and her less widely known daughters, are common property among the natives of the beautiful little city of Hilo. One of these legends of more than ordinary interest finds its location in the three small hills back of Hilo toward the mountains.

These hills are small craters connected with some ancient lava flow of unusual violence. The eruption must have started far up on the slopes of Mauna Loa. As it sped down toward the sea, it met some obstruction which, although overwhelmed, checked the flow and caused a great mass of cinders and ashes to be thrown out until a large hill with a hollow crater was built up, covering many acres of ground.

Soon the lava found another vent and then another obstruction and a second, and then a third, hill were formed nearer the sea. These hills or extinct craters bear the names Halai, Opeapea, and Puu Honu. They are not far from the Wailuku River, famous for its picturesque waterfalls and also for the legends which are told along its banks.

Hina had several daughters, four of whose names are given: Hina Keahi, Hina Kekai, Hina Mahuia, and Hina Kuluua. Each name marked the peculiar mana or divine gift which Hina, the mother, had bestowed upon her daughters.

Hina Keahi meant the Hina who had control of fire. This name is sometimes given to Hina the mother. Hina Kekai was the daughter who had power over the sea. She was said to have been in a canoe with her brother Maui when he fished up Coconut Island, his line breaking before he could pull it up to the mainland and make it fast. Hina Kuluua was the mistress over the forces of rain. The winds and the storms were supposed to obey her will. Hina Mahuia is peculiarly a name connected with the legends of the other island groups of the Pacific; Mahuia or Mafuie was a god or goddess of fire all through Polynesia.

The legend of the Hilo hills pertains especially to Hina Keahi and Hina Kuluua. Hina the mother gave the hill Halai to Hina Keahi and the hill Puuhonu to Hina Kuluua for their families and dependents.

The hills were of rich soil and there was much rain. Therefore, for a long time, the two daughters had plenty of food for themselves and their people. But at last the days were like fire and the sky had no rain to it. The taro planted on the hillsides died. The bananas and sugar cane and sweet potatoes withered and the fruit on the trees was blasted. The people were faint because of hunger, and the shadow of death was over the land.

Hina Keahi pitied her suffering friends and determined to provide food for them. Slowly her people labored at her command. Over they went to the banks of the river course, which was only the bed of an ancient lava stream, over which no water was flowing. The famished laborers toiled, gathering and carrying back whatever wood they could find, then went up the mountainside to the great koa and ohia forests, gathering their burdens of fuel according to the wishes of the chiefess.

Their sorcerers planted charms along the way and uttered incantations to ward off the danger of failure. The priests offered sacrifices and prayers for the safe and successful return of the burden bearers. After many days, the great quantity of wood desired by the goddess was piled up by the side of the Halai Hill.

Then came the days of digging out the hill and making a great imu or cooking oven, and preparing it with stones and wood. Large quantities of wood were thrown into the place. Stones best fitted for retaining heat were gathered and the fires kindled. When the stones were hot, Hina Keahi directed the people to arrange the imu in its proper order for cooking the materials for a great feast. A place was made for sweet potatoes, another for taro, another for pigs, and another for dogs. All the forms of preparing the food for cooking were passed through, but no real food was laid on the stones.

Then Hina told them to make a place in the imu for a human sacrifice. Probably, out of every imu of the long ago, a small part of the food was offered to the gods, and there may have been a special place in the imu for that part of the food to be cooked. At any rate, Hina had this oven so built that the people understood that a remarkable sacrifice would be offered in it to the gods, who for some reason had sent the famine upon the people.

Therefore it was in quiet despair that the workmen obeyed Hina Keahi and prepared the place for sacrifice.

27

It might mean their own holocaust as an offering to the gods. At last Hina Keahi bade the laborers cease their work and stand by the side of the oven, ready to cover it with the dirt which had been thrown out and piled up by the side. The people stood by, not knowing upon whom the blow might fall.

But Hina Keahi was "Hina the Kind," and although she stood before them robed in royal majesty and power, still her face was full of pity and love. Her voice melted the hearts of her retainers as she bade them carefully follow her directions.

"O my people! Where are you? Will you obey and do as I command? This imu is my imu. I shall lie down in its bed of burning stones. I shall sleep under its cover. But deeply cover me, or I may perish. Quickly throw the dirt over my body. Fear not the fire. Watch for three days. A woman will stand by the imu. Obey her will."

Hina Keahi was very beautiful, and her eyes flashed light like fire as she stepped into the great pit and lay down on the burning stones. A great smoke arose and gathered over the imu. The men toiled rapidly, placing the imu mats over their chiefess and throwing the dirt back into the oven until it was all thoroughly covered and the smoke was quenched.

Then they waited for the strange, mysterious thing which must fallow the sacrifice of this divine chiefess.

Halai hill trembled and earthquakes shook the land round about. The great heat of the fire in the imu withered the little life that was still left from the famine. Meanwhile, Hina Keahi was carrying out her plan for securing aid for her people. She could not be injured by the heat, for she was a goddess of fire. The waves of heat raged around her as she sank down through the stones of the imu into the underground paths which belonged to the spirit world.

The legend says that Hina made her appearance in the form of a gushing stream of water which would always supply the wants of her adherents. The second day passed. Hina was still journeying underground, but this time she came to the surface as a pool named Moe-waa (Canoe Sleep), much nearer the sea. The third day came and Hina caused a great spring of sweet water to burst forth from the seashore in the very path of the ocean surf. This received the name of Auauwai. Here Hina washed away all traces of her journey through the depths.

This was the last of the series of earthquakes and the appearance of new water springs. The people waited, feeling that some more wonderful event must follow the remarkable experience of the three days. Soon a woman stood by the imu, who commanded the laborers to dig away the dirt and remove the mats. When this was done, the hungry people found a very great abundance of food, enough to supply their wants until the food plants should have time to ripen and the days of the famine should be over.

The joy of the people was great when they knew that their chiefess had escaped death and would still dwell among them in comfort. Many were the songs sung and stories told about the great famine and the success of the goddess of fire.

The second sister, Hina Kuluua, the goddess of rain, was always very jealous of her beautiful sister Hina Keahi, and many times sent rain to put out fires which her sister tried to kindle. Hina Keahi could not stand the rain and so fled with her people to a home by the seaside.

Hina Kuluua could control rain and storms, but for some reason failed to provide a food supply for her people, and the famine wrought havoc among them. She thought of the stories told and songs sung about her sister, and wished for the same honor for herself. She commanded her people to make a great imu for her in the hill Puu Honu. She knew that a strange power belonged to her and yet, blinded by jealousy, forgot that rain and fire could not work together. She planned to furnish a great supply of food for her people in the same way in which her sister had worked.

The oven was dug. Stones and wood were collected and the same ghostly array of potatoes, taro, pig and dog prepared as had been done before by her sister.

The kahunas or priests knew that Hina Kuluua was going out of her province in trying to do as her sister had done, but there was no use in attempting to change her plans. Jealousy is self-willed and obstinate, and no amount of reasoning from her dependents could have any influence over her.

The ordinary incantations were observed, and Hina Kuluua gave the same directions as those her sister had given. The imu was to be well heated. The make-believe food was to be put in and a place left for her body. It was the goddess of rain making ready to lie down on a bed prepared for the goddess of fire. When all was ready, she lay down on the heated stones and the oven mats were thrown over her and the ghostly provisions. Then the covering of dirt was thrown back upon the mats and heated stones, filling the pit which had been dug. The goddess of rain was left to prepare a feast for her people as the goddess of fire had done for her followers.

Some of the legends have introduced the demi-god Maui into this story. The natives say that Maui came to "burn or cook the rain" and that he made the oven very hot, but that the goddess of rain escaped and hung over the hill in the form of a cloud. At least this is what the people saw — not a cloud of smoke over the imu, but a rain cloud. They waited and watched for such evidences of underground labor as attended the passage of Hina Keahi through the earth from the hill to the sea, but the only strange appearance was the dark rain cloud. They waited three days and looked for their chiefess to come in the form of a woman. They waited another day and still another, and no signs or wonders were manifest.

Meanwhile, Maui, changing himself into a white bird, flew up into the sky to catch the ghost of the goddess of rain that had escaped from the burning oven. Having caught this spirit, he rolled it in some kapa cloth that he kept for food to be placed in an oven, and carried it to a place in the forest on the mountainside, where again the attempt was made to "burn the rain"; but a great drop escaped and sped upward into the sky.

Again Maui caught the ghost of the goddess and carried it to a pali or precipice below the great volcano Kilauea, where he again tried to destroy it in the heat of a great lava oven. But this time the spirit escaped and found a safe refuge among kukui trees on the mountainside, from which she sometimes rises in clouds that the natives say are the sure sign of rain.

The ghosts of Hina Keahi and Hina Kuluua sometimes draw near to the old hills in the form of the fire of flowing lava or clouds of rain, while the old men and women tell the story of the Hinas, the sisters of Maui, who were laid upon the burning stones of the imus of a famine.

II. Pele and Her Family

Ai-laau, the Forest Eater

WHEN PELE came to the island of Hawaii, seeking a permanent home, she found another god of fire already in possession of the territory. "Ai" means "the one who eats or devours." "Laau" means "tree" or "a forest." Ai-laau was, therefore, the fire god who devours forests. Time and again he laid the districts of South Hawaii desolate by the lava he poured out from his fire pits.

He was the god with the insatiable appetite, the continual eater of trees, whose path through forests was covered with black smoke fragrant with burning wood, and sometimes burdened with the smell of human flesh charred into cinders in the lava flow.

Ai-laau seemed to be destructive and was so named by the people, but his fires were a part of the forces of creation. He built up the islands for future life. The process of creation demanded volcanic activity. The flowing lava made land. The lava disintegrating made earth deposits and soil. Upon this land, storms fell and through it multitudes of streams found their way to the sea. Flowing rivers came from the cloud-capped mountains. Fruitful fields and homes made this miniature world-building complete.

Ai-laau still poured out his fire. It spread over the fertile fields, and the people feared him as the destroyer giving no thought to the final good.

He lived, the legends say, for a long time in a very ancient part of Kilauea, on the large island of Hawaii, now separated by a narrow ledge from the great crater and called Kilauea-iki (Little Kilauea). This seems to be the first and greatest of a number of craters extending in a line from the great lake of fire in Kilauea to the seacoast, many miles away. They are called "the pit craters" because they are not hills of lava but a series of pits going deep down into the earth, some of them still having blowholes of sputtering steam and smoke.

After a time, Ai-laau left these pit craters and went into the great crater. He was said to be living there when Pele came to the seashore far below.

In one of the Pele stories is the following literal translation of the account of her taking Kilauea:

"When Pele came to the island of Hawaii, she first stopped at a place called Keahialaka in the district of Puna. From this place she began her inland journey toward the mountains. As she passed on her way, there grew within her an intense desire to go at once and see Ai-laau, the god to whom Kilauea belonged, and find a resting place with him at the end of her journey.

"She came up, but Ai-laau was not in his house. Of a truth, he had made himself thoroughly lost. He had vanished because he knew that this one coming toward him was Pele. He had seen her toiling down by the sea at Keahialaka. Trembling dread and heavy fear overpowered him. He ran away and was entirely lost.

"When Pele came to that pit, she laid out the plan for her abiding home, beginning at once to dig up the foundations. She dug day and night and found that this place fulfilled all her desires. Therefore, she fastened herself tight to Hawaii for all time."

These are the words in which the legend disposes of this ancient god of volcanic fires. He disappears from Hawaiian thought, and Pele from a foreign land finds a satisfactory crater in which her spirit power can always dig up everlastingly.

How Pele Came to Hawaii

THE SIMPLEST, most beautiful legend does not mention the land from which Pele started. In this legend her father was Moe-moea-au-lii (The Chief Who Dreamed of Trouble). Her mother was Haumea, or Papa, who personified Mother Earth. Moemoea apparently is not mentioned in any other of the legends. Haumea is frequently named as the mother of Pele, as well as the heroine of many legendary experiences.

Pele's story is that of wanderlust. She was living in a happy home in the presence of her parents, and yet for a long time she was "stirred by thoughts of faraway lands." At last she asked her father to send her away. This request meant that he must provide a seagoing canoe with mat sails, sufficiently large to carry a number of persons and food for many days.

"What will you do with your little egg sister?" asked her father.

Pele caught the egg, wrapped it in her skirt to keep it warm near her body, and said that it should always be with her. Evidently, in a very short time the egg was changed into a beautiful little girl who bore the name of Hii-aka-i-ka-poli-o-Pele (Hiiaka-in-the-Bosom-of-Pele), the youngest one of the Pele family.

After the care of the helpless one had been provided for, Pele was sent to her oldest brother, Kamohoalii, the king of dragons, or, as he was later known in Hawaiian mythology, "the god of sharks." He was a sea god who would provide the great canoe for the journey. While he was getting all things ready, he asked Pele where she was going. She replied: "I am going to Bolabola; to Kuai-he-lani; to Kane-huna-moku; then to Moku-mana-mana; then to see a queen, Kaoahi her name and Niihau her island." Apparently her journey would be first to Borabora in the Society Islands, then

37

among the mysterious ancestral islands, and then to the northwest until she found Niihau, the most northerly of the Hawaiian group.

The god of sharks prepared his large canoe and put it in the care of some of their relatives, Kane-pu-a-hio-hio (Kane the Whirlwind), Ke-au-miki (The Strong Current), and Ke-au-ka (Moving Seas).

Pele was carried from land to land by these wise boatmen until at last she landed on the island of Niihau. Then she sent back the boat to her brother the shark god. It is said that after a time he brought all the brothers and sisters to Hawaii.

Pele was welcomed and entertained. Soon she went over to Kauai, the large, beautiful garden island of the Hawaiian group. There is a story of her appearance as a dream maiden before the king of Kauai, whose name was Lohiau. She married him, but could not stay until she had found a place where she could build a permanent home for herself and all who belonged to her.

She had a magic digging tool called Paoa. When she struck this down into the earth it made a fire pit. It was with this Paoa that she was to build a home for herself and Lohiau. She dug along the lowlands of Kauai, but water drowned the fires she kindled. She went from island to island, but could only dig along the beach near the sea. All her fire pits were so near the water that they burst out in great explosions of steam and sand and quickly died, until at last she found Kilauea on the large island of Hawaii. There she built a mighty, enduring place of fire, but her dream marriage was at an end. The little sister Hiiaka, after many adventures, married Lohiau and lived on Kauai.

Again and again the legends give Kuwahailo as the father and Haumea as the mother of the Pele family. Hina is sometimes said to be Kuwahailo's sister in these legends. She quarreled with him because he devoured all the people. The Hawaiians as a nation, even in their traditions, have never been cannibals, although their legends give many individual instances of cannibalism. The Pele stories say that "Kuwahailo was a cannibal" and "Haumea was a pali (precipice or a prominent part of the earth)."

A greater sorcerer married Namakaokahai, Pele's sister who was goddess of the sea. After a time he saw Pele and her beautiful young sister Hiiaka. He took them secretly to be his wives. This sorcerer was Au-kele-nui-a-iku (The Great Smoothly Swimming Son of Iku). He could fly through the heavens, swim through the seas, or run swiftly over the earth. By magic power he conquered enemies, visited strange lands, found the fountain of the water of life, sprinkled that water over his dead brothers, brought them back to life, and did many marvelous deeds. But he could not deliver Pele and Hiiaka from the wrath of their sister.

High tides and floods from the seas destroyed Pele's home and lands. Then the elder brother of Pele—Kamohoalii, the shark god—called for all the family to aid Pele. Namakaokahai fought the whole family and defeated them. She broke down their houses and drove them into the ocean. There Kamohoalii provided them with the great boat Honua-i-a-kea (The Great Spread-out-World) and carried them away to distant islands.

Namakaokahai went to the highest of all the mythical lands of the ancestors, Nuu-mea-lani (The Raised Dais of Heaven). There she could look over all the seas from Kalakeenui-a-Kane to Kauai (from a legendary land in the south to the most northerly part of the Hawaiian Islands). Pele carried her Paoa, the magic spade. Wherever they landed she struck the earth, thus opening a crater in which volcanic fires burned. As the smoke rose to the clouds, the angry watching one rushed from Nuu-mea-lani and tried to slay the family. Again and again they escaped. Farther and farther from the homeland were they driven until they struck far out into the ocean.

Namakaokahai went back to her lookout mountain.

After a long time she saw the smoke of earth fires far away on the island of Kauai. Pele had struck her Paoa into the earth, dug a deep pit, and thrown up a large hill known to this day as the Puu-o-Pele (The Hill of Pele). It seemed as if an abiding place had been found.

But the sister came and fought Pele. There is no long account of the battle. Pele was broken and smashed and left for dead. She was not dead, but she left Kauai and went to Oahu, to a place near Honolulu, to Moanalua, a beautiful suburb. There she dug a fire pit. The earth, or rather the eruption of lava, was forced up into a hill which later bore the name of Ke-alia-manu (The Bird White Like a Salt Bed or The White Bird). The crater which she dug filled up with salt water and was named Ke-alia-paa-kai (The White Bed of Salt, or Salt Lake).

Pele was not able to strike her Paoa down into a mountainside and dig deep for the foundations of her home. She could find fire only in the lowlands near the seashore. The best place on Oahu was just back of Leahi, the ancient Hawaiian name for Diamond Head. Here she threw up a great quantity of fire rock, but at last her fires were drowned by the water she struck below.

Thus she passed along the coast of each island, the family watching and aiding until they came to the great volcano of Haleakala. There Pele dug with her Paoa, and a great quantity of lava was thrown out of her fire pit.

Namakaokahai saw enduring clouds day after day, rising with the colors of the dark dense smoke of the underworld, and knew that her sister was still living.

Pele had gained strength and confidence; therefore she entered alone into a conflict unto death. The battle was fought by the two sisters hand to hand. The conflict lasted for a long time along the western slope of the mountain Haleakala. Namakaokahai tore the body of Pele and broke her lava bones into great pieces which lie to this day along the seacoast of the district called Kahikinui. The masses of broken lava are called Na-iwi-o-Pele (The Bones of Pele).

40

Pele and the Owl Ghost-god

MANY, MANY years after Pele's angry sister Nama-kaokahai had driven her from the island of Kauai, and after the land had many dwellers therein, a quarrel arose between two of the highest chiefs of the island. They were named Koa and Kau. It did not become an open conflict immediately, but Koa was filled with such deep hatred that he was ready to employ any means to destroy his enemy.

There was a mighty kapua, or dragon of the Pii family, at that time on Kauai. These dragons had come, according to the legends, to the Hawaiian Islands from the faraway lands of Kuai-he-lani as attendants on the first young chief Kahanai-a-ke-akua (The Boy Brought Up by the Gods). These dragons had the mana, or magic power, of appearing as men or as dragons, according to their desire.

This dragon was named Pii-ka-Lalau (Pili Dwelling at Kalalau). He was supposed to be semi-divine. His home was on the crest of an almost inaccessible precipice up which he would rush with incredible speed. Koa, the angry chief, came to this precipice and called Pii to come to him. There they plotted the death of Kau, the enemy. Assuming the appearance of a splendidly formed young man, Pii went down among the people with Koa to watch for an opportunity to seize Kau.

After a time, Kau was lured to go at night to a house far from his own home. As he entered the door, he received a heavy blow that smashed the bones of one shoulder and laid him prostrate. A great giant leaped out, thrusting an enormous spear at him. Kau was one of the most skillful of all chiefs in what was known as "spear practice." He avoided the thrusts and leaped to his feet. He had a wooden dagger as his only weapon, but could not get near enough to the giant to use it.

41

Just as he was becoming too weary to move, his wife, who had followed him, hurled rocks, striking the giant's face. Then, seizing her husband, she fled with him homeward.

There followed a great battle, in which Pii attacked all the warriors belonging to the wounded chief. The legends say that "this giant was twelve feet high; he had eyes as large as a man's fist, and an immense mouth full of tusks like those of a wild hog. His legs were as large as trees, and his weight was such that wherever he stepped there were great holes in the ground."

The warriors fled as this mighty giant charged upon them. Suddenly they stopped and rushed back. Their chief's wife had caught an ikoi, a heavy piece of wood fastened to a long, stout cord. This she hurled so that it twisted around him and bound his arms to his sides. Stones and spears beat upon him, but he broke the coco-nut-fiber cords of the ikoi and again drove the warriors before him, trying to gain the house where the wounded chief Kau was lying.

There was an old prophetess who had rushed to the side of her master when he was brought to his home. She was one of the worshippers of Pele, the fire goddess of the island of Hawaii. Powerful were her prayers and incantations.

Soon, out of the clear sky above the conflict, appeared Pele hurling a fierce bolt of lightning at the giant. It struck the ground at his feet, almost overthrowing him. A second flash of lightning blinded and stunned him.

Pii, smitten by this new danger, called for Pueo, his most mighty ghost-god. Pele's fire darts were falling upon him and he was near death. Then came Pueo flying down from the steep places of the mountain. Pueo was a great owl in which dwelt one of the most powerful of Pii's ancestors.

Pueo hovered over the head of Pii facing Pele. Whenever Pele hurled her fiery darts, the owl swiftly thrust his head from side to side, catching them in his beak, and with a shake of the head tossing them off to the ground.

Then came the warriors in a great body around the giant and his ghost-god. Thickly flew their spears and darts. Great clouds of stones were hurled, and both Pii and his owl-god were grievously wounded. Pele's flashes of lightning were coming with great rapidity.

The giant called to his aumakua to fly to the mountains, and then, suddenly changing himself into his dragon form, he dashed up the precipice toward his home.

The warriors were so surprised at the wonderful change that they forgot to fight, and only realized that this dragon was their enemy when they saw him far out of reach of their best weapons. They could see that dragon leaping from stone to stone, and swiftly gliding up the steep precipice. He escaped to his home in the mountain recesses and nevermore troubled the chief by the sea. His employer was killed in a later battle. Pele returned to her home in the volcano of Kilauea.

Pele and Kama-Puaa

KAMA-PUAA was born on the island of Oahu, where he was known as a very powerful and destructive monster, also as a peculiarly handsome and even lovable chief. He was a kupua — a being who could appear at will as an animal or man. He usually appeared as a man, but when his brutal desires to destroy overcame him, or when he wished to hide from anyone, he adopted the form of a hog. He had the two natures, human and brutal. He had been endowed with superhuman powers, according to the legends, and was many times called Puaa-akua (Hog-god) of Oahu.

There is a curiously marked fish with an angular body

and very thick skin, which is said by the Hawaiians to sometimes utter a grunting sound. It is named the Humuhumu-nukunuku-a-puaa (The-grunting-angular pig). It was claimed that the hog-man could change himself into this fish as easily as into a hog.

An ancient chant thus described him:

> O Kama-puaa!
> You are the one with rising bristles.
> O Rooter! O Wallower in ponds!
> O remarkable fish of the sea!
> O youth divine!

Kama-puaa had a beautiful magic shell—the leho. This was a fairy boat in which he usually journeyed from island to island. When he landed he took this shell in his hands and it grew smaller and smaller until he could tuck it away in his loincloth. When he sailed away alone it was just large enough to satisfy his need. If some of his household traveled with him, the canoe became the large ocean boat for the family.

Some of the legends say that as a fish Kama-puaa swam through the seas to Hawaii, but others say that he used his leho boat, visited the different islands, and passed slowly to the southeastern point of Hawaii, to Cape Kumu-kahi.

He crossed the rough beds of lava, left by recent eruptions. He threaded his way through forests of trees and ferns and at last stood on the hills looking down upon the lake of fire. Akani-kolea was the hill upon which he stood clearly outlined against the sky.

Here was Ka-lua-Pele (The-Pit-of-Pele), the home of the goddess of fire. Here she rested among glorious fountains of fire; or, rising in sport, dashed the flaming clouds in twisted masses around the precipices guarding her palace. Here Kama-puaa looked down upon a fire dance, wherein Pele and her sisters, wrapped in filmy gowns of bluish haze, swept back and forth over the lake of fire, the pressure of their footfalls marked by hundreds of boiling bubbles rising and bursting under their

44

tread, until the entire surface was a restless sea covered with choppy waves of fire.

Suddenly a great cloud concealed the household, then rolled away, and all the surrounding cliffs were clearly revealed. One of the sisters looking up saw Kama-puaa and cried out: "Oh, see that fine-looking man standing on Akani-kolea. He stands as straight as a precipice. His face is bright like the moon. Perhaps if our sister frees him from her kapu, he can be the husband of one of us."

The sisters looked. They heard the tum-tum-tum of a small hand-gourd drum; they saw a finely formed athletic stranger who was dancing on the hilltop, gloriously outlined in the splendor of the morning light.

Pele scorned him and said: "That is not a man, but a hog. If I ridicule him he will be angry." Then she started the war of taunting words with which chiefs usually began a conflict. She called to him, giving him all the characteristics of a hog. He was angry and boasted of his power to overcome and destroy the whole Pele family. Pele thought she could easily frighten him and drive him off; she sent clouds of sulphur smoke and a stream of boiling lava against him. To her surprise he brushed the clouds away, with a few words checked the eruption, and stood before them unharmed.

The sisters begged Pele to send for the handsome stranger and make him a member of their family. At last she sent her brother Kane-hoa-lani to speak to him. There were many hindrances before a thorough reconciliation took place.

For a time Pele and Kama-puaa lived together as husband and wife, in various parts of the district of Puna. The places where they dwelt are pointed out even at this day by the natives who know the traditions. It is said that a son was born and named Opelu-haa-lii and that the fiery life of his mother was so strenuous that he lived only a little while. Some say he became the fish "opelu."

This marriage did not endure. Kama-puaa had too many of the habits and instincts of a hog to please Pele, and she was too quickly angry to suit the overbearing Kama-puaa. Pele was never patient even with her sisters. With Kama-puaa she would burst into fiery rage, while taunts and bitter words were freely hurled back and forth.

A sarcastic chant has been handed down among the Hawaiians as one of the taunts hurled at Pele by Kama-puaa.

Oh, look at that one with the sore eyes!
Tell her to go to the sea of Pikeha.
(To wash her eyes and cure them.)
What food makes her fair as the moonlight?
Even her eyebrows were shaved off by some god.

Pele was bitterly angry and tried her best to destroy her tormentor. She stamped on the ground, the earth shook, cracks opened in the surface, and sometimes clouds of smoke and steam arose around Kama-puaa. He was unterrified and matched his divine powers against hers. It was demi-god against demi-goddess. It was the goddess-of-fire of Hawaii against the hog-god of Oahu. Pele's home life was given up; the bitterness of strife swept over the black sands of the seashore.

When the earth seemed ready to open its doors and pour out mighty streams of flowing lava in the defence of Pele, Kama-puaa called for the waters of the ocean to rise up. Then flood met fire and quenched it. Pele was driven inland. Her former lover, hastening after her and striving to overcome her, followed her upward until at last, amid clouds of poisonous gases, she went back into her spirit home in the pit of Kilauea.

Then Kama-puaa as a god of the sea gathered the waters together in great masses and hurled them into the fire-pit. Violent explosions followed the inrush of waters. The sides of the great crater were torn to pieces by fierce earthquakes. Masses of fire expanded the water into steam, and Pele gathered the forces of the underworld to aid in driving back Kama-puaa. The lavas rose in many lakes and fountains. Rapidly the surface was cooled and the fountains were checked by the water thrown in by Kama-puaa; but just as rapidly were new openings made and new streams of fire hurled at the demi-god of Oahu. It was a mighty battle of the elements.

The legends say that the hog-man, Kama-puaa, poured water into the crater until its fires were driven back to their lowest depths and Pele was almost drowned by the floods. The clouds of the skies dropped their burden of rain. All the waters of the sea that Kama-puaa could collect were poured into the crater.

Pele sent Lono-makua, who had charge of the earth fires. He kindled eruptions manifold, but they were overwhelmed by the vast volumes of water hurled against them by Kama-puaa.

Kama-puaa raised his voice in the great ancient chant:

> O gods in the skies!
> Let the rain come, let it fall.
> Let Paoa (Pele's spade) be broken.
> Let the rain be separated from the sun.
> O clouds in the skies!
> O great clouds of Iku! black as smoke!
> Let the heavens fall on earth,
> Let the heavens roll open for the rain,
> Let the storm come

The storm fell in torrents from black clouds gathered right over the pit. The water filled the crater, according to the Hawaiian, ku-ma-waho, rising until it overflowed the walls of the crater. The fires were imprisoned and drowned—the home of Pele seemed to be destroyed. There remained, however, a small spark of fire hidden in the breast of Lono-makua.

Pele prayed for:

> The bright gods of the underworld.
> Shining in Wawao (Vavau) are the gods of the night,
> The gods thick clustered for Pele.

Kama-puaa thought he had destroyed Pele's resources, but just as his wonderful storms had put forth their greatest efforts, Lono-makua kindled the flames of fierce eruptions once more. The gods of the underworld lent their aid to the Pele family. The new attack was more than Kama-puaa could endure. The lua-pele (pit of Pele) was full of earth fire. Streams of lava poured out against Kama-puaa.

He changed his body into a kind of grass now known as ku-kae-puaa, filling a large field with it. When the grass lay in the pathway of the fire, the lava was turned aside for a time; but Pele, inspired by the beginning of victory, called anew upon the gods of the underworld for strong reinforcements.

Out from the pits of Kilauea came vast masses of lava piling up against the field of grass in its pathway, and soon the grass began to burn. Then Kama-puaa assumed the shape of a man; the hair or bristles on his body were singed, and the smart of many burns began to cause agony. Apparently the grass represented the bristles on the front of his hog-body which were scorched and burned. The legends say that since this time hogs have had very little hair on the stomach.

Down he rushed to the sea, but the lava spread out on either side, cutting off retreat along the beach. Pele followed close behind, striving to overtake him before he could reach the water. The side streams had poured into the sea and the water was rapidly heated into tossing, boiling waves. Pele threw great masses of lava at Kama-puaa, striking and churning the sea into which he leaped amidst the swirling, heated mass. Kama-puaa gave up the battle, and, thoroughly defeated, changed himself into a fish. To that fish he gave the tough skin which he assumed when roaming over the islands as a hog. It was thick enough to withstand the boiling waves through which he swam out into the deep sea. The Hawaiians say that this fish has always been able to make a noise like the grunting of a small hog.

It was said that Kama-puaa fled to foreign lands, where he married a high chiefess and lived with his family for many years.

Sometime during this adventure of Kama-puaa in the domains of Pele, the islands were divided between the two demi-gods, and an oath of divine solemnity was taken by them. They set apart a large portion of the island of Hawaii for Pele, and the eastern shore from Hilo to Kohala and all the islands northwest of Hawaii as the kingdom over which Kama-puaa might establish rulers. It is said that the oath has never been broken.

Pele and the Snow Goddess

THERE were four maidens with white mantles in the mythology of the Hawaiians. They were all queens of beauty, full of wit and wisdom, lovers of adventure, and enemies of Pele. They were the goddesses of the snow-covered mountains. They embodied the mythical ideas of spirits carrying on eternal warfare between heat and cold, fire and frost, burning lava and stony ice. They ruled the mountains north of Kilauea and dwelt in the cloud-capped summits. They clothed themselves against the bitter cold with snow mantles. They all had the power of laying aside the white garment and taking in its place clothes made from the golden sunshine. Their stories are nature myths derived from the power of snow and cold to check volcanic action and sometimes clothe the mountain tops and upper slopes with white, which melted as the maidens came down closer to the sea through lands made fertile by flowing streams and blessed sunshine.

It is easy to see how the story arose of Pele and Poliahu, the snow goddess of Mauna Kea. But it is not easy to understand the different forms which the legend takes, while the legends concerning the other three maidens of the white mantle are very obscure indeed.

Lilinoe was sometimes known as the goddess of the mountain Haleakala. In her hands lay the power to hold in check the eruptions which might break forth through the old cinder cones in the floor of the great crater. She was the goddess of dead fires and desolation. She sometimes clothed the long summit of the mountain with a glorious garment of snow several miles in length.

Waiau was another snow maiden of Mauna Kea, whose record in the legends has been almost entirely forgotten. There is a beautiful lake glistening in one of the crater cones of the summit of the mountain. This was sometimes called "The Bottomless Lake," and was supposed to go down deep into the heart of the mountain. It is really forty feet at its greatest depth—deep enough for the bath of the goddess. The name Wai-au means water of sufficient depth to bathe. Somewhere, buried in the memory of some old Hawaiian, is a legend worth exhuming, probably connecting Waiau, the maiden, with Wai-au, the lake.

Kahoupokane was possibly the goddess of the mountain Hualalai, controlling the snows which after long intervals fall on its desolate summits. At present but little more than the name is known about this maiden of the snow garment.

Poliahu, the best known among the maidens of the mountains, loved the eastern cliffs of the great island of Hawaii, the precipices which rise from the raging surf that beats against the coast known now as the Hamakua district. Here she sported among mortals, meeting the chiefs in their many and curious games of chance and skill. Sometimes she wore a mantle of pure white kapa and rested on the ledge of rock overhanging the torrents of water which in various places fell into the sea.

There is a legend of Kauai woven into the fairy tale of the maiden of the mist—Laieikawai—and in this story Poliahu for a short time visits Kauai as the bride of one of the high chiefs, who bore the name Aiwohikupua. The story of the betrothal and marriage suggests the cold of the snow mantle and shows the inconstancy of human hearts.

Aiwohikupua, passing near the cliffs of Hamakua, saw a beautiful woman resting on the rocks above the sea. She beckoned with most graceful gestures for him to approach the beach. Her white mantle lay on the rocks beside her. He landed and proposed marriage, but she made a betrothal with him by the exchange of the cloaks which they were wearing. Aiwohikupua went away to Kauai, but he soon returned clad in the white cloak and wearing a beautiful helmet of red feathers. A large retinue of canoes attended him, filled with musicians and singers and his intimate companions. The three mountains belonging to the snow goddesses were clothed with snow almost down to the seashore.

Poliahu and the three other maidens of the white robe came down to meet the guests from Kauai. Cold winds swayed their garments as they drew near to the sea. The blood of the people of Kauai chilled in their veins. Then the maidens threw off their white mantles and called for the sunshine. The snow went back to the mountaintops, and the maidens, in the beauty of their golden sun garments, gave hearty greeting to their friends. After the days of the marriage festival, Poliahu and her chief went to Kauai.

A queen of the island of Maui had also a promise given by Aiwohikupua. In her anger she hastened to Kauai and in the midst of the Kauai festivities revealed herself and charged the chief with his perfidy. Poliahu turned against her husband and forsook him.

The chief's friends made reconciliation between the Maui chiefess and Aiwohikupua, but when the day of marriage came, the chiefess found herself surrounded by an invisible atmosphere of awful cold. This grew more and more intense as she sought aid from the chief.

At last he called to her: "This cold is the snow mantle of Poliahu. Flee to the place of fire!" But down by the fire

51

the sun mantle belonging to Poliahu was thrown around her and she cried out, "He wela e, he wela!" ("The heat! Oh, the heat!"). Then the chief answered, "This heat is the anger of Poliahu." The Maui chiefess hastened away from Kauai to her own home.

Then Poliahu and her friends of the white mantle threw their cold wave over the chief and his friends and, while they shivered and were chilled almost to the verge of death, appeared before all the people standing in their shining robes of snow, glittering in the glory of the sun. Then, casting once more their cold breath upon the multitude, they disappeared forever from Kauai, returning to their own home on the great mountains of the southern islands.

It may have been before or after this strange legendary courtship that the snow maiden met Pele, the maiden of volcanic fires. Pele loved the holua coasting—the race of sleds, long and narrow, down sloping, grassy hillsides. She usually appeared as a woman of wonderfully beautiful countenance and form—a stranger unknown to any of the different companies entering into the sport. The chiefs of the different districts of the various islands had their favorite meeting places for any sport in which they desired to engage.

There were sheltered places where gambling reigned, or open glades where boxing and spear throwing could best be practiced, or coasts where the splendid surf made riding the waves on surfboards a scene of intoxicating delight. There were hillsides where sled riders had opportunity for the exercise of every atom of skill and strength.

Poliahu and her friends had come down Mauna Kea to a sloping hillside south of Hamakua. Suddenly in their midst appeared a stranger of surpassing beauty. Poliahu welcomed her and the races were continued. Some of the legend tellers think that Pele was angered by the superiority, real or fancied, of Poliahu. The ground began to grow warm and Poliahu knew her enemy.

Pele threw off all disguise and called for the forces of fire to burst open the doors of the subterranean caverns of Mauna Kea. Up toward the mountain she marshalled her fire fountains. Poliahu fled toward the summit. The snow mantle was seized by the outbursting lava and began to burn up. Poliahu grasped the robe, dragging it away and carrying it with her. Soon she regained strength and threw the mantle over the mountain.

There were earthquakes upon earthquakes, shaking the great island from sea to sea. The mountains trembled while the tossing waves of the conflict between fire and snow passed through and over them. Great rock precipices staggered and fell down the sides of the mountains. Clouds gathered over the mountain summit at the call of the snow goddess. Each cloud was gray with frozen moisture and the snows fell deep and fast on the mountain. Farther and farther down the sides the snow mantle unfolded, until it dropped on the very fountains of fire. The lava chilled and hardened and choked the flowing, burning rivers.

Pele's servants became her enemies. The lava, becoming stone, filled up the holes out of which the red melted mass was trying to force itself. Checked and chilled, the lava streams were beaten back into the depths of Mauna Loa and Kilauea. The fire rivers, already rushing to the sea, were narrowed and driven downward so rapidly that they leaped out from the land, becoming immediately the prey of the remorseless ocean.

Thus the ragged mass of laupahoehoe was formed, and the great ledge of the arch of Onomea, and the different sharp and torn lavas in the edge of the sea which mark the various eruptions of centuries past.

Poliahu in legendary battles has met Pele many times. She has kept the upper part of the mountain desolate under her mantle of snow and ice, but down toward the sea, most fertile and luxuriant valleys and hillside slopes attest the gifts of the goddess to the beauty of the island and the welfare of men.

Out of Mauna Loa, Pele has stepped forth again and again, and has hurled eruptions of mighty force and great extent against the maiden of the snow mantle, but the people say that in this battle Pele has been and always will be defeated. Pele's kingdom has been limited to the southern half of the island Hawaii, while the snow maidens rule the territory to the north.

Pele's Long Sleep

PELE and her family dwelt in the beauty of Puna. On a certain day there was a fine, clear atmosphere and Pele saw the splendid surf with its white crests and proposed to her sisters to go down for bathing and surf-riding.

Pele, as the high chiefess of the family, first entered the water and swam far out, then returned, standing on the brink of the curling wave, for the crest was her surfboard, which she rode with great skill. Sometimes her brother, Kamohoalii, the great shark god, in the form of a shark would be her surfboard. Again and again she went out to the deep pit of the waves, her sisters causing the country inland to resound with their acclamation, for she rode as one born of the sea.

At last she came to the beach and, telling the sisters that the kapu on swimming was lifted and they could enter upon their sport, went inland with her youngest sister, Hiiaka, to watch while she slept. They went to a house thatched with ti leaves, a house built for the goddess. There Pele lay down, saying to her sister Hiiaka:

"I will sleep, giving up to the shadows of the falling evening — dropping into the very depths of slumber. Very hard will be this sleep. I am jealous of it. Therefore it is kapu. This is my command to you, O my little one.

Wait you without arousing me nine days and eight nights. Then call me and chant the 'Hulihia'" (a chant supposed to bring life back and revive the body).

Then Pele added: "Perhaps this sleep will be my journey to meet a man — our husband. If I shall meet my lover in my dreams, the sleep will be of great value. I will sleep."

Hiiaka moved softly about the head of her sister Pele, swaying a kahili fringed and beautiful. The perfume of the hala, the fragrance of Keaau, clung to the walls of the house. From that time Puna has been famous as the land fragrant with perfume of the leaves and flowers of the hala tree.

Whenever Pele slept she lost the appearance which she usually assumed, of a beautiful and glorious young woman, surpassing all the other women in the islands. Sleep brought out the aged hag that she really was. Always when any worshipper saw the group of sisters and Pele asleep in their midst, they saw a weary old woman lying in the fire bed in the great crater.

While Pele was sleeping her spirit heard the sound of a hula drum skillfully played, accompanied by a chant sung by a wonderful voice. The spirit of Pele arose from her body and listened to that voice. She thought it was the hula of Laka, who was the goddess of the dance. Then she clearly heard male voices, strong and tender, and a great joy awoke within her, and she listened toward the east, but the hula was not there. Then westward, and there were the rich tones of the beaten drum and the chant. Pele's spirit cried: "The voice of love comes on the wind. I will go and meet it."

Pele then forsook Keaau and went to Hilo, but the drum was not there. She passed from place to place, led by the call of the drum and dance, following it along the palis (precipices) and over the deep ravines, through forest shadows and along rocky beaches, until she came to the upper end of Hawaii. There she heard the call coming across the sea from the island of Maui. Her spirit crossed the channel and listened again. The voices of the dance were louder and clearer and more beautiful.

She passed on from island to island until she came to Kauai, and there the drumbeat and the song of the dance did not die away or change, so she knew she had found the lover desired in her dream.

Pele's spirit now put on the body of strong, healthful youth. Nor was there any blemish in her beauty and symmetry from head to foot. She was anointed with all the fragrant oils of Puna. Her dress was the splendid garland of the red lehua flower and maile leaf and the fern from the dwelling places of the gods. The tender vines of the deep woods veiled this queen of the crater. In glorious young womanhood she went to the halau. The dark body of a great mist enveloped her.

The drum and the voice had led her to Haena, Kauai, to the house of Lohiau, the highborn chief of that island. The house for dancing was long, and was beautifully draped with mats of all kinds. It was full of chiefs engaged in the sports of that time. The common people were gathered outside the house of the chief.

The multitude saw a glorious young woman step out of the mist. Then they raised a great shout, praising her with strong voices. It seemed as if the queen of sunrise had summoned the beauty of the morning to rest upon her. The countenance of Pele was like the clearest and gentlest moonlight. The people made a vacant space for the passage of this wonderful stranger, casting themselves on the ground before her.

An ancient chant says:

O the passing of that beautiful woman.
Silent are the voices on the plain.
No medley of the birds is in the forest;
There is quiet, resting in peace.

Pele entered the long house, passed by the place of the drums, and seated herself on a restingplace of soft royal mats.

The chiefs were astonished, and after a long time

asked her if she came from the far-off sunrise of foreign lands.

Pele replied, smiling, "Ka! I belong to Kauai."

Lohiau, the high chief, said: "O stranger, child of a journey, you speak in riddles. I know Kauai from harbor to clustered hills, and my eyes have never seen any woman like you."

"Ka!" said Pele, "the place where you did not stop, there I was."

But Lohiau refused her thought, and asked her to tell truly whence she had come. At last Pele acknowledged that she had come from Puna, Hawaii, "the place beloved by the sunrise at Haehae."

The chiefs urged her to join them in a feast, but she refused, saying she had recently eaten and was satisfied, but she "was hungry for the hula — the voices and the drum."

Then Lohiau told her that her welcome was all that he could give. "For me is the island, inland, seaward, and all around Kauai. This is your place. The home you have in Puna you will think you see again in Kauai. The name of my house for you is Ha-laau-ola" (Tree of Life).

Pele replied: "The name of your house is beautiful. My home in Puna is Mauli-ola (Long Life). I will accept this house of yours."

Lohiau watched her while he partook of the feast with his chiefs, and she was resting on the couch of mats. He was thinking of her marvelous, restful beauty, as given in the ancient chant known as "Lei Mauna Loa."

Lei of Mauna Loa, beautiful to look upon.
The mountain honored by the winds.
Known by the peaceful motion.
Calm becomes the whirlwind.
Beautiful is the sun upon the plain.
Dark-leaved the trees in the midst of the hot sun.
Heat rising from the face of the moist lava.
The sunrise mist lying on the grass,

Free from the care of the strong wind.
The bird returns to rest at Palaau.
He who owns the right to sleep is at Palaau.
I am alive for your love —
For you indeed.

Then Lohiau proposed to his chiefs that he should take this beautiful chiefess from Kauai as his queen, and his thought seemed good to all. Turning to Pele, he offered himself as her husband and was accepted.

Then Lohiau arose and ordered the sports to cease while they all slept. Pele and Lohiau were married and dwelt together several days, according to the custom of the ancient time.

After this time had passed Lohiau planned another great feast and a day for the hula dance and the many sports of the people. When they came together, beautiful were the dances and sweet the voices of Lohiau and his aikane (closest friend).

Three of the women of Kauai who were known as "the guardians of Haena" had come into the halau and taken their places near Lohiau. The people greeted their coming with great applause, for they were very beautiful and were also possessed of supernatural power. Their beauty was like that of Pele save for the paleness of their skins, which had come from their power to appear in different forms, according to their pleasure. They were female mo-o, or dragons. Their human beauty was enhanced by their garments of ferns and leaves and flowers.

Pele had told Lohiau of their coming and had charged him in these words: "Remember, you have been set apart for me. Remember, and know our companionship. Therefore I place upon you my law, 'Ke kai okia' (Cut off by the sea) are you — separated from all for me."

Lohiau looked on these beautiful women. The chief of the women, Kilinoe, was the most interesting. She refused to eat while others partook of a feast before the dancing should begin, and sat watching carefully with large, bright, shining eyes the face of Lohiau, using magic power to make him pay attention to her charms. Pele did not wish these women to know her, so placed a shadow between them and her so that they looked upon her as through a mist.

Some legends say that Pele danced the Hula of the Winds of Kauai, calling their names until strong winds blew and storms of rain beat upon the house in which the chiefs were assembled, driving the common people to their homes.

There the chiefs took their hula drums and sat down, preparing to play for the dancers. Then up rose Kilinoe and, taking ferns and flowers from her skirts, made fragrant wreaths wherewith to crown Lohiau and his fellow hula drummers, expecting the chief to see her beauty and take her for his companion. But the law of Pele was upon him and he called to her for a chant before the dance should commence.

Pele threw aside her shadow garments and came out clothed in her beautiful pa-u (skirt) and fragrant with the perfumes of Puna. She said, "It is not for me to give an olioli mele (a chant) for your native dance, but I will call the guardian winds of your islands Niihau and Kauai, O Lohiau, and they will answer my call."

Then she called for the gods who came to Hawaii; the gods of her old home now known through all Polynesia; the great gods Lono and his brothers, coming in the winds of heaven. Then she called on all the noted winds of the island Niihau, stating the directions from which they came, the points of land struck when they touched the island and their gentleness or wrath, their weakness or power, and their helpfulness or destructiveness.

For a long time she chanted, calling wind after wind, and while she sang, soft breezes blew around and through the house. Then came stronger winds whistling through the trees outside. As the voice of the singer rose or fell, so also danced the winds in strict harmony. While she sang, the people outside the house cried out, "The sea grows rough and white, the waves are tossed by strong winds and clouds are flying, the winds are gathering the clouds and twisting the heavens."

But one of the dragon women sitting near Lohiau said: "The noise you think is from the sea or rustling through the leaves of the trees is only the sound of the people talking outside the great building. Their murmur is like the voice of the wind."

Then Pele chanted for the return of the winds to Niihau and its small islands, and the day was at peace as the voice of the singer softened toward the end of the chant. Hushed were the people and wondering were the eyes turned upon Pele by the chiefs who were seated in the great halau. Pele leaned on her couch of soft mats and rested.

Very angry was Kilinoe, the dragon woman. Full of fire were her eyes and dark was her face with hot blood, but she only said: "You have seen Niihau. Perhaps also you know the winds of Kauai." By giving this challenge she thought she would overthrow the power of Pele over Lohiau. She did not know who Pele was, but supposed she was one of the women of high rank native to Kauai.

Pele again chanted, calling for the guardian winds of the island Kauai:

O Kauai, great island of the lehua,
Island moving in the ocean,
Island moving from Tahiti,
Let the winds rattle the branches to Hawaii.
Let them point to the eye of the sun.
There is the wind of Kane at sunset —
The hard night wind for Kauai.

Then she called for kite-flying winds when the birds sport in the heavens and the surf lies quiet on incoming waves, and then she sang of the winds kolonahe, softly blowing; and the winds hunahuna, breaking into fragments; and the winds which carry the mist, the sprinkling shower, the falling rain and the severe storm; the winds which touch the mountaintops and those which creep along the edge of the precipices, holding on by their fingers; and those which dash over the plains and along the sea beach, blowing the waves into mist.

Then she chanted how the caves in the seacoast were opened and the guardians of the winds lifted their calabashes and let loose evil winds, angry and destructive, to sweep over the homes of the people and tear in pieces their fruit trees and houses. Then Pele's voice rang out while she made known the character of the beautiful dragon women, the guardians of the caves of Haena, calling them the mocking winds of Haena.

The people did not understand, but the dragon women knew that Pele only needed to point them out as they sat near Lohiau, to have all the chiefs cry out against them in scorn. Out of the house they rushed, fleeing back to their home in the caves.

When Pele ceased chanting, winds without number began to come near, scraping over the land. The surf on the reef was roaring. The white sand of the beach rose up. Thunder followed the rolling, rumbling tongue of branching lightning. Mist crept over the precipices. Running water poured down the face of the cliffs. Red water and white water fled seaward, and the stormy heart of the ocean rose in tumbled heaps. The people rushed to their homes. The chiefs hastened from the house of pleasure. The feast and the day of dancing were broken up. Lohiau said to Pele: "How great indeed have been your true words, telling the evil of this day. Here have come the winds and destructive storms of Haena. Truly this land has had evil today."

When Pele had laid herself down on the soft mats of Puna for her long sleep, she had charged her little sister, who had been carried in her bosom, to wake her if she had not returned to life before nine days were past.

The days were almost through to the last moment when Lohiau lamented the evil which his land had felt. Then as the winds died away and the last strong gust journeyed out toward the sea, Pele heard Hiiaka's voice calling from the island Hawaii in the magic chant Pele had told her to use to call her back to life.

Hearing this arousing call, she bowed her head and wept. After a time she said to Lohiau: "It is not for me to remain here in pleasure with you. I must return because of the call of my sister. Your care is to obey my law, which is upon you. Calm will take the place of the storm, the winds will be quiet, the sea will ebb peacefully, cascades will murmur on the mountainsides, and sweet flowers will be among the leaves. I will send my little sister; then come quickly to my home in Puna."

Hiiaka knew that the time had come when she must arouse her goddess sister from that deep sleep. So she commenced the incantation which Pele told her to use. It would call the wandering spirit back to its home, no matter where it might have gone. This incantation was known as "hulihia ke au" (the current is turning). This was a call carried by the spirit power of the one who uttered it into faraway places to the very person for whom it was intended. The closing lines of the incantation were a personal appeal to Pele to awake.

"*E Pele e! The milky way turns.*
E Pele e! The night changes.
E Pele e! The red glow is on the island.
E Pele e! The red dawn breaks.
E Pele e! Shadows are cast by the sunlight.
E Pele e! The sound of roaring is in your crater.
E Pele e! The uhi-uha is in your crater (this means the sound of
wash of lava is in the crater).
E Pele e! Awake, arise, return."

The spirit of Pele heard the wind, Naue, passing down to the sea, and soon came the call of Hiiaka over the waters. Then she bowed down her head and wept.

When Lohiau saw the tears pouring down the face of his wife, he asked why in this time of gladness she wept.

For a long time she did not reply. Then she spoke of the winds with which she had danced that night—the guardians of Niihau and Kauai, a people listening to her call, under the ruler of all the winds, the great Lono, dwelling on the waters.

Then she said: "You are my husband and I am your wife, but the call has come and I cannot remain with you. I will return to my land—to the fragrant blossoms of the hala, but I will send one of my younger sisters to come after you. Before I forsook my land for Kauai, I put a charge upon my young sister to call me before nine days and nights had passed. Now I hear this call and I must not abide by the great longing of your thought."

Then the queen of fire ceased speaking and began to be lost to Lohiau, who was marveling greatly at the fading away of his loved one. As Pele disappeared, peace came to him and all the land of Kauai was filled with calm and rest.

Pele's spirit passed at once to the body lying in the house thatched with ti leaves in Puna. Soon she arose and told Hiiaka to call the sisters from the sea and they would go inland.

Then they gathered around the house in which Pele had slept. Pele told them they must dance the hula of the lifted kapu, and asked them, one after the other, to dance, but they all refused until she came to Hiiaka, who had guarded her during her long sleep. Hiiaka desired to go down to the beach and bathe with a friend, Hopoe, while the others went inland.

Pele said, "You cannot go unless you first dance for the lifted kapu."

Hiiaka arose and danced gloriously before the hula god and chanted while she danced—

Puna dances in the wind.
The forest of Keaau is shaken.
Haena moves quietly.
There is motion on the beach of Nanahuki.
The hula-lea danced by the wife,
Dancing with the sea of Nanahuki.
Perhaps this is a dance of love,
For the friend loved in the sleep.

Pele rejoiced over the skill of her younger sister and was surprised by the chanted reference to the experiences at Haena. She granted permission to Hiiaka to remain by the sea with her friend Hopoe, bathing and surfriding until a messenger should be sent to call her home to Kilauea. Then Pele and the other sisters went inland.

Hopoe, the Dancing Stone

Moving back and forth in the wind,
Softly moving in the quiet breeze,
Rocking by the side of the sea.

ON THE southeastern seacoast of the island of Hawaii, near a hamlet called Keaau, is a large stone which was formerly so balanced that it could be easily moved. One of the severe earthquake shocks of the last century overthrew the stone, and it now lies a great black mass of lava rock near the seashore.

This stone in the long ago was called by the natives Hopoe, because Hopoe, the graceful dancer of Puna who taught Hiiaka, the youngest sister of Pele, how to dance, was changed into this rock. The story of the jealousy and anger of Pele, which resulted in overwhelming Hopoe in a flood of lava and placing her in the form of a balanced rock to dance by the sea to the music of the eternally moving surf, is a story which must be kept on record for the lovers of Hawaiian folklore.

Pele had come from the islands of the South Seas and had found the Hawaiian Islands as they are at the present day. After visiting all the other islands she settled in Puna, on the large island of Hawaii. There she had her long sleep, in which she went to the island of Kauai and found her lover Lohiau, whom she promised to send for that he might come to her home in the volcano of Kilauea.

Pele called her sisters one by one and told them to go to Kauai, but they feared the uncertainty of Pele's jealousy and wrath and refused to go. At last she called for Hiiaka, but she was down by the seashore with her friend Hopoe. There in a beautiful garden spot grew the fine food plants of the old Hawaiians. There were ohias (mountain apples) and the brilliant red, feathery blossoms of the lehua trees, and there grew the hala, from which sweet-scented skirts and mats were woven.

Hopoe was very graceful and knew all the dances of the ancient people. Hour after hour she taught Hiiaka the oldest hulas known among the Hawaiians until Hiiaka excelled in all beautiful motions of the human form. Hopoe taught Hiiaka how to make leis from the most fragrant and splendid flowers. Together they went out into the white-capped waves, bathing and swimming and seeking the fish of the coral caves. Thus they learned to have great love for each other. The girl from the South Seas promised to care for the Hawaiian girl whose home was in the midst of volcanic fires, and the Hawaiian gave pledge to aid and serve as best she could.

Together they were making life happy when Pele called for Hiiaka. Out from the fumes of the crater, echoing from hill to hill through Puna, rustling the leaves of the forest trees, that insistent voice came to the younger sister.

Hiiaka by her magic power quickly passed from the seashore to the volcano. Some of the native legends say that Pele had slept near the seashore where she had commenced to build a volcanic home for herself and her sisters, and that while longing for the coming of her lover Lohiau she had dug feverishly, throwing up hills and digging some of the many pit craters which are famous in the district of Puna.

At last she determined to visit Ai-laau, the god residing in Kilauea, but he had fled from her and she had taken his place and found a home in the earthquake-shaken pit of molten lava, leaping fire, and overwhelming sulphur smoke. Here she felt that her burning love could wait no longer and she must send for Lohiau.

To her came Hiiaka fresh from the clear waters of the sea and covered with leis made by her friend Hopoe. For a few minutes she stood before her sisters. Then, untwisting the wreaths one by one, she danced until all the household seemed to be overcome by her grace and gladness. She sent the influence of her goodwill deep into the hearts of her sisters.

Pele alone looked on with scowling, dissatisfied face. As soon as she could she said to Hiiaka: "Go far away; go to Kauai; get a husband for us, and bring him to Hawaii. Do not marry him. Do not even embrace him. He is kapu to you. Go forty days only—no longer for going or coming back.

Hiiaka looked upon the imperious goddess of fire and said: "That is right. I go after your husband but I lay my charge upon you: You must take care of my lehua forest and not permit it to be injured. You may eat all other places of ours, but you must not touch my own lehua grove, my delight. You will be waiting here. Anger will arise in you. You will destroy inland; you will destroy toward the sea; but you must not touch my friend—my Hopoe. You will eat Puna with your burning wrath, but you must not go near Hopoe. This is my covenant with you, O Pele."

Pele replied: "This is right; I will care for your forest and your friend. Go you for our husband." As Pele had charged Hiiaka, so had Hiiaka laid her commandment on Pele. Hiiaka, like the other sisters, knew how uncertain Pele was in all her moods and how suddenly and unexpectedly her wrath would bring destruction upon anything appearing to oppose her. Therefore she laid upon Pele the responsibility for and protecting Hopoe. This was ceremonial oath-taking between the two.

Hiiaka rose to prepare for the journey, but Pele's impatience at every moment's delay was so great that she forced Hiiaka away without food or extra clothing. Hiiaka slowly went forth catching only a magic pa-u, or skirt, which had the death-dealing power of flashing lightning.

As she climbed the walls of the crater, she looked down on her sisters and chanted:

The traveler is ready to go for the loved one,
The husband of the dream.
I stand, I journey while you remain,
O women with bowed heads.
O my lehua forest — inland at Kaliu.
The longing traveler journeys many days
For the lover of the sweet dreams,
    For Lohiau ipo.

When Pele heard this chant from the forgiving love of her little sister, she relented somewhat and gave Hiiaka a portion of her divine power with which to wage battle against the demons and dragons and sorcerers innumerable whom she would meet in her journey. She also sent Pauopalae, the woman of supernatural power who cared for the ferns of all kinds around the volcano, to be her companion.

As Hiiaka went up to the highlands above the volcano, she looked down over Puna. Smoke from the volcano fell toward the sea, making dark the forest along the path to Keaau, where Hopoe dwelt. Hiiaka, with a heavy heart, went on her journey, fearing that this smoke might be prophetic of the wrath of the goddess of fire, visited at the suggestion of some sudden jealousy or suspicion upon Hopoe and her household.

What the Hawaiians called mana, or supernatural power able to manifest itself in many ways, had come upon Hiiaka. She found this power growing within her as she overcame obstacle after obstacle in the progress of her journey. Thus Hiiaka, from time to time as she passed over the mountains of the different islands, was able to look back over the dearly loved land of Puna.

At last she saw the smoke, which had clouded the forests along the way to the home of her friend, grow darker and blacker and then change into the orange hues of outbreaking fire. She felt Pele's unfaithfulness and chanted:

The smoke bends over Kaliu.
I thought my lehuas were tabu.
The birds of fire are eating them up.
They are picking my lehuas
Until they are gone.

Then from that far-off island of Kauai she looked over her burning forest toward the sea and again chanted:

O my friend of the steep ridges above Keaau,
My friend who made garlands
Of the lehua blossoms of Kaliu,
Hopoe is driven away to the sea —
The sea of Lanahiku.

Fiercer and more devouring were the lava floods hurled out over the forest so loved by Hiiaka. Heavier were the earthquake shocks shaking all the country around the volcano. Then Hiiaka bowed her head and said:

Puna is shaking in the wind,
Shaking is the hala grove of Keaau.
Tumbling are Haena and Hopoe,
Moving is the land — moving is the sea.

Thus by her spirit-power she looked back to Hawaii and saw Puna devastated and the land covered by the destructive floods of lava sent out by Pele.

Hopoe was the last object of Pele's anger at her younger sister, but there was no escape. The slow torrent of lava surrounded the beach where Hopoe waited death. She placed the garlands Hiiaka had loved over her head and shoulders. She wore the finest skirt she had woven from lauhala leaves. She looked out over the death-dealing seas into which she could not flee, and then began the dance of death.

There Pele's fires caught her but did not devour her.

The angry goddess of fire took away her human life and gave her goblin power. Pele changed Hopoe into a great block of lava and balanced it on the seashore. Thus Hopoe was able to dance when the winds blew or the earth shook, or some human hand touched her and disturbed her delicate poise. It is said that for centuries she has been the dancing stone of Puna.

Hiiaka fulfilled her mission patiently and faithfully, bringing Lohiau even from a grave in which he had been placed back to life, and at last presenting him before Pele, although all along the journey she was filled with bitterness because of the injustice of Pele in dealing death to Hopoe.

Hiiaka's Battle with Demons

HIIAKA, the youngest sister of Pele, the goddess of fire, is the central figure of many a beautiful Hawaiian myth. She was sent on a wearisome journey over all the islands to find Lohiau, the lover of Pele.

Out of the fire-pit of the volcano of Kilauea she climbed. Through a multitude of cracks and holes, out of which poured fumes of foul gases, she threaded her way until she stood on the highest plateau of lava the volcano had been able to build.

Pele was impatient and angry at the slow progress of Hiiaka and at first ordered her to hasten alone on her journey, but as she saw her patiently climbing along the rough way, she relented and gave to her supernatural power to aid in overcoming great difficulties, as well as a magic skirt which had the power of lightning in its folds. But she saw that this was not enough. She called on the divine guardians of plants to come with garments and bear a burden of skirts with which to drape Hiiaka on her journey. At last the goddess of ferns, Pau-o-palae, came with a skirt of ferns which pleased Pele. It was thrown over Hiiaka, the most beautiful drapery which could be provided.

Pau-o-palae was clothed with a network of most delicate ferns. She was noted because of her magic power over all the ferns of the forest, and for her skill in using the most graceful fronds for clothing and garlands.

Pele ordered Pau-o-palae to go with Hiiaka as her kahu, or guardian servant. She was very beautiful in her fern skirt and garland, but Hiiaka was of higher birth and nobler form and was more royal in her beauty than her follower, the goddess of ferns. It was a queen of highest legendary honor, with one of her most worthy attendants, setting forth on a strange quest through lands abounding in dangers and adventures.

Everywhere in ancient Hawaii were eepas, kupuas, and mo-os. Eepas were the deformed inhabitants of the Hawaiian gnomeland. They were twisted and defective in mind and body. They were the deceitful, treacherous fairies, living in the most beautiful places of the forest or glen, often appearing as human beings but always having some defect in some part of the body. Kupuas were gnomes or elves of supernatural power, able to appear in some nature form as well as like a human being. They came to the Hawaiian Islands only as the legendary memories of the crocodiles and great snakes of the lands from which the first Hawaiian natives emigrated.

Throughout Polynesia the mo-o, or moko, remained for centuries in the minds of the natives of different island groups as their most dreadful enemy, living in deep pools and sluggish streams.

Hiiaka's first test of patient endurance came in a battle with the kupuas of a forest lying between the volcano and the ocean.

The land of the island of Hawaii slopes down from the raging fire-pit, mile after mile, through dense tropical forests and shining lava beds, until it enfolds, in black lava shores, the ceaselessly moving waters of the bay of Hilo. In this forest dwelt Pana-ewa, a reptile man. He was very strong and could make the change in a moment. He watched the paths through the forest, hoping to catch strangers, robbing them and sometimes devouring them. Some he permitted to pass, but for others he made much trouble, bringing fog and rain and wind until the road was lost to them.

He ruled all the evil forces of the forest above Hilo. Every wicked sprite who twisted vines to make men stumble over precipices or fall into deep lava caves was his servant. Every demon wind, every foul fiend dwelling in dangerous branches of falling trees, every wicked gnome whirling clouds of dust or fog and wrapping them around a traveler, in fact every living thing which could in any way injure a traveler was his loyal subject. He was the kupua chief of the vicious sprites and cruel elves of the forest above Hilo. Those who knew about Pana-ewa brought offerings of awa to drink, taro and red fish to eat, tapa for mats, and malos, or girdles. Then the way was free from trouble.

There were two bird-brothers of Pana-ewa; very little birds, swift as a flash of lightning, giving notice of any one coming through the forest of Pana-ewa.

Hiiaka, entering the forest, threw aside her fern robes, revealing her beautiful form. Two birds flew around her and before her. One called to the other, "This is one of the women of ka lua (the pit)." The other answered, "She is not as strong as Pana-ewa; let us tell our brother."

Hiiaka heard the birds and laughed; then she chanted, and her voice rang through all the forest:

Pana-ewa is a great lehua island;
A forest of ohias inland.
Fallen are the red flowers of the lehua,
Spoiled are the red apples of the ohia,
Bald is the head of Pana-ewa;
Smoke is over the land;
The fire is burning.

71

Hiiaka hoped to make Pana-ewa angry by reminding him of seasons of destruction by lava eruptions, which left bald lava spots in the midst of the upland forest.

Pana-ewa, roused by his bird watchmen and stirred by the taunt of Hiiaka, said: "This is Hiiaka, who shall be killed by me. I will swallow her. There is no road for her to pass."

The old Hawaiians said that Pana-ewa had many bodies. He attacked Hiiaka in his fog body, Kino-ohu, and threw around her his twisting fog-arms, chilling her and choking her and blinding her. He wrapped her in the severe cold mantle of heavy mists.

Hiiaka told her friend to hold fast to her girdle while she led the way, sweeping aside the fog with her magic skirt. Then Pana-ewa took his body called the bitter rain, ua-awa, the cold freezing rain which pinches and shrivels the skin. He called also for the strong winds to bend down trees and smite his enemy, and lie in tangled masses in her path. So the way was hard.

Hiiaka swiftly swept her lightning skirt up against the beating rain and drove it back. Again and again she struck against the fierce storm and against the destructive winds. Sometimes she was beaten back, sometimes her arms were so weary that she could scarcely move her skirt; but she hurled it over and over against the storm until she drove it deeper into the forest and gained a little time for rest and renewal of strength.

On she went into the tangled woods, and the gods of the forest rose up against her. They tangled her feet with vines. They struck her with branches of trees. The forest birds in multitudes screamed around her, dashed against her, tried to pick out her eyes and confuse her every effort. The god and his followers brought all their power and enchantments against Hiiaka. Hiiaka made an incantation against these enemies:

Night is at Pana-ewa and bitter is the storm;
The branches of the trees are bent down;

> Rattling are the flowers and leaves of the lehua;
> Angrily growls the god Pana-ewa,
> Stirred up inside by his wrath.
> Oh, Pana-ewa!
> I give you hurt,
> Behold, I give the hard blows of battle.

She told her friend to stay far back in the places already conquered, while she fought with a bamboo knife in one hand and her lightning skirt in the other. Harsh noises were on every hand. From each side she was beaten and sometimes almost crushed under the weight of her opponents. Many she cut down with her bamboo knife and many she struck with her lightning skirt. The two little birds flew over the battlefield and saw Hiiaka nearly dead from wounds and weariness, and their own gods of the forest lying as if asleep. They called to Pana-ewa:

> Our gods are tired from fighting,
> They sleep and rest.

Pana-ewa came and looked at them. He saw that they were dead without showing deep injury, and wondered how they had been killed. The birds said, "We saw her skirt moving against the gods, up and down, back and forth."

Again the hosts of that forest gathered around the young chiefess. Again she struggled bitterly against the multitudes of foes, but she was very, very tired, and her arms sometimes refused to lift her knife and skirt. The discouraged woman felt that the battle was going against her, so she called for Pele, the goddess of fire.

Pele heard the noise of the conflict and the voice of her sister. She called for a body of her own servants to go down and fight the powerful kupua.

The Hawaiian legends give the name Ho-ai-ku to these reinforcements. This means "standing for food" or "devourers." Lightning storms were hurled against Pana-ewa, flashing and cutting and eating all the gods of the forest.

Hiiaka in her weariness sank down among the foes she had slain.

The two little birds saw her fall and called to Pana-ewa to go and take the one he had said he would "swallow." He rushed to the place where she lay. She saw him coming and wearily arose to give battle once more.

A great thunderstorm swept down on Pana-ewa. As he had fought Hiiaka with the cold forest winds, so Pele fought him with the storms from the pit of fire. Lightning drove him down through the forest. A mighty rain filled the valleys with red water. The kupuas were swept down the river beds and out into the ocean, where Pana-ewa and the remnant of his followers were devoured by the sharks.

The Ho-ai-ku, as the legends say, went down and swallowed Pana-ewa, eating him up. Thus the land above Hilo became a safe place for the common people. To this day it is known by the name Pana-ewa.

How Hiiaka Found Wahine-omao

THE STORY of the journey of the youngest sister of Pele, the goddess of volcanic fires, when seeking a husband for her oldest sister, has a simple and yet exceedingly human element in the incidents which cluster around the finding of a faithful follower and friend. It is a story of two girls attracted to each other by lovable qualities. Hiiaka was a goddess with an attendant from the old Hawaiian fairyland — the Guardian of the Ferns. Then there was added the human helper, Wahine-omao, or "the light-colored woman."

While Hiiaka was journeying through the lower part of the forest which she had freed from demons, the Guardian of Ferns said: "I hear the grunting of a pig, but cannot tell whether it is before us or on one side. Where is it — from the sea or inland?"

Hiiaka said: "This is a pig from the sea. It is the humu-humu-nukunuku-a-puaa. It is the grunting, angular pigfish. There is also a pig from the land. There are two pigs. They are before us. They belong to a woman and are for a gift — a sacrifice to the sister goddess who is over us two. This is Wahine-omao."

They walked on through the restful shadows of the forest and soon met a beautiful woman carrying a little black pig and a striped, angular fish. Humuhumu means "grunting." Nukunuku means "cornered." Puaa means "pig." The humuhumu-nukunuku-a-puaa was a fish with a sharp-pointed back, grunting like a pig. It was the fish into which the fabled demi-god Kamapuaa changed himself when fleeing from the destructive fires of Pele.

Hiiaka greeted the stranger, "Love to you, O Wahine-omao."

The woman replied: "It is strange that you two have my name while your eyes are unknown to me. What are your names and where do you go?"

The sister of Pele concealed their names. "I am Ku, and Ka is the name of my friend. A troublesome journey is before us beyond the waters of Hilo and the kupuas (demons) dwelling there and along the hard paths over the cliffs of the seacoast even to the steady blowing winds of Kohala."

The newcomer looked longingly into the eyes of the young chiefess and said: "I have a great desire for that troublesome journey, but this pig is a sacrifice for the goddess of the crater. Shall I throw away the pig and go with you?"

Hiiaka told her to hurry on, saying: "If your purpose is strong to go with us, take your sacrifice pig to the woman of the pit. Then come quickly after us. You will find us. While you go say continually, 'O Ku! O Ka! O Ku! O Ka!' When you arrive at the pit throw the pig down into the fire and return quickly, saying, 'O Ku! O Ka!' until you find us."

The woman said: "I will surely remember your words,

but you are so beautiful and have such power that I think you are Pele. Take my pig now and end my trouble." Then she started to throw herself and her offerings on the ground before Hiiaka.

Hiiaka forbade this and explained that the offering must be taken as had been vowed.

Then the woman took her sacred gifts and went up through the woods to the crater, saying over and over, "O Ku! O Ka!" all the time realizing that the new activity and life were coming to her and that she was moving as swiftly as the wind. In a little while she stood on the high point above the crater called Kolea—the place where birds rested. Before her lay a great circular plain, black-walled, full of burning lava leaping up in wonderful fire-dances and boiling violently around a group of beautiful women. She called to Pele:

> E Pele e! Here is my sacrifice—a pig.
> E Pele e! Here is my gift—a pig.
> Here is a pig for you.
> O goddess of the burning stones.
> Life for me. Life for you.
> The flowers of fire wave gently.
> Here is your pig.

The woman threw the pig and the fish over the edge into the mystic fires beneath and leaned over, looking down into the deadliness of the fire and smoke which received the sacrifice. Flaming hands leaped up, caught the gifts, and drew them down under the red surface. But in a moment there was a rush upward of a fountain of lava, and hurled up with it she saw the body of the little black pig tossing in the changing jets of fire.

Down it went again into the whirling, groaning fires of the underworld. Then she knew that the sacrifice had been accepted and that she was free from her vow of service to Pele. Every kapu upon her free action had been removed and she was free—free to do according to her own wish. Then she saw one of the women of the pit slowly changing into an old woman lying on a mat of fire apart from the others. It was Pele, who was always growing more and more jealous and angry with Hiiaka.

Pele called from the pit of fire, "O woman! Have you seen two travelers?"

When she learned that they had been seen going on their journey, she charged her new worshipper to go with Hiiaka and always spy upon her movements.

Wahine-omao became angry and cried out: "When I came here I thought you were beautiful with the glory of fire resting on you. Your sisters are beautiful, but you are a harsh old woman. Your eyes are red. Your eyebrows and hair are burned. You are the woman with the scorched eyelids." Then she ran from the crater, saying, "O Ku! O Ka!" Her feet seemed to be placed on a swift-moving cloud, and in a few moments she was dropped by the side of Hiiaka.

The three women — Hiiaka, the powerful; Pau-o-palae, the fairy of the ferns; and Wahine-omao, the brave and beautiful young woman of the forest — went on toward Hilo. They came to a grove of ohia, or native apple, trees, and the new friend begged them to rest for a little while in this place, for it was her father's home.

Hiiaka hesitated, saying: "I am afraid that you would entangle me, O friend! Someone is waiting below whom I must see. Our journey cannot end."

"Oh," said the woman, "I intend not to stay. Stepping sideways was my thought, to see my family dwelling in this house — then journey on."

They turned aside through the red-fruited, tall ohia trees to a resting-place called Papa-lau-ahi, or the fireleaf of lava spread out flat like a board. This has always been a resting-place for travelers coming across the island to Hilo Bay. There they greeted friends and rested, but Hiiaka thought lovingly of another friend, Hopoe, far dearer to her than anyone else. Tears rolled down her cheeks.

Wahine-omao said, "Why do you weep, O friend?" The reply came: "Because of my friend who lives over by that sea far below us. The smoke of the fire-anger of our sister-lord is falling over toward my friend Hopoe."

Wahine-omao said: "One of our people truly lives over there. We know and love her well, but her name is Nana-huki. The name is given because when looking at you her eyes are like a cord pulling you to her."

"Yes," said Hiiaka, "that is her name, but for me she had the sweet-scented hala wreaths and the beautiful wreaths of the red blossoms of the lehua and baskets of the most delicious treasures of the sea. So my name for her is Hopoe."

The name Hopoe may mean "one encircled," as with leis, or wreaths, or as with loving arms, or possibly it might convey the idea of one set apart in a special class or company. Both thoughts might well be included in the deep love of the young goddess for a human friend.

The time came for the three women to hasten on their way. The final alohas were said. The friends rubbed noses in the old Hawaiian way and went down to Hilo.

Hiiaka looked again from the upland over to the distant seacoast and wailed:

> My journey opens to Kauai.
> Loving is my thought for my aikane,
> My bosom friend —
> Hopoe — my sweet-scented hala.
> Far will we go;
> Broad is the land;
> Perhaps Kauai is the end.

Thus Hiiaka sent her loving thoughts over forest and rugged lava plains to her dearest friend, even while she opened her heart to another friend who served her with the utmost faithfulness and love all the rest of her eventful journey.

Hiiaka Catching a Ghost

HIIAKA, the sister of Pele; the goddess of ferns; and their new friend, Wahine-omao, were hastening through the forests above the bay of Hilo. They came near a native house. Two girls were lying on a mat near the doorway. The girls saw the strangers and with hearts full of hospitality cried: "O women strangers, stop at our house and eat. Here are dried fish and the kilu-ai (a-little-calabash-full-of-poi, the native food)." It was all the food the girls had, but they offered it gladly.

Hiiaka said: "One of us will stop and eat. Two of us will pass on. We are not hungry." The truth was that Wahine-omao of the light skin needed food like anyone not possessing semi-divine powers.

So Wahine-omao stopped and ate. She saw that the girls were kupilikia (stirred-up-with-anxiety) and asked them why they were troubled.

"Our father," they said, "went to the sea to fish in the night and has not returned. We fear that he is in trouble."

Hiiaka heard the words and looked toward the sea. She saw the spirit of that man coming up from the beach with an ipu-holoholona (a-calabash-for-carrying-fish-lines) in his hands.

She charged the girls to listen carefully while she told them about their father, saying: "You must not let tears fall or wailing tones come into your voices. Your father has been drowned in the sea during the dark night. The canoe filled with water. The swift-beating waters drove your father on to the reef of coral and there his body lies. The spirit was returning home, but now sees strangers and is turning aside. I will go and chase that spirit from place to place until it goes back to the place where it left its house — the body supposed to be dead. Let no one eat until my work is done."

Hiiaka looked again toward the sea. The spirit was

wandering aimlessly from place to place with its calabash thrown over its shoulder. It was afraid to come near the strangers and yet did not want to go back to the body. Hiiaka hastened after the ghost and drove it toward the house where the girls were living. She checked it as it turned to either side and tried to dash away into the forest. She pushed it into the door and called the girls in. They saw the ghost as if it were the natural body. They wept and began to beseech Hiiaka to bring him back to life.

She told them she would try, but they must remember to keep the bundle of tears inside the eyes. She told them that the spirit must take her to the body and they must wait until the rainbow colors of a divine chief came over their house. Then they would know that their father was alive. But if a heavy rain should fall they would know he was not alive and need not restrain their cries.

As Hiiaka rose to pass out of the door, the ghost leaped and disappeared. Hiiaka rushed out and saw the ghost run to the sea. She leaped after it and followed it to a great stone lying at the foot of a steep precipice. There the heana (dead body) was lying. It was badly torn by the rough coral and the face had been bitten by eels. Around it lay the broken pieces of the shattered canoe. Hiiaka washed the body in the sea and then turned to look for the ghost, but it was running away as if carried by a whirlwind.

Hiiaka thrust out her "strong hand of Kilauea." This meant her power as one of the divine family living in the fire of the volcano. She thrust forth this power and turned the spirit back to the place where the body was lying. She drove the ghost to the side of the body and ordered it to enter, but the ghost thought that it would be a brighter and happier life if it could be free among the blossoming trees and fragrant ferns of the forest. It tried again to slip away from the house in which it had lived.

Hiiaka slapped the ghost back against the body and told it to go in at the bottom of a foot. She slapped the feet again and again, but it was very hard to push the ghost inside. It tried to come out as fast as Hiiaka pushed it in. Then Hiiaka uttered an incantation, while she struck the feet and limbs. The incantation was a call for the gift of life from her friends of the volcano.

O the top of Kilauea!
O the five ledges of the pit!
The kapu fire of the woman.
When the heavens shake,
When the earth cracks open (earthquakes),
Man is thrown down,
Lying on the ground.
The lightning of Kane (a great god) wakes up.
Kane of the night, going fast.
My sleep is broken up.
E ala e! Wake up!
The heaven wakes up.
The earth inland is awake.
The sea is awake.
 Awake you!
 Here am I.

By the time this chant was ended Hiiaka had forced the ghost up to the hips. There was a hard struggle — the ghost trying to go back and yet yielding to the slapping and going further and further into the body.

Then Hiiaka put forth her hand and took fresh water, pouring it over the body, chanting again:

I make you grow, O Kane!
Hiiaka is the prophet.
This work is hers.
She makes the growth.
Here is the water of life.
E ala e! Awake! Arise!
Let life return.
The kapu (of death) is over.
It is lifted,
It has flown away.

These were ancient chants for the restoration of life.

All this time she was slapping and pounding the spirit into the body. It had gone up as far as the chest. Then she took more fresh water and poured it over the eyes, dashing it into the face. The ghost leaped up to the mouth and eyes — choking noises were made — the eyes opened faintly and closed again, but the ghost was entirely in the body. Slowly life returned. The lips opened and breath came back.

The healing power of Hiiaka restored the places wounded by coral rocks and bitten by eels. Then she asked him how he had been overcome. He told her he had been fishing when a great kupua came in the form of a mighty wave falling upon the boat, filling it full of water.

The fisherman said that he had tried to bail the water out of his canoe, when it was hurled down into the coral caves, and he knew nothing more until the warm sun shone in his face and his eyes opened. Hiiaka told him to stand up, and putting out her strong hand lifted him to his feet.

He stood shaking and trembling, trying to move his feet. Little by little the power of life came back and he walked slowly to his house.

Hiiaka called for the glory of a divine chief to shine around them. Among the ancient Hawaiians it was believed that the eyes of prophets could tell the very family to which a high chief belonged by the color or peculiar appearance of the light around the individual even when a long distance away. Thus the watching anxious girls and the friends of Hiiaka knew that the ghost had gone back into the body and the fisherman had been brought back to life.

Lohiau

THE STORY of Hiiaka's journey over the seas which surround the Hawaiian Islands, and through dangers and perplexities, cannot be fully told in the limits of these short stories. There are several versions, so that only the substance of all can be given.

On each island she slew dragons which had come from the ancient traditional home of the Polynesians, India. She destroyed many evil-minded gnomes and elves; fought the aumakuas and the demi-gods of land and sea; found the body of Lohiau put away in a cave and watched over by the dragon-women who had been defeated by Pele when in her long sleep she chanted the songs of the Winds of Kauai. She slew the guardians of the cave and carried the body to a house where she used powerful chants for restoration. She captured the wandering ghost of Lohiau and compelled it again to take up its home in the body, and then with Lohiau and Wahine-omao made the long journey to her home in the volcano. From the island of Hawaii to the island Kauai and along the return journey, Hiiaka's path was marked with experiences beneficial to the people whom she passed. This must all be left untold except the story of Lohiau's restoration to life and the conflict with Pele.

As Hiiaka and her friend came near the island of Kauai, Hiiaka told Wahine-omao that Lohiau was dead and that she saw the spirit standing by the opening of a cave out on the pali of Haena.

Then she chanted to Lohiau:

> The lehua is being covered by the sand,
> A little red flower remains on the plain,
> The body is hidden in the stones,
> The flower is lying in the path.
> Very useful is the water of Kaunu.

Thus she told the ghost that she would give new life

even as dew on a thirsty flower. They landed and met Lohiau's sisters and friends.

Hiiaka asked about the death of Lohiau, and one sister said, "His breath left him and the body became yellow."

Hiiaka said: "There was no real reason for death, but the two women dragons took his spirit and held it captive. I will try to bring him back. Great is the magic power and strength of the two dragons, and I am not a man and may not win the victory. I will have something to eat, and then will go. You must establish a kapu for twenty days, and there must be quiet. No one can go to the mountains, nor into the sea. You must have a house made of ti leaves for the dead body and make it very tight on all sides."

The next day they made the house. Hiiaka commanded that a door be made toward the east. Then Hiiaka said, "Let us open the door of the house." When this was done, Hiiaka said: "Tomorrow let the kapu be established on land and sea. Tomorrow we commence our work."

She made arrangements to go to the cave in the precipice at dawn. Rain came down in floods and a strong wind swept the face of the precipice. A fog clung fast to the hills. The water rushed in torrents to the sea. It was an evil journey to Lohiau.

At sunrise they went on through the storm. Hiiaka uttered this incantation:

Our halas greet the inland precipice,
In the front of the calling hill.
Let it call,
You are calling to me.
Here is the great hill outside.
It is cold,
Cold for us.

The dragons shouted for them to stay down, or they would destroy them on the rocks. But the small spirit voice of Lohiau called for Hiiaka to come and get him.

Hiiaka chanted to Lohiau, telling him they would save him. As they went up, stones in showers fell around and upon them. One large stone struck Hiiaka in the breast,

84

and she fell off the pali. Then they began to get up and sticks of all kinds fell upon them again, forcing Hiiaka over the precipice.

The dragons leaped down on Hiiaka, trying to catch her in their mouths and strike her with their tails. Hiiaka struck them with her magic skirt, and their bodies were broken.

The spirits of the dragons went into other bodies and leaped upon Hiiaka, roaring and biting and tearing her body. She swung her skirt up against the dragons, and burned their bodies to ashes. The dragons again took new bodies for the last and most bitter battle.

Hiiaka told Wahine-omao to cover her body with leaves and sticks near the pali, and in the event of her death to return with the tidings to Hawaii.

One dragon caught Hiiaka and bent her over. The other leaped upon Hiiaka, catching her around the neck and arm. One tried to pull off the pa-u and tear it to pieces.

Pau-o-palae saw the danger. From her home on the island of Hawaii, she saw the dragons shaking Hiiaka. Then she sent her power and took many kinds of trees and struck the dragons. The roots twisted around the dragons, entangling their feet and tails and scratching eyes and faces.

The dragons tried to shake off the branches and roots — the leaf bodies of the wilderness. One let go the pa-u of Hiiaka, and the other let go the neck. Pau-o-palae called all the wind bodies of the forest and sent them to aid Hiiaka, the forces of the forest, and the wind spirits.

At last Hiiaka turned to say farewell to Wahine-omao, because the next fight with the dragons in their new bodies might prove fatal.

The dragons were now stronger than before. They leaped upon her, one on each side. The strong winds blew and the storm poured upon her, while the dragons struck her to beat her down. But all kinds of ferns were leaping up rapidly around the place where the dragons renewed the fight. The ferns twisted and twined around the legs and bodies of the dragons.

Hiiaka shook her magic skirt and struck them again and again, and the bodies of these dragons were broken in pieces. Then the wind ceased, the storm passed away, and the sky became clear. But it was almost evening and darkness was falling fast.

The people have for many years claimed that Hiiaka found the time too short to climb the precipice, catch the ghost of Lohiau, and carry it and the body down to the house prepared for her work. Therefore she uttered this incantation:

O gods! Come to Kauai, your land.
O pearl-eyed warrior (an idol) of Halawa!
O Kona! guardian of our flesh!
O the great gods of Hiiaka!
Come, ascend, descend,
Let the sun stop over the river of Hea.
Stand thou still, O sun!

The sun waited and its light rested on the precipice and pierced the deep shadows of the cave in which the body lay, while Hiiaka sought Lohiau.

Hiiaka heard the spirit voice saying, "Moving, moving, you will find me in a small coconut calabash fastened in tight." Hiiaka followed the spirit voice and soon saw a coconut closed up with feathers. Over the coconut a little rainbow was resting. She caught the coconut and went back to the body of Lohiau. It had become very dark in the cave, but she did not care. She took the bundle of the body of Lohiau and said: "We have the body and the spirit; we are ready now to go down to our house."

Then she called the spirits of the many kinds of ferns of Pau-o-palae to take the body down. The fern servants of Pau-o-palae carried the bundle of the body down to the house.

Hiiaka said to her friend: "You ask how the spirit can be restored into the body. It is hard and mysterious and a work of the gods. We must gather all kinds of ferns and maile and lehua and flowers from the mountains. We must take wai-lua (flowing water) and wai-lani (rain) and put them into new calabashes to use in washing the body. Then pray. If my prayer is not broken (interrupted or a mistake made), he will be alive. If the prayer is broken four times, life will not return."

The servants of Pau-o-palae, the goddess of ferns, brought all manner of sweet-scented ferns, flowers, and leaves to make a bed for the body of Lohiau, and to place around the inside of the house as fragrant paths by which the gods could come to aid the restoration to life.

There were many prayers, sometimes to one class of gods and sometimes to another. The following prayer was offered to the aumakuas, or ghost-gods, residing in cloud-land and revealing themselves in different cloud forms:

> Dark is the prayer rising up to Kanaloa,
> Rising up to the ancient home, Kealohilani.
> Look at the kupuas above sunset!
> Who are the kupuas above?
> The black dog of the heavens,
> The yellow dog of Ku in the small cloud,
> Ku is in the long cloud,
> Ku is in the short cloud,
> Ku is in the cloud of red spots in the sky.
> Listen to the people of the mountains,
> The friends of the forest,
> The voices of the heavens.
> The water of life runs, life is coming,
> Open with trembling, to let the spirit in,
> A noise rumbling,
> The sound of Ku.
> The lover sent for is coming.
> I, Hiiaka, am coming.
> The lover of my sister Pele,
> The sister of life,
> Is coming to life again.
> Live! Live!

After each one of the prayers and incantations the body was washed in the kind of water needed for each special ceremony. Thus days passed by; some legends say ten days, some say a full month. At last the body was ready for the incoming of the spirit.

The coconut shell in which the spirit had been kept was held against the body, the feet and limbs were slapped, and the body rubbed by Wahine-omao while Hiiaka continued her necessary incantations until the restoration to life was complete.

Many, many days had passed since the fiery and impetuous Pele had sent her youngest sister after the lover, Lohiau. In her restlessness Pele had torn up the land in all directions around the pit of fire with violent earthquakes. She had poured her wrath in burning floods of lava over all the southern part of the island. She had broken her most solemn promise to Hiiaka.

Whenever she became impatient at the delay of the coming of Lohiau, she would fling her scorching smoke and foul gas over Hiiaka's beautiful forests — and sometimes would smite the land with an overflow of burning lava.

Sometimes she would look down over that part of Puna where Hopoe dwelt and hurl spurts of lava toward her home. At last she had yielded to her jealous rage and destroyed Hopoe and her home and then burned the loved spots of restful beauty belonging to Hiiaka.

Hiiaka had seen Pele's action as she had looked back from time to time on her journey to Kauai. Even while she was bringing Lohiau back to life, her love for her own home revealed to her the fires kindled by Pele, and she chanted many songs of complaint against her unfaithful sister.

Hiiaka loyally fulfilled her oath until she stood with Lohiau on one of the high banks overlooking Ka-lua-Pele, the pit of Pele in the volcano of Kilauea. Down below in the awful majesty of fire were the sisters.

Wahine-omao went down to them as a messenger

from Hiiaka. One of the legends says that Pele killed her. Another says that she was repulsed and driven away. Others say that Pele refused to listen to any report of the journey to Kauai and hurled Wahine-omao senseless into a hole near the fire-pit, and raved against Hiiaka for the long time required in bringing Lohiau.

Hiiaka at last broke out in fierce rebellion against Pele.. On the hill where they stood were some of the lehua trees with their brilliant red blossoms. She plucked the flowers, made wreaths, and going close to Lohiau hung them around his neck.

All through the long journey to the crater Lohiau had been gaining a full appreciation of the bravery, the unselfishness, and the wholly lovable character of Hiiaka. He had proposed frequently that they be husband and wife. Now, as they stood on the brink of the crater with all the proof of Pele's oath-breaking around them, Hiiaka gave way entirely. She chanted while she fastened flowers tightly around him and while her arms were playing around his neck:

Hiiaka is the wife,
Caught in the embrace with the flowers.
The slender thread is fast.
Around him the leis from the land of the lehuas are fastened.
I am the wife. The clouds are blown down,
Hiding the sea at Hilo.

Lohiau had no longer any remnant of affection for Pele. Hiiaka had fulfilled her vow and Pele had broken all her promises. Lohiau and Hiiaka were now husband and wife. Pele had lost forever her husband of the long sleep.

Pele was uncontrollable in her jealous rage. One of the legends says that even while Lohiau and Hiiaka were embracing each other, Pele ran up the hill and threw her arms around his feet and black lava congealed over them. Then she caught his knees and then his body. Lava followed every clasp of the arms of Pele, until at last his whole body was engulfed in a lava flow. His spirit leaped from the body into some clumps of trees and ferns not far away.

Another legend says that Pele sent her brother Lono-makua, with his helpers, to kindle eruptions around Lohiau and Hiiaka. This could not harm Hiiaka, for she was at home in the worst violence of volcanic flames, but it meant death to Lohiau.

Lono-makua kindled fires all around Lohiau, but for a long time refrained from attacking him.

Hiiaka could not see the pit as clearly as Lohiau. She asked if Pele's fires were coming. He chanted:

> Hot is the mountain of the priest.
> Rain is weeping on the awa.
> I look over the rim of the crater.
> Roughly tossing is the lava below.
> Coming up to the forest —
> Attacking the trees —
> Clouds of smoke from the crater.

The lava came up, surrounding them. Tossing fountains of lava bespattered them. Wherever any spit of his body was touched, Lohiau became stone. He uttered incantations and used all his powers as a sorcerer-chief. The lava found it difficult to overwhelm him. Pele sent increased floods of burning rock upon him. Lohiau's body was all turned to stone. His spirit fled from the pit to the cool places of a forest on a higher part of the surrounding mountains.

Hiiaka was crazed by the death of Lohiau. She had fought against the eruption; now she caught the lava, tore it to pieces, and broke down the walls toward the innermost depths of their lava home. She began to open the pit for the coming of the sea.

Pele and her sisters were frightened. Pele called Wahine-omao from her prison and listened to the story of Hiiaka's faithfulness. Chagrined and full of self-blame, she told Wahine-omao how to restore happiness to her friend.

Wahine-omao went to Hiiaka and softly chanted by

the side of the crazy one who was breaking up the pit. She told the story of the journey after Lohiau and the possibility of seeking the wandering ghost.

Hiiaka turned from the pit and sought Lohiau. Many were the adventures in ghost-land. At last the ghost was found. Lohiau's body was freed from the crust of lava and healed and the ghost put back in its former home. A second time Hiiaka had given life to Lohiau.

Hiiaka and Lohiau went to Kauai, where, as chief and chiefess, they lived happily until real death came to Lohiau.

Then Hiiaka returned to her place in the Pele family. It was said that Wahine-omao became the wife of Lono-makua, the one kindling volcanic fire.

III. Ghosts and Ghost-gods

Maluae and the Underworld

THIS IS a story from Manoa Valley, back of Honolulu. In the upper end of the valley, at the foot of the highest mountains on the island of Oahu, lived Maluae. He was a farmer, and had chosen this land because rain fell abundantly on the mountains, and the streams brought down fine soil from the decaying forests and disintegrating rocks, fertilizing his plants.

Here he cultivated bananas, taro, and sweet potatoes. His bananas grew rapidly by the sides of the brooks, and yielded large bunches of fruit from their tree-like stems. His taro filled small walled-in pools, growing in the water like water lilies, until the roots were matured, when the plants were pulled up and the roots boiled and prepared for food. His sweet potatoes were planted on the drier uplands.

Thus he had plenty of food continually growing, and ripening from time to time. Whenever he gathered any of his food products, he brought a part to his family temple and placed it on an altar before the gods Kane and Kanaloa. Then he took the rest to his home for his family to eat.

He had a boy whom he dearly loved, whose name was Kaa-lii (Rolling Chief). This boy was a careless, rollicking child.

One day the boy was tired and hungry. He passed by the temple of the gods and saw bananas, ripe and sweet, on the little platform before the gods. He took these bananas and ate them all.

The gods looked down on the altar expecting to find food, but it was all gone and there was nothing for them. They were very angry, and ran out after the boy. They caught him eating the bananas, and killed him. The body they left lying under the trees, and taking out his ghost threw it into the Underworld.

The father toiled hour after hour cultivating his food plants, and when wearied returned to his home. On the way he met the two gods. They told him how his boy had robbed them of their sacrifices and how they had punished him. They said, "We have sent his ghost body to the lowest regions of the Underworld."

The father was very sorrowful and heavy-hearted as he went on his way to his desolate home. He searched for the body of his boy, and at last he found it. He saw too that the story of the gods was true, for partly eaten bananas filled the mouth, which was set in death.

He wrapped the body very carefully in kapa cloth made from the bark of trees. He carried it into his rest house and laid it on the sleeping mat. After a time he lay down beside the body, refusing all food, and planning to die with his boy. He thought if he could escape from his own body he would be able to go down where the ghost of his boy had been sent. If he could find that ghost, he hoped to take it to the other part of the Underworld, where they could be happy together.

He placed no offerings on the altar of the gods. No prayers were chanted. The afternoon and evening passed slowly. The gods waited for their worshipper, but he came not. They loooked down on the altar of sacrifice, but there was nothing for them.

The night passed and the following day. The father lay by the side of his son, neither eating nor drinking, and longing only for death. The house was tightly closed.

Then the gods talked together, and Kane said: "Maluae eats no food, he prepares no awa to drink, and there is no water by him. He is near the door of the Underworld. If he should die, we would be to blame."

Kanaloa said: "He has been a good man, but now we do not hear any prayers. We are losing our worshipper. We in quick anger killed his son. Was this the right reward? He has called us morning and evening in his worship. He has provided fish and fruits and vegetables for our altars. He has always prepared awa from the juice of the yellow awa root for us to drink. We have not paid him well for his care."

Then they decided to go and give life to the father, and permit him to take his ghost body and go down into Po, the dark land, to bring back the ghost of the boy. They went to Maluae and told him they were sorry for what they had done.

The father was very weak from hunger and longing for death, and could scarcely listen to them.

When Kane said, "Have you love for your child?" the father whispered: "Yes. My love is without end."

"Can you go down into the dark land and get that spirit and put it back in the body which lies here?"

"No," the father said, "no, I can only die and go to live with him and make him happier by taking him to a better place."

Then the gods said, "We will give you the power to go after your boy and we will help you to escape the dangers of the land of ghosts."

Then the father, stirred by hope, rose up and took food and drink. Soon he was strong enough to go on his journey.

The gods gave him a ghost body and also prepared a hollow stick like bamboo, in which they put food, battle weapons, and a piece of burning lava for fire.

Not far from Honolulu is a beautiful modern estate with fine roads, lakes, running brooks, and interesting valleys extending back into the mountain range. This is called by the very ancient name of Moanalua (two lakes). Near the seacoast of this estate was one of the most noted ghost localities of the islands. The ghosts after wandering over the island of Oahu would come to this place to find a way into their real home, the Underworld or Po.

Here was a ghostly breadfruit tree named Lei-walo, possibly meaning the "eight wreaths" or "the eighth wreath"—the last wreath of leaves from the land of the living which would meet the eyes of the dying.

The ghosts would leap or fly or climb into the branches of this tree, trying to find a rotten branch upon which they could sit until it broke and threw them into the dark sea below.

Maluae climbed up the breadfruit tree. He found a branch where ghosts were sitting waiting for it to fall. His weight was so much greater than theirs that the branch broke at once, and down they all fell into the land of Po.

He needed merely to taste the food in his hollow cane to have new life and strength. This he had done when he climbed the tree; thus he had been able to push past the fabled guardians of the pathway of the ghosts in the Upperworld. As he entered the Underworld, he again tasted the food of the gods and he felt himself growing stronger and stronger.

He took a magic war club and a spear out of the cane given by the gods. Ghostly warriors tried to hinder his entrance into the different districts of the dark land. The spirits of dead chiefs challenged him when he passed their homes. Battle after battle was fought. His magic club struck the warriors down, and his spear tossed them aside.

Sometimes he was warmly greeted and aided by ghosts of kindly spirits. Thus he went from place to place, searching for his boy. He found him at last, as the Hawaiians quaintly expressed it, "down in the papa-ku" (the established foundation of Po), choking and suffocating from the bananas of ghost-land which he was compelled to continually force into his mouth.

The father caught the spirit of the boy and started back toward the Upperworld, but the ghosts surrounded him. They tried to catch him and take the spirit away from him. Again the father partook of the food of the gods. Once more he wielded his war club, but the hosts of enemies were too great. Multitudes arose on all sides, crushing him by their overwhelming numbers.

At last he raised his magic hollow cane and took the

last portion of food. The he poured out the portion of burning lava which the gods had placed inside. It fell upon the dry floor of the Underworld. The flames dashed into the trees and the shrubs of ghost-land. Fire holes opened and streams of lava burst out.

Backward fled the multitude of spirits. The father thrust the spirit of the boy quickly into the empty magic cane and rushed swiftly up to his homeland. He brought the spirit to the body lying in the rest house and forced it to find again its living home.

Afterward the father and the boy took food to the altars of the gods, and chanted the accustomed prayers heartily and loyally all the rest of their lives.

A Giant's Rock-Throwing

A POINT of land on the northwestern coast of the island Oahu is called Kalae-o-Kaena, which means "The Cape of Kaena."

A short distance from this cape lies a large rock which bears the name of Pohaku-o-Kauai, or rock of Kauai, a large island northwest of Oahu. This rock is as large as a small house.

There is an interesting legend told on the island of Oahu which explains why these names have for generations been fastened to the cape and to the rock. A long time ago there lived on Kauai a man of wonderful power, Hau-pu. When he was born, the signs of a demi-god were over the house of his birth. Lightning flashed through the skies, and thunder reverberated — a rare event in the Hawaiian Islands, and supposed to be connected with the birth or death or some very unusual occurrence in the life of a chief.

Mighty floods of rain fell and poured in torrents down

the mountainsides, carrying the red soil into the valleys in such quantities that the rapids and the waterfalls became the color of blood, and the natives called this a blood rain.

During the storm, and even after sunshine filled the valley, a beautiful rainbow rested over the house in which the young chief was born. This rainbow was thought to come from the miraculous powers of the newborn child shining out from him, instead of from the sunlight around him. Many chiefs throughout the centuries of Hawaiian legends were said to have had this rainbow around them all their lives.

Hau-pu while a child was very powerful, and after he grew up was widely known as a great warrior. He would attack and defeat armies of his enemies without aid from any person. His spear was like a mighty weapon, sometimes piercing a host of enemies and sometimes putting aside all opposition when he thrust it into the ranks of his opponents.

If he had thrown his spear and if fighting with his bare hands did not vanquish his foes, he would leap to the hillside, tear up a great tree, and with it sweep away all before him as if he were wielding a huge broom. He was known and feared throughout all the Hawaiian Islands. He became angry quickly and used his great powers very rashly.

One night he lay sleeping in his royal resthouse on the side of a mountain which faced the neighboring island of Oahu. Between the two islands lay a broad channel about thirty miles wide. When clouds were on the face of the sea, these islands were hidden from each other; but when they lifted, the rugged valleys of the mountains on one island could be clearly seen from the other. Even by moonlight the shadowly lines would appear.

This night the strong man stirred in his sleep. Indistinct noises seemed to surround his house. He turned over and dropped off into slumber again.

Soon he was aroused a second time, and he was awake

enough to hear shouts of men far, far away. Louder rose the noise, mixed with the roar of the great surf waves. He realized that it came from the sea, and he then forced himself to rise and stumble to the door.

He looked out toward Oahu. A multitude of lights were flashing on the sea before his sleepy eyes. A low murmur of many voices came from the place where the dancing lights seemed to be. His confused thoughts made it appear to him that a great fleet of warriors was coming from Oahu to attack his people.

He blindly rushed out to the edge of a high precipice which overlooked the channel. Evidently, many boats and many people were out in the sea below.

He laughed, and stooping down tore a huge rock from its place. This he swung back and forth, back and forth, back and forth, until he gave it great impetus which, added to his own miraculous power, sent it far out over the sea. Like a great cloud it rose in the heavens and, as if blown by swift winds, sped on its way.

Over on the shores of Oahu a chief whose name was Kaena had called his people out for a night's fishing. Canoes large and small came from all along the coast. Torches without number had been made and placed in the canoes. The largest fish nets had been brought.

There was no need of silence. Nets had been set in the best places. Fish of all kinds were to be aroused and frightened into the nets. Flashing lights, splashing paddles, and clamor from hundreds of voices resounded all around the nets.

Gradually the canoes came nearer and nearer the centre. The shouting increased. Great joy ruled the tumult which drowned the roar of the waves.

Across the channel and up the mountainsides of Kauai swept the shouts of the fishing party. Into the ears of drowsy Hau-pu the noise forced itself. Little dreamed the excited fishermen of the effect of this on faraway Kauai.

Suddenly, something like a bird as large as a mountain

seemed to be above, and then with a mighty sound like the roar of winds it descended upon them.

Smashed and submerged were the canoes when the huge boulder thrown by Hau-pu hurled itself upon them.

The chief Kaena and his canoe were in the centre of this terrible mass of wreckage, and he and many of his people lost their lives.

The waves swept sand upon the shore until in time a long point of land was formed. The remaining followers of the dead chief named this cape "Kaena."

The rock thrown by Hau-pu embedded itself in the depths of the ocean, but its head rose far above the water, even when raging storms dashed turbulent waves against it. To this death-dealing rock the natives gave the name "Rock of Kauai."

Thus for generations has the deed of the man of giant force been remembered on Oahu, and so have a cape and a rock received their names.

Lau-ka-ieie

Waipio Valley, the beautiful:
Precipices around it,
The sea on one side;
The precipices are hard to climb;
Not to be climbed
Are the sea precipices.

KAKEA (The White One) and Kaholo (The Runner) were the children of the Valley. Their parents were the precipices which were sheer to the sea, and could only be passed by boats. They married, and Kaholo conceived. The husband said, "If a boy is born, I will name it; if a girl, you give the name."

He went up to see his sister Pokahi, and asked her to go

swiftly to see his wife. Pokahi's husband was Kaukini, a bird catcher. He went out into the forest for some birds. Soon he came back and prepared them for cooking. Hot stones were put inside the birds, which were packed in calabashes, carefully covered over with wet leaves which made steam inside, so that the birds were well cooked. Then they were brought to Kaholo for a feast.

On their way they went down to Waipio Valley, coming to the foot of the precipice. Pokahi wanted some sea moss and some shellfish. She told the two men to go on while she secured these things to take to Kaholo. She gathered the soft lipoa moss and went up to the waterfall, to Ulu (Kaholo's home).

The baby was born, wrapped in the moss, and thrown into the sea, making a shapeless bundle, but a kupua (sorcerer) saw that a child was there. The child was taken and washed clean in the soft lipoa, and cared for. All around were the signs of the birth of a chief.

They named him Hiilawe, and from him the Waipio waterfall has its name, according to the saying, "Falling into mist is the water of Hiilawe."

Pokahi took up her package in which she had brought the moss and shellfish, but the moss was gone. Hina-ulu-ohia (Hina-the-Growing-Ohia-Tree) was the sorcerer who took the child in the lipoa moss. She was the aumakua, or ancestor goddess, of the boat builders.

Pokahi dreamed that a beautiful woman appeared, her body covered with the leaves of ohia trees. "I know that you have not had any child. I will now give you one. Awake, and go to the Waipio River; watch thirty days, then you will find a girl wrapped in soft moss. This shall be your adopted child. I will show you how to care for it. Your brother and his wife must not know. Your husband alone may know about this adopted girl."

Pokahi and her husband went down at once to the mouth of the river, heard an infant cry in the midst of red-colored mist, and found a child wrapped in the fragrant moss. She wished to take it up, but was held back by magic powers. She saw an ohia tree rising up from the water—branches, leaves, and flowers—and iiwi (birds) coming to pick the flowers. The red birds and red flowers were very beautiful. This tree was Hina. The birds began to sing, and quietly the tree sank down into the water and disappeared, the birds flying away to the west.

Pokahi returned to her brother's house. Going down to the sea every day, she saw the human form of the child growing in the shelter of that red mist on the surface of the sea. At the end of the thirty days Pokahi told her friends and her husband that they must go back home. On their way they went to the river. She told her husband to look at the red mist, but he wanted to hurry on. As they approached their house, cooking odors welcomed them, and they found plenty of food prepared outside. They saw something moving inside. The trees seemed to be walking as if with the feet of men. Steps were heard, and voices were calling for the people of the house.

Kaukini prepared a lamp, and Pokahi in a vision saw the same fine tree she had seen before. There was also a hala tree with its beautiful yellow blossoms. As they looked they saw leaves of different kinds falling one after another, making in one place a soft fragrant bed.

Then a woman and a man came with an infant. They were the god Ku and Hina his wife. They said to Pokahi and her husband, "We have accepted your sacrifices and have seen that you are childless, so now we have brought you this child to adopt." Then they disappeared among the trees of the forest, leaving the child, Lau-ka-ieie (Leaf of the Ieie Vine). She was well cared for, and grew up into a beautiful woman without fault or blemish. Her companions and servants were the birds and the flowers.

Lau-ka-pali (Leaf of the Precipice) was one of her friends. One day she made whistles of ti leaves and blew them. The Leaf-of-the-Morning-glory saw that the young chiefess liked this game. She went out and found Pupu-kani-oi (The Singing Land Shell), whose home was on the leaves of the forest trees. Then she found another Pupu-hina-hina-ula (Shell-Beautiful-with-Rainbow-Colors). In the night the shells sang, and their voices stole their way into the love of Lau-ka-ieie, so that she gently sang with them.

Nohu-ua-palai (a fern), one of the old residents of that place, went out into the forest and, hearing the voices of the girl and the shells, came to the house. She chanted her name, but there was no reply. All was silent. At last, Pua-ohelo (The Blossom of the Ohelo), one of the flowers in the house, heard and, opening the door, invited her to come in and eat.

Nohu-ua-palai went in and feasted with the girls. Lau-ka-ieie dreamed about Kawelona (The Setting of the Sun) at Lihue, a fine young man, the first-born of one of the high chiefs of Kauai. She told her kahu (guardian) all about her dream and the distant island. The kahu asked who should go to find the man of the dream. All the girl friends wanted to go. She told them to raise their hands and the one who had the longest fingers could go. This was Pupu-kani-oi (The Singing Shell). The leaf family all sobbed as they bade farewell to the shell.

The shell said: "Oh, my leaf sisters Laukoa (Leaf of the Koa Tree) and Lauanau (Leaf of the Paper-mulberry Tree), arise, go with me on my journey! Oh, my shell sisters of the blue sea, come to the beach, to the sand! Come and show me the path I am to go! Oh, Pupu-mokalau (The Land Shell Clinging to the Mokihana Leaf), come and look at me, for I am one of your family! Call all the shells to aid me in my journey! Come to me!"

Then she summoned her brother, Makani-kau, chief of the winds, to waft them away in their wind bodies. They journeyed all around the island of Hawaii to find some man who would be like the man of the dream. They found no one there, nor on any of the other islands up to Oahu, where the Singing Shell fell in love with a chief and turned from her journey. But Makani-kau went on to Kauai.

Ma-eli-eli, the dragon woman of Heeia, tried to persuade him to stop, but on he went. She ran after him. Limaloa, the dragon of Laiewai, also tried to catch Makani-kau, but he was too swift.

On the way to Kauai, Makani-kau saw some people in a boat chased by a big shark. He leaped on the boat and told them he would play with the shark and they could stay near but need not fear. Then he jumped into the sea. The shark turned over and opened its mouth to seize him; he climbed on it, caught its fins, and forced it to flee through the water. He drove it to the shore and made it fast among the rocks. It became the great shark stone, Koa-mano (Warrior Shark), at Haena. He leaped from the shark to land, the boat following.

He saw the hill of "Fire-Throwing," a place where burning sticks were thrown over the precipices, a very beautiful sight at night. He leaped to the top of the hill in his shadow body. Far up on the hill was a vast number of iiwi (birds). Makani-kau went to them as they were flying toward Lehua. They only felt the force of the winds, for they could not see him or his real body. As he drew near, he saw that the birds were carrying a fine man.

This was the one Lau-ka-ieie desired for her husband. They carried this boy on their wings easily and gently over the hills and sea toward the sunset island, Lehua. There they slowly flew to earth. They were the bird guardians of Kawelona, and when they travelled from place to place they were under the direction of the bird sorcerer, Kukala-a-ka-manu.

Kawelona had dreamed of a beautiful girl who had visited him again and again, so that he was prepared to meet Makani-kau. He told his parents and adopted guardians and bird priests about his dreams and the beautiful girl he wanted to marry.

Makani-kau met the winds of Niihau and Lehua, and at last was welcomed by the birds. He told Kawelona his mission. Kawelona prepared to go to Hawaii, asking how

106

they should go. Makani-kau went to the seaside and called for his many bodies to come and give him the boat for the husband of their great sister, Lau-ka-ieie. Thus he made known his mana, or spirit power, to Kawelona. He called on the great cloud gods to send the long white cloud boat, and it soon appeared. Kawelona entered the boat with fear, and in a few minutes lost sight of the island of Lehua and his bird guardians as he sailed out into the sea. Makani-kau dropped down by the side of a beautiful shell boat, entered it, and stopped at Mana. There he took several girls and put them in a double canoe, or au-waa-olalua (spirit boat).

Meanwhile the sorcerer ruler of the birds agreed to find out where Kawelona was, to satisfy the longing of his parents, whom he had left without showing them where he was going or what dangers he might meet. The sorcerer poured water into a calabash and threw in two lehua flowers, which floated on the water. Then he turned his eyes toward the sun and prayed: "Oh, great sun, to whom belongs the heavens, turn your eyes downward to look on the water in this calabash, and show us what you see therein! Look upon the beautiful young woman. She is not one from Kauai. There is no one more beautiful than she. Her home is under the glowing east, and a royal rainbow is around her. There are beautiful girls attending her."

The sorcerer saw the sun pictures in the water, and interpreted to the friends the journey of Kawelona, telling them it was a long, long way, and they must wait patiently many days for any word. In the signs he saw the boy in the cloud boat, Makani-kau in his shell boat, and the three girls in the spirit boat.

The girls were carried to Oahu, and there found the shell girl, Pupu-kani-oi, left by Makani-kau on his way to Lehua. They took her with her husband and his sisters in the spiritboat. There were nine in the company of travelers to Hawaii: Kawelona in his cloudboat; two girls from Kauai; Kaiahe, a girl from Oahu; three from Molokai; one from Maui; and a girl called Lihau. Makani-kau himself was the leader; he had taken the girls away.

On this journey he turned their boats to Kahoolawe to visit Ka-moho-alii, the ruler of the sharks. There Makani-kau appeared in his finest human body, and they all landed. Makani-kau took Kawelona from his cloud boat, went inland, and placed him in the midst of the company, telling them he was the husband for Lau-ka-ieie. They were all made welcome by the ruler of the sharks.

Ka-moho-alii called his sharks to bring food from all the islands over which they were placed as guardians. They quickly brought prepared food, fish, flowers, leis, and gifts of all kinds. The company feasted and rested. Then Kamoho-alii called his sharks to guard the travelers on their journey. Makani-kau went in his shell boat and Kawelona in his cloud boat, and they were all carried over the sea until they landed under the mountains of Hawaii.

Makani-kau, in his wind body, carried the boats swiftly on their journey to Waipio. Lau-ka-ieie heard her brother's voice calling her from the sea. Hina answered. Makani-kau and Kawelona went up to Waimea to cross over to Lau-ka-ieie's house, but were taken by Hina to the top of Mauna Kea. Poliahu and Lilinoe saw the two fine young men and called to them, but Makani-kau passed by, without a word, to his own wonderful home in the caves of the mountains resting in the heart of mists and fogs, and placed all his travelers there. Makani-kau went down to the sea and called the sharks of Ka-moho-alii. They appeared in their human bodies in the valley of Waipio, leaving their shark bodies resting quietly in the sea. They feasted and danced near the ancient temple of Kahuku-welo-welo, which was the place where the wonderful shell, Kiha-pu, was kept.

Makani-kau put seven shells on the top of the precipice and they blew until sweet sounds floated over all the land. Thus was the marriage of Lau-ka-ieie and Kawelona celebrated.

All the shark people rested, soothed by the music. After the wedding they bade farewell and returned to Kahoolawe, going around the southern side of the island, for it was counted bad luck for them to turn back. They must go straight ahead all the way home. Makani-kau went to his sister's house, and met the girls and Lau-ka-ieie. He told her that his house was full of strangers, as the people of the different kupua bodies had assembled to celebrate the wedding. These were the kupua people of the Hawaiian Islands. The eepa people were more like fairies and gnomes, and were usually somewhat deformed.

After the marriage, Pupu-kani-oi (The Singing Shell) and her husband entered the shell boat and started back to Molokai. On their way they heard sweet bird voices. Makani-kau had a feather house covered with rainbow colors. Later he went to Kauai, and brought back the adopted parents of Kawelona to dwell on Hawaii, where Lau-ka-ieie lived happily with her husband.

Hiilawe became very ill, and called his brother Makani-kau and his sister Lau-ka-ieie to come near and listen. He told them that he was going to die, and they must bury him where he could always see the eyes of the people, and then he would change his body into a wonderful new body.

The beautiful girl took his malo and leis and placed them along the sides of the valley, where they became trees and clinging vines, and Hina made him live again; so Hiilawe became an aumakua of the waterfalls. Makani-kau took the body in his hands and carried it in the thunder and lightning, burying it on the brow of the highest precipice of the valley. Then his body was changed into a stone, which has been lying there for centuries. But his ghost was made by Hina into a kupua, so that he could always appear as the wonderful misty falls of Waipio, looking into the eyes of his people.

After many years had passed Hina assumed permanently the shape of the beautiful ohia tree, making her home in the forest around the volcanoes of Hawaii. She still had magic power, and was worshipped under the name of Hina-ula-ohia.

Makani-kau watched over Lau-ka-ieie, and when the time came for her to lay aside her human body she came to him as a slender, graceful woman, covered with leaves, her eyes blazing like fire. Makani-kau said: "You are a vine; you cannot stand alone. I will carry you into the forest and place you by the side of Hina. You are the ieie vine. Climb trees! Twine your long leaves around them! Let your blazing red flowers shine between the leaves like the eyes of fire! Give your beauty to all the ohia trees of the forest!"

Carried hither and thither by Makani-kau (Great Wind), and dropped by the side of splendid tall trees, the ieie vine has for centuries been one of the most graceful tree ornaments in all the forest life of the Hawaiian Islands.

Makani-kau in his spirit form blew the golden clouds of the islands into the light of the sun, so that the Rainbow Maiden, Anuenue, might lend her garments to all her friends of the ancient days.

Kauhuhu, the Shark God of Molokai

THE STORY of the shark god Kauhuhu has been told under the legend of "Aikanaka (Man-eater)," which was the ancient name of the little harbor of Pukoo, which lies at the entrance to one of the beautiful valleys of the island of Molokai. The better way is to take the legend as revealing the great man-eater in one of his most kindly aspects.

The shark god appears as the friend of a priest who is seeking revenge for the destruction of his children. Kamalo was the name of the priest. His heiau, or temple, was at Kaluaaha, a village which faced the channel between the islands of Molokai and Maui. Across the channel the rugged red-brown slopes of the mountain Eeke (Iao Needle) were lost in the masses of clouds which continually hung around its sharp peaks.

The two boys of the priest delighted in the glorious revelations of sunrise and sunset tossed in shattered fragments of cloud color, and rejoiced in the reflected tints which danced to them over the swift channel currents. It is no wonder that the courage of sky and sea entered into the hearts of the boys, and that many deeds of daring were done by them. They were taught many of the secrets of the temple by their father, but were warned that certain things were sacred to the gods and must not be touched.

The high chief, or alii, of that part of the island had a temple a short distance from Kaluaaha, in the valley of the harbor which was called Aikanaka. The name of this chief was Kupa. The chiefs always had a house built within the temple walls as their own residence, to which they could retire at certain seasons of the year. Kupa had two remarkable drums, which he kept in his house at the heiau. His skill in beating his drums was so great that they could reveal his thoughts to the waiting priests.

One day Kupa sailed far away over the sea to his favorite fishing grounds. Meanwhile the boys were tempted to go to Kupa's heiau and try the wonderful drums. The valley of the little harbor Aikanaka bore the musical name Mapulehu. Along the beach and over the ridge hastened the two sons of Kamalo. Quickly they entered the heiau, found the high chief's house, took out his drums, and began to beat upon them. Some of the people heard the familiar tones of the drums. They dared not enter the sacred doors of the heiau, but watched until the boys became weary of their sport and returned home.

When Kupa returned they told him how the boys had beaten upon his sacred drums. Kupa was very angry, and ordered his mu, or temple sacrifice seekers, to kill the boys and bring their bodies to the heiau to be placed on the altar.

When the priest Kamalo heard of the death of his sons, in bitterness of heart he sought revenge. His own power was not great enough to cope with his high chief; therefore he sought the aid of the seers and prophets of highest repute throughout Molokai. But they feared Kupa the chief, and could not aid him; and therefore sent him on to another kaula, or prophet, or sent him back to consult someone the other side of his home. All this time he carried with him fitting presents and sacrifices, by which he hoped to gain the assistance of the gods through their priests. At last he came to the steep precipice which overlooks Kalaupapa and Kalawao. At the foot of this precipice was a heiau, in which the great shark god was worshipped. Down the sides of the precipice he climbed and at last found the priest of the shark god. The priest refused to give assistance, but directed him to go to a great cave in the bold cliffs south of Kalawao. The name of the cave was Anaopuhi, the cave of the eel. Here dwelt the great shark god Kauhuhu and his guardians or watchers, Waka and Mo-o, the great dragons or reptiles of Polynesian legends. These dragons were mighty warriors in the defense of the shark god, and were his kahus, or caretakers, while he slept or when his cave needed watching during his absence.

Kamalo, tired and discouraged, plodded along through the rough lava fragments piled around the entrance to the cave. He bore across his shoulders a black pig, which he had carried many miles as an offering to whatever power he could find to aid him. As he came near to the cave the watchmen saw him and said:

"E, here comes a man, food for the great [shark] Mano. Fish for Kauhuhu." But Kamao came nearer and for some reason aroused sympathy in the dragons. "E hele! E hele!" they cried to him. "Away, away! It is death to you. Here's the kapu place."

"Death it may be — life it may be. Give me revenge for my sons — and I have no care for myself."

Then the watchmen asked about his trouble and he

112

told them how the chief Kupa had slain his sons as a punishment for beating the drums. Then he narrated the story of his wanderings all over Molokai, seeking for some power strong enough to overcome Kupa. At last he had come to the shark god, as the final possibility of aid. If Kauhuhu failed him, he was ready to die; indeed, he had no wish to live.

The mo-o assured him of their kindly feelings, and told him that it was a very good thing that Kauhuhu was away fishing, for if he had been home there would have been no way for him to go before the god without suffering immediate death. There would have been not even an instant for explanations. Yet they ran a very great risk in aiding him, for they must conceal him until the way was opened by the favors of the great god. If he should be discovered and eaten before gaining the aid of the shark god, they, too, must die with him.

They decided that they would hide him in the rubbish pile of taro peelings which had been thrown on one side when they had pounded taro. Here he must lie in perfect silence until the way was made plain for him to act. They told him to watch for the coming of eight great surf waves rolling in from the sea, and then wait in his place of concealment for some opportunity to speak to the god, because he would come in the last great wave.

Soon the surf began to roll in and break against the cliffs. Higher and higher rose the waves until the eighth reared far above the waters and met the winds from the shore, which whipped the curling crest into a shower of spray. It raced along the water and beat far up into the cave, breaking into foam out of which the shark god emerged.

At once he took his human form and walked around the cave. As he passed the rubbish heap he cried out: "A man is here. I smell him."

The dragons earnestly denied that anyone was there, but the shark god said, "There is surely a man in this cave. If I find him, dead men you are. If I find him not, you

113

shall live." Then Kauhuhu looked along the walls of the cave and into all the hiding places, but could not find him. He called with a loud voice, but only the echoes answered, like the voices of ghosts. After a thorough search he was turning away to attend to other matters when Kamalo's pig squealed. Then the giant shark god leaped to the pile of taro leavings and thrust them apart. There lay Kamalo and the black pig which had been brought for sacrifice.

Oh, the anger of the god!

Oh, the blazing eyes!

Kauhuhu instantly caught Kamalo and lifted him from the rubbish up toward his great mouth. Now the head and shoulders were in Kauhuhu's mouth. So quickly had this been done that Kamalo had no time to think. Kamalo spoke quickly as the teeth were coming down upon him. "E Kauhuhu, listen to me. Hear my prayer! Then perhaps eat me."

The shark god was astonished and did not bite. He took Kamalo from his mouth and said: "Well for you that you spoke quickly! Perhaps you have a good thought. Speak."

Then Kamalo told about his sons and their death at the hands of the executioners of the great chief, and that no one dared avenge him. All the prophets of the different gods had sent him from one place to another but could give him no aid. Sure now was he that Kauhuhu alone could give him aid!

Pity came to the shark god as it had come to his dragon watchers when they saw the sad condition of Kamalo. All this time Kamalo had held the hog which he had carried with him for sacrifice. This he now offered to the shark god. Kauhuhu, pleased and compassionate, accepted the offering, and said: "E Kamalo. If you had come for any other purpose I would eat you, but your cause is sacred. I will stand as your kahu, your guardian, and sorely punish the high chief Kupa."

Then he told Kamalo to go to the heiau of the priest who told him to see the shark god, take this priest on his shoulders, carry him over the steep precipices to his own heiau at Kaluaaha, and there live with him as a fellow priest. They were to build a kapu fence around the heiau and put up the sacred kapu staffs of white kapa cloth. They must collect black pigs by the four hundred, red fish by the four hundred, and white chickens by the four hundred. Then they were to wait patiently for the coming of Kauhuhu.

It was to be a strange coming. On the island of Lanai, far to the west of the Maui channel, they should see a small cloud, white as snow, increasing until it covered the little island. Then that cloud would cross the channel against the wind and climb the mountains of Molokai until it rested on the highest peaks over the valley where Kupa had his temple.

"At that time," said Kauhuhu, "a great rainbow will span the valley. I shall be in the care of that rainbow, and you may clearly understand that I am there and will speedily punish the man who has injured you. Remember that because you came to me for this sacred cause, therefore I have spared you, the only man who has ever stood in the presence of the shark god and escaped alive."

Swiftly did Kamalo go up and down precipices and along the rough hard ways to the heiau of the priest of the shark god. Gladly did he carry him up from Kalaupapa to the mountain ridge above. Quickly did he carry him to his home and there provide for him while he gathered together the black pigs, the red fish, and the white chickens within the sacred enclosure he had built. Here he brought his family, those who had the nearest and strongest claims upon him.

When his work was done, his eyes burned with watching the clouds of the little western island of Lanai. Ah, the days passed by so slowly! The weeks and the months came, so the legends say, and still Kamalo waited in patience. At last one day a white cloud appeared. It was unlike all the other white clouds he had anxiously watched during the dreary months. Over the channel it came. It spread over the hillsides and climbed the mountains and rested at the head of the valley belonging to Kupa. Then the watchers saw the glorious rainbow and knew that Kauhuhu had come according to his word.

The storm arose at the head of the valley. The winds struggled into a furious gale. The clouds gathered in heavy black masses, dark as midnight, and were pierced through with terrific flashes of lightning. The rain fell in floods, sweeping the hillside down into the valley, and rolling all that was below onward in a resistless mass toward the ocean. Down came the torrent upon the heiau belonging to Kupa, tearing its walls into fragments and washing Kupa and his people into the harbor at the mouth of the valley. Here the shark god had gathered his people. Sharks filled the bay and feasted upon Kupa and his followers until the waters ran red and all were destroyed. Hence came the legendary name for that little harbor — Aikanaka, the place for man-eaters.

It is said in the legends that "when great clouds gather on the mountains and a rainbow spans the valley, look out for furious storms of wind and rain which come suddenly, sweeping down the valley." It is also said in the legends that this strange storm which came in such awful power upon Kupa spread out over the adjoining lowlands, carrying great destruction everywhere, but it paused at the kapu staff of Kamalo, and rushed on either side of the sacred fence, not daring to touch anyone who dwelt therein. Therefore Kamalo and his people were spared.

The legend has been called "Aikanaka" because of the feast of the sharks on the human flesh that swept down into that harbor by the storm, but it seems more fitting to name the story after the shark god Kauhuhu, who sent mighty storms and wrought great destruction.

The Shark Man of Waipio Valley

THIS IS A story of Waipio Valley, the most beautiful of all the valleys of the Hawaiian Islands, and one of the most secluded. It is now, as it has always been, very difficult of access. The walls are a sheer descent of over a thousand feet. In ancient times a narrow path slanted along the face of the bluffs wherever foothold could be found. In these later days the path has been enlarged, and horse and rider can descend into the valley's depths. In the upper end of the valley is a long silver ribbon of water falling fifteen hundred feet from the brow of a precipice, over which a mountain torrent swiftly hurls itself to the fertile valley below. Other falls show the convergence of several mountain streams to the ocean outlet offered by the broad plains of Waipio.

Here in the long-ago, high chiefs dwelt and sacred temples were built. From Waipio Valley, Moikeha and Laa-Mai-Kahiki sailed away on their famous voyages to distant foreign lands. In this valley dwelt the priest who in the times of Maui was said to have the winds of heaven concealed in his calabash. Raising the cover a little, he sent gentle breezes in the direction of the opening. Severe storms and hurricanes were granted by swiftly opening the cover widely and letting a chaotic mass of fierce winds escape. The stories of magical powers of bird and fish as well as of the strange deeds of powerful men are almost innumerable. Not the least of the myths of Waipio Valley is the story of Nanaue, the shark man, who was one of the cannibals of the ancient time.

Ka-moho-alii was the king of all the sharks which frequent Hawaiian waters. When he chose to appear as a man, he was always a chief of dignified, majestic appearance. One day, while swimming back and forth just beneath the surface of the waters at the mouth of the valley, he saw an exceedingly beautiful woman coming to bathe in the white surf.

That night Ka-moho-alii came to the beach black with lava sand, crawled out of the water, and put on the form of a man. As a mighty chief he walked through the valley and mingled with the people. For days he entered into their sports and pastimes and partook of their bounty, always looking for the beautiful woman whom he had seen bathing in the surf. When he found her he came to her and won her to be his wife.

Kalei was the name of the woman who married the strange chief. When the time came for a child to be born to them, Ka-moho-alii charged Kalei to keep careful watch of it and guard its body continually from being seen of men, and never allow the child to eat the flesh of any animal. Then he disappeared, never permitting Kalei to have the least suspicion that he was the king of the sharks.

When the child was born, Kalei gave to him the name "Nanaue." She was exceedingly surprised to find an opening in his back. As the child grew to manhood, the opening developed into a large shark mouth with rows of fierce sharp teeth.

From infancy to manhood, Kalei protected Nanaue by keeping his back covered with a fine kapa cloth. She was full of fear as she saw Nanaue plunge into the water and become a shark. The mouth on his back opened for any kind of prey. But she kept the terrible birthmark of her son a secret hidden in the depths of her own heart.

For years she prepared for him the common articles of food, always shielding him from the temptation to eat meat. But when he became a man, his grandfather took him to the men's eating house, where his mother could no longer protect him. Meats of all varieties were given to him in great abundance, yet he always wanted more. His appetite was insatiable.

While under his mother's care he had been taken to the pool of water into which the great Waipio Falls poured its cascade. There he bathed and, changing himself into a

118

shark, caught the small fish which were playing around him. His mother was always watching him to give an alarm if any of the people came near to the bathing place.

As he became a man he avoided his companions in all bathing and fishing. He went away by himself. When the people were out in the deep sea bathing or fishing, suddenly a fierce shark would appear in their midst, biting and tearing their limbs and dragging them down in the deep water. Many of the people disappeared secretly, and great terror filled the homes of Waipio.

Nanaue's mother alone was certain that he was the cause of the trouble. He was becoming very bold in his depredations. Sometimes he would ask when his friends were going out in the sea; then he would go to a place at some distance, leap into the sea, and swiftly dash to intercept the return of his friends to the shore. Perhaps he would allay suspicion by appearing as a man and challenging someone to a swimming race. Diving suddenly, he would in an instant become a shark and destroy his fellow swimmer.

The people felt that he had some peculiar power, and feared him. One day, when their high chief had called all the men of the valley to prepare the taro patches for their future supply of food, a fellow workman standing by the side of Nanaue tore his kapa cape from his shoulders. The men behind cried out, "See the great shark mouth!" All the people came running together, shouting "A shark man! A shark man!"

Nanaue became very angry and snapped his shark teeth together. Then with bitter rage he attacked those standing near him. He seized one by the arm and bit it in two. He tore the flesh of another in ragged gashes. Biting and snapping from side to side, he ran toward the sea.

The crowd of natives surrounded him and blocked his way. He was thrown down and tied. The mystery had now passed from the valley. The people knew the cause of the troubles through which they had been passing, and all crowded around to see this wonderful thing, part

119

man and part shark.

The high chief ordered their largest oven to be prepared, that Nanaue might be placed therein and burned alive. The deep pit was quickly cleaned out by many willing hands and, with much noise and rejoicing, fire was placed within and the stones for heating were put in above the fire. "We are ready for the shark man," was the cry.

During the confusion Nanaue quietly made his plans to escape. When he suddenly changed himself into a shark, the cords which bound him fell off and he rolled into one of the rivers which flowed from the falls in the upper part of the valley.

None of the people dared to spring into the water for a hand-to-hand fight with the monster. They ran along the bank, throwing stones at Nanaue and bruising him. They called for spears that they might kill him, but he made a swift rush to the sea and swam away, never again to return to Waipio Valley.

Apparently Nanaue could not live long in the ocean. The story says that he swam over to the island of Maui and landed near the village of Hana. There he dwelt for some time, and married a chiefess. Meanwhile he secretly killed and ate some of the people. At last his appetite for human flesh made him so bold that he caught a beautiful young girl and carried her out into the deep waters. There he changed himself into a shark and ate her body in the sight of the people.

The Hawaiians became very angry. They launched their canoes and, throwing in all kinds of weapons, pushed out to kill their enemy. But he swam swiftly away, passing around the island until at last he landed on Molokai.

Again he joined himself to the people, and again one by one those who went bathing and fishing disappeared. The priests (kahunas) of the people at last heard from their fellow priests of the island of Maui that there was a dangerous shark man roaming through the islands.

They sent warnings to the people, urging all trusty fishermen to keep strict watch.

At last they saw Nanaue change himself into a great fish. The fishermen waged a fierce battle against him. They entangled him in their nets, they pierced him with spears and struck him with clubs until the waters were red with his blood. They called on the gods of the sea to aid them. They uttered prayers and incantations. Soon Nanaue lost strength and could not throw off the ropes which were tied around him, nor could he break the nets in which he was entangled.

The fishermen drew him to the shore, and the people dragged the great shark body up the hill of Puu-mano. Then they cut the body into small pieces and burned them in a great oven.

Thus died Nanaue, whose cannibal life was best explained by giving to him in mythology the awful appetite of an insatiable man-eating shark.

The Strange Banana Skin

KUKALI, according to the folklore of Hawaii, was born at Kalapana, the most southerly point of the largest island of the Hawaiian group. Kukali lived hundreds of years ago in the days of the migrations of Polynesians from one group of islands to another throughout the length and breadth of the great Pacific Ocean. He visited strange lands, now known under the general name of Kahiki, or Tahiti. Here he killed the great bird Halulu, found the deep bottomless pit in which was a pool of the fabled water of life, married the sister of Halulu, and returned to his old home. All this he accomplished through the wonderful power of a banana skin.

Kukali's father was a priest, or kahuna, of great wisdom and ability, who taught his children how to exercise strange and magical powers. To Kukali he gave a banana with the impressive charge to preserve the skin whenever he ate the fruit, and be careful that it was always under his control. He taught Kukali the wisdom of the makers of canoes and also how to select the fine-grained lava for stone knives and hatchets, and fashion the blade to the best shape. He instructed the young man in the prayers and incantations of greatest efficacy and showed him charms which would be more powerful than any charms his enemies might use in attempting to destroy him. He taught him those omens which were too powerful to be overcome. Thus Kukali became a wizard, having great confidence in his ability to meet the craft of the wise men of distant islands.

Kukali went inland through the forests and up the mountains, carrying no food save the banana which his father had given him. Hunger came, and he carefully stripped back the skin and ate the banana, folding the skin once more together. In a little while the skin was filled with fruit. Again and again he ate, and as his hunger was satisfied the fruit always again filled the skin, which he was careful never to throw away or lose.

The fever of sea-roving was in the blood of the Hawaiian people in those days, and Kukali's heart burned within him with the desire to visit the faraway lands about which other men told marvelous tales and from which came strangers like to the Hawaiians in many ways.

After a while he went to the forests and selected trees approved by the omens, and with many prayers fashioned a great canoe in which to embark upon his journey. The story is not told of the days passed on the great stretches of water as he sailed on and on, guided by the sun in the day and the stars in the night, until he came to the strange lands about which he had dreamed for years.

His canoe was drawn up on the shore and he lay down for rest. Before falling asleep he secreted his magic banana in his malo, or loincloth, and then gave himself to deep slumber. His rest was troubled with strange dreams, but his weariness was great and his eyes heavy, and he could not rouse himself to meet the dangers which were swiftly surrounding him.

A great bird which lived on human flesh was the god of the land to which he had come. The name of the bird was Halulu. Each feather of its wings was provided with talons and seemed to be endowed with human powers. Nothing like this bird was ever known or seen in the beautiful Hawaiian Islands. But here in the mysterious foreign land it had its deep valley, walled in like the valley of the Arabian Nights, over which the great bird hovered looking into the depths for food. A strong wind always attended the coming of Halulu when he sought the valley for his victims.

Kukali was lifted on the wings of the bird god, carried to this hole, and quietly laid on the ground to finish his hour of deep sleep.

When Kukali awoke he found himself in the shut-in valley with many companions who had been captured by the great bird and placed in this prison hole. They had been without food and were very weak. Now and then one of the number would lie down to die. Halulu, the bird god, would perch on a tree which grew on the edge of the precipice and let down its wing to sweep across the floor of the valley and pick up the victims lying on the ground. Those who were strong could escape the feathers as they brushed over the bottom and hide in the crevices in the walls; but day by day the weakest of the prisoners were lifted out and prepared for Halulu's feast.

Kukali pitied the helpless state of his fellow prisoners and prepared his best incantations and prayers to help him overcome the great bird. He took his wonderful banana and fed all the people until they were very strong. He taught them how to seek stones best fitted for the manufacture of knives and hatchets. Then for days they worked until they were all well armed with sharp stone weapons.

While Kukali and his fellow prisoners were making preparation for the final struggle, the bird god had often come to his perch and put his wing down into the valley, brushing the feathers back and forth to catch his prey. Frequently the search was fruitless. At last he became very impatient, and sent his strongest feathers along the precipitous walls, seeking for victims.

Kukali and his companions then ran out from their hiding places and fought the strong feathers, cutting them off and chopping them into small pieces.

Halulu cried out with pain and anger, and sent feather after feather into the prison. Soon one wing was entirely destroyed. Then the other wing was broken to pieces and the bird god in his insane wrath put down a strong leg armed with great talons. Kukali uttered mighty invocations and prepared sacred charms for the protection of his friends.

After a fierce battle, they cut off the leg and destroyed the talons. Then came the struggle with the remaining leg and claws, but Kukali's friends had become very bold. They fearlessly gathered around this enemy, hacking and pulling until the bird god, screaming with pain, fell into the pit among the prisoners, who quickly cut the body into fragments.

The prisoners made steps in the walls, and by the aid of vines climbed out of their prison. When they had fully escaped, they gathered great piles of branches and trunks of trees and threw them into the prison until the body of the bird god was covered. Fire was thrown down and Halulu was burned to ashes. Thus Kukali taught by his charms that Halulu could be completely destroyed.

But two of the breast feathers of the burning Halulu flew away to his sister, who lived in a great hole which had no bottom. The name of this sister was Namakaeha. She belonged to the family of Pele, the goddess of volcanic fires, who had journeyed to Hawaii and taken up her home in the crater of the volcano of Kilauea.

Namakaeha smelled smoke on the feathers which

came to her, and knew that her brother was dead. She also knew that he could have been conquered only by one possessing great magical powers. So she called to his people: "Who is the great kupua (wizard) who has killed my brother? Oh, my people, keep careful watch."

Kukali was exploring all parts of the strange land in which he had already found marvelous adventures. By and by he came to the great pit in which Namakaeha lived. He could not see the bottom. He told his companions he was going down to see what mysteries were concealed in this hole without a bottom. They made a rope of the hau tree bark. Fastening one end around his body, he ordered his friends to let him down. Uttering prayers and incantations, he went down and down until, owing to counter-incantations of Namakaeha's priests, who had been watching, the rope broke and he fell.

Down he went swiftly, but, remembering the prayer which a falling man must use to keep him from injury, he cried, "O Ku! Guard my life!"

In the ancient Hawaiian mythology there was frequent mention of "the water of life." Sometimes the sick bathed in it and were healed. Sometimes it was sprinkled upon the unconscious, bringing them back to life. Kukali's incantation was of great power, for it threw him into a pool of the water of life and he was saved.

One of the kahunas (priests) caring for Namakaeha was a very great wizard. He saw the wonderful preservation of Kukali and became his friend. He warned Kukali against eating anything that was ripe, because it would be poison; and even the most powerful charms could not save him.

Kukali thanked him and went out among the people. He had carefully preserved his wonderful banana skin, and was able to eat apparently ripe fruit and yet be perfectly safe.

The kahunas of Namakaeha tried to overcome him and destroy him, but he conquered them, killed those who were bad, and entered into friendship with those who were good.

At last he came to the place where the great chiefess dwelt. Here he was tested in many ways. He accepted the fruits offered him, but always ate the food in his magic banana. Thus he preserved his strength and conquered even the chiefess and married her.

After living with her for a time, he began to long for his old home in Hawaii. Then he persuaded her to do as her relative Pele had already done, and the family, taking their large canoe, sailed away to Hawaii, their future home.

Hawaiian Ghost Testing

MANOA VALLEY for centuries has been to the Hawaiians the royal palace of rainbows. The mountains at the head of the valley were gods, whose children were the divine wind and rain from whom was born the beautiful rainbow-maiden who plays in and around the valley day and night whenever misty showers are touched by sunlight or moonlight.

The natives of the valley usually give her the name of Kahalaopuna, or The Hala of Puna. Sometimes, however, they call her Kaikawahine Anuenue, or The Rainbow Maiden. The rainbow, the anuenue, marks the continuation of the legendary life of Kahala.

The legend of Kahala is worthy of record in itself, but connected with the story is a very interesting account of an attempt to discover and capture ghosts according to the methods supposed to be effective by the Hawaiian witch doctors or priests of the long, long ago.

The legends say that the rainbow maiden had two lovers, one from Waikiki and one from Kamoiliili, half-way between Manoa and Waikiki. Both wanted the beautiful arch to rest over their homes and the maiden, the descendant of the gods, to dwell therein.

Kauhi, the Waikiki chief, was of the family of Mohoalii, the shark god, and partook of the shark's cruel nature. He became angry with the rainbow maiden and killed her and buried the body. But her guardian god, Pueo, the owl, scratched away the earth and brought her to life. Several times this occurred, and the owl each time restored the buried body to the wandering spirit. At last the chief buried the body deep down under the roots of a large koa tree. The owl god scratched and pulled, but the roots of the tree were many and strong. His claws were entangled again and again. At last he concluded that life must be extinct and so deserted the place.

The spirit of the murdered girl was wandering around hoping that it could be restored to the body, and not be compelled to descend to Milu, the Underworld of the Hawaiians. Po was sometimes the Underworld, and Milu was the god ruling over Po. The Hawaiian ghosts did not go to the home of the dead as soon as they were separated from the body. Many times, as when rendered unconscious, it was believed that the spirit had left the body, but for some reason had been able to come back into it and enjoy life among friends once more.

Kahala, the rainbow maiden, was thus restored several times by the owl god, but with this last failure it seemed to be certain that the body would grow cold and stiff before the spirit could return. The spirit hastened to and fro in great distress, trying to attract attention.

If a wandering spirit could interest someone to render speedy aid, the ancient Hawaiians thought that a human being could place the spirit back in the body. Certain prayers and incantations were very effective in calling the spirit back to its earthly home.

The spirit of Kahala was almost discouraged. The shadows of real death were encompassing her, and the feeling of separation from the body was becoming more and more permanent. At last she saw a noble young chief approaching. He was Mahana, the chief of Kamoiliili.

127

The spirit hovered over him and around him and tried to impress her anguish upon him.

Mahana felt the call of distress and attributed it to the presence of a ghost, or aumakua, a ghost-god. He was conscious of an influence leading him toward a large koa tree. There he found the earth disturbed by the owl god. He tore aside the roots and discovered the body bruised and disfigured, and yet recognized it as the body of the rainbow maiden whom he had loved.

Mahana's elder brother was a kahuna, or witch doctor, of great celebrity. He was called at once to announce the prayers and invocations necessary for influencing the spirit and the body to reunite. Long and earnestly the kahuna practiced all the arts with which he was acquainted and yet completely failed. In his anxiety he called upon the spirits of two sisters who, as aumakuas, watched over the welfare of Mahana's clan. These spirit sisters brought the spirit of the rainbow maiden to the bruised body and induced it to enter the feet. Then, by using the forces of spirit land, while the kahuna chanted and used his charms, they pushed the spirit of Kahala slowly up to the body until "the soul was once more restored to its beautiful tenement."

The spirit sisters then aided Mahana in restoring the wounded body to its old vigor and beauty. Thus many days passed in close comradeship between Kahala and the young chief, and they learned to care greatly for one another.

But while Kauhi lived it was unsafe for it to be known that Kahala was alive. Mahana determined to provoke Kauhi to personal combat; therefore he sought the places which Kauhi frequented for sport and gambling. Bitter words were spoken and fierce anger aroused until at last, by the skillful use of Kahala's story, Mahana led Kauhi to admit that he had killed the rainbow maiden and buried her body.

Mahana said that Kahala was now alive and visiting his sisters. Kauhi declared that if there was any one visiting

Mahana's home it must be an imposter. In his anger against Mahana he determined a more awful death than could possibly come from any personal conflict. He was so sure that Kahala was dead that he offered to be baked alive in one of the native imus, or ovens, if she should be produced before the king and the principal chiefs of the district. Akaaka, the grandfather of Kahala, one of the mountain gods of Manoa Valley, was to be one of the judges.

This proposition suited Mahana better than a conflict, in which there was a possibility of losing his own life.

Kauhi now feared that some deception might be practiced. His proposition had been so eagerly accepted that he became suspicious; therefore he consulted the sorcerers of his own family. They agreed that it was possible for some powerful kahuna to present the ghost of the murdered maiden and so deceive the judges. They decided that it was necessary to be prepared to test the ghosts.

If it could be shown that the ghosts were present, then the aid of "spirit catchers" from the land of Milu could be invoked. Spirits would seize these venturesome ghosts and carry them away to the spirit land, where special punishments should be meted out to them. It was supposed that spirit catchers were continually sent out by Milu, king of the Underworld.

How could these ghosts be detected? They would certainly appear in human form and be carefully safeguarded. The chief sorcerer of Kauhi's family told Kauhi to make secretly a thorough test. This could be done by taking the large and delicate leaves of the ape plant and spreading them over the place where Kahala must walk and sit before the judges. A human being could not touch these leaves so carefully placed without tearing and bruising them. A ghost walking upon them could not make any impression. Untorn leaves would condemn Mahana to the ovens to be baked alive, and the spirit catchers would be called by the sorcerers to seize the escaped ghost and carry it back to spirit land. Of course, if some other maid of the islands had pretended to be Kahala, that could be easily determined by her divine ancestor Akaaka. The trial was really a test of ghosts, for the presence of Kahala as a spirit in her former human likeness was all that Kauhi and his chief sorcerer feared.

The leaves were selected with great care and secretly placed so that no one should touch them but Kahala. There was great interest in this strange contest for a home in a burning oven. The imus had been prepared. The holes had been dug, and the stones and wood necessary for the sacrifice laid close at hand.

The king and judges were in their places. The multitude of retainers stood around at a respectful distance. Kauhi and his chief sorcerer were placed where they could watch closely every movement of the maiden who should appear before the judgment seat.

Kahala, the rainbow maiden, with all the beauty of her past girlhood restored to her, drew near, attended by the two spirit sisters who had saved and protected her. The spirits knew at once the ghost test by which Kahala was to be tried. They knew also that she had nothing to fear, but they must not be discovered. The test applied to Kahala would only make more evident the proof that she was a living human being, but that same test would prove that they were ghosts. The spirit catchers would be called at once and they would be caught and carried away for punishment. The spirit sisters could not try to escape. Any such attempt would arouse suspicion and they would be surely seized. The ghost testing was a serious ordeal for Kahala and her friends.

The spirit sisters whispered to Kahala, telling her the purpose attending the use of the ape leaves and asking her to break as many of them on either side of her as she could without attracting undue attention. Thus she could aid her own cause and also protect the sister spirits. Slowly and with great dignity the beautiful rainbow maiden passed through the crowds of eager attendants to their places before the king. Kahala bruised and broke as many of the leaves as she could quietly. She was recognized at once as the child of the divine rain and wind of Manoa Valley. There was no question concerning her bodily presence. The torn leaves afforded ample and indisputable testimony.

Kauhi, in despair, recognized the girl whom he had several times tried to slay. In bitter disappointment at the failure of his ghost test, the chief sorcerer, as the Kalakaua version of this legend says, "declared that he saw and felt the presence of spirits in some manner connected with her." These spirits, he claimed, must be detected and punished.

A second form of ghost testing was proposed by Akaaka, the mountain god. This was a method frequently employed throughout all the islands of the Hawaiian group. It was believed that any face reflected in a pool or calabash of water was a spirit face. Many times had ghosts been discovered in this way. The face in the water had been grasped by the watcher, crushed between his hands, and the spirit destroyed.

The chief sorcerer eagerly ordered a calabash of water to be quickly brought and placed before him. In his anxiety to detect and seize the spirits who might be attending Kahala, he forgot about himself and leaned over the calabash. His own spirit face was the only one reflected on the surface of the water. This spirit face was believed to be his own true spirit escaping for the moment from the body and bathing in the liquid before him. Before he could leap back and restore his spirit to his body, Akaaka leaped forward, thrust his hands down into the water, and seized and crushed this spirit face between his mighty hands. Thus it was destroyed before it could return to its home of flesh and blood.

The chief sorcerer fell dead by the side of the calabash by means of which he had hoped to destroy the friends of the rainbow maiden.

In this trial of the ghosts, the two most powerful methods of making a test, as far as known among the ancient Hawaiians, were put in practice.

Kauhi was punished for his crimes against Kahala. He was baked alive in the imu prepared on his own land at Waikiki. His lands and retainers were given to Kahala and Mahana.

The story of Kahala and her connection with the rainbows and waterfalls of Manoa Valley has been told from time to time in the homes of the nature-loving residents of the valley.

How Milu Became the King of Ghosts

LONO WAS a chief living on the western side of the island of Hawaii. He had a very red skin and strange-looking eyes. His choice of occupation was farming. This man had never been sick. One time he was digging with the o-o, a long sharp-pointed stick or spade. A man passed and admired him. The people said, "Lono has never been sick." The man said, "He will be sick."

Lono was talking about that man and at the same time struck his o-o down with force and cut his foot. He shed much blood and fainted, falling to the ground. A man took a pig, went after the stranger, and let the pig go, which ran to this man. The stranger was Kamaka, a god of healing. He turned and went back at the call of the messenger, taking some popolo fruit and leaves in his cloak. When he came to the injured man he asked for salt, which he pounded into the fruit and leaves. He placed the mixture in coco cloth and bound it on the wound, leaving it a long time. Then he went away.

As he journeyed on he heard heavy breathing, and turning saw Lono, who said, "You have helped me, and

132

so I have left my lands in the care of my friends, directing them what to do, and have hastened after you to learn how to heal other people."

The god said, "Lono, open your mouth!" This Lono did, and the god spat in his mouth, so that the saliva could be taken into every part of Lono's body. Thus a part of the god became a part of Lono, and he became very skillful in the use of all healing remedies. He learned about the various diseases and the medicines needed for each. The god and Lono walked together, Lono receiving new lessons along the way, passing through the districts of Kau, Puna, and Hilo, and then going to Hamakua.

The god said, "It is not right for us to stay together. You can never accomplish anything by staying with me. You must go to a separate place and give yourself up to healing people."

Lono turned aside to dwell in Waimanu and Waipio Valleys and there began to practice healing, becoming very noted, while the god Kamaka made his home at Ku-kui-haele.

This god did not tell the other gods of the medicines that he had taught Lono. One of the other gods, Kalae, was trying to find some way to kill Milu, and was always making him sick. Milu, chief of Waipio, heard of the skill of Lono. Some had been sick even to death, and Lono had healed them. Therefore Milu sent a messenger to Lono. He responded at once, came and slapped Milu all over the body, and said, "You are not ill. Obey me and you shall be well."

Then he healed him from all the sickness inside the body caused by Kalae. But since there was danger from outside, he said: "You must build a ti-leaf house and dwell there quietly for some time, letting your disease rest. If a company should come by the house making sport, with a great noise, do not go out, because when you go they will come up and get you for your death. Do not open the ti leaves and look out. The day you do this you shall die."

Some time passed and the chief remained in the house, but one day there was the confused noise of many people talking and shouting around his house. He did not forget the command of Lono. Two birds were sporting in a wonderful way in the sky above the forest. This continued all day until it was dark.

Then another long time passed and again Waipio was full of resounding noises. A great bird appeared in the sky, resplendent in all kinds of feathers, swaying from side to side over the valley, from the top of one precipice across to the top of another, in grand flights passing over the heads of the people, who shouted until the valley re-echoed with the sound.

Milu became tired of that great noise and could not patiently obey his physician. He pushed aside some of the ti leaves of his house and looked out upon the bird. That was the time when the bird swept down upon the house, thrusting a claw under Milu's arm, tearing out his liver.

Lono saw this and ran after the bird, but it flew swiftly to a deep pit in the lava on one side of the valley and dashed inside, leaving blood spread on the stones. Lono came, saw the blood, took it and wrapped it in a piece of tapa cloth, and returned to the place where the chief lay almost dead. He poured some medicine into the wound and pushed the kapa and blood inside. Milu was soon healed.

The place where the bird hid with the liver of Milu is called to this day Ke-ake-o-Milu (The Liver of Milu). When this death had passed away he felt very well, even as before his trouble.

Then Lono told him that another death threatened him and would soon appear. He must dwell in quietness.

For some time Milu was living in peace and quiet after this trouble. Then one day the surf of Waipio became very high, rushing from far out even to the sand, and the people entered into the sport of surfriding with great joy and loud shouts. This noise continued day by day, and Milu was impatient of the restraint and forgot the words of Lono. He went out to bathe in the surf.

When he came to the place of the wonderful surf, he let the first and second waves go by, and as the third came near he launched himself upon it while the people along the beach shouted uproariously. He went out again into deeper water, and again came in, letting the first and second waves go first. As he came to the shore the first and second waves were hurled back from the shore in a great mass against the wave upon which he was riding. The two great masses of water struck and pounded Milu, whirling and crowding him down, while the surfboard was caught in the raging, struggling waters and thrown out toward the shore. Milu was completely lost in the deep water.

The people cried: "Milu is dead! The chief is dead!" The god Kalae thought he had killed Milu. With the other poison gods he went on a journey to Mauna Loa. Kapo and Pua, the poison gods, or gods of death of the island of Maui, found them as they passed, and joined the company. They discovered a forest on Molokai, and there as kupua spirits, or ghost bodies, entered into the trees of that forest, so that the trees became the kupua bodies. They were the medicinal or poison qualities in the trees.

Lono remained in Waipio Valley, becoming the ancestor and teacher of all the good healing priests of Hawaii. But Milu became the ruler of the Underworld, the place where the spirits of the dead had their home after they were driven away from the land of the living.

Many people came to him from time to time. He established ghostly sports like those which his subjects had enjoyed before death. They played the game kilu with polished coconut shells, spinning them over a smooth surface to strike a post set up in the center. He taught konane, a game commonly called "Hawaiian checkers" but more like the Japanese game of "Go." He permitted them to gamble, betting all the kinds of property found in ghost-land. They boxed and wrestled; they leaped from precipices into ghostly swimming pools; they feasted and fought, sometimes attempting to slay each other. Thus they lived the ghost life as they had lived on earth. Sometimes the ruler was forgotten and the ancient Hawaiians called the Underworld by his name — Milu.

A Visit to the King of Ghosts

WHEN ANY person lay in an unconscious state, it was supposed by the ancient Hawaiians that death had taken possession of the body and opened the door for the spirit to depart. Sometimes if the body lay like one asleep, the spirit was supposed to return to its old home. One of the Hawaiian legends weaves their deep-rooted faith in the spirit world into the expressions of one who seemed to be permitted to visit that ghost-land and its king. This legend belonged to the island of Maui and the region near the village of Lahaina. Thus was the story told:

Ka-ilio-hae (The Wild Dog) had been sick for days and at last sank into a state of unconsciousness. The spirit of life crept out of the body and finally departed from the left eye into a corner of the house, buzzing like an insect. Then he stopped and looked back over the body he had left. It appeared to him like a massive mountain. The eyes were deep caves, into which the ghost looked. Then the spirit became afraid and went outside and rested on the roof of the house.

The people began to wail loudly and the ghost fled from the noise to a coconut tree and perched like a bird in the branches. Soon he felt the impulse of the spirit land moving him away from his old home. He leaped from tree to tree and flew from place to place, wandering toward Kekaa, the place from which the ghosts leave the island of Maui for their home in the permanent spirit land — the Underworld.

As he came near this doorway to the spirit world, he met the ghost of a sister who had died long before, and to whom was given the power of sometimes turning a ghost back to its body again. She was an aumakua-ho-ola (a spirit making alive). She called to Ka-ilio-hae and told him to come to her house and dwell for a time. But she warned him that when her husband was at home he must not yield to any invitation from him to enter their house, nor could he partake of any of the food which her husband might urge him to eat. The home and the food would be only the shadows of real things, and would destroy his power of becoming alive again.

The sister said, "When my husband comes to eat the food of the spirits and to sleep the sleep of ghosts, then I will go with you and you shall see all the spirit land of our island and see the king of ghosts."

The ghost sister led Ka-ilio-hae into the place of whirl-winds, a hill where he heard the voices of many spirits planning to enjoy all the sports of their former life. He listened with delight and drew near to the multitude of happy spirits. Some were making ready to go down to the sea for the hee-nalu (surfriding). Others were al-ready rolling the ulu-maika (the round stone discs for rolling along the ground). Some were engaged in the mokomolo or umauma (boxing) and the kulakulai (wrest-ling), as well as the honuhonu (pulling with the hands), the loulou (pulling with hooked fingers), and other athletic sports.

Some of the spirits were already grouped in the shade of trees, playing the gambling games in which they had delighted when alive. There were the stone konane board (somewhat like checkers); the puepue-one (a small sand mound in which was concealed some object); the puhenehene (the hidden stone under piles of kapa); and the many other trials of skill which permitted betting. Then in another place crowds were gathered around the hulas (the many forms of dancing). These sports were all in the open air and seemed to be full of interest.

137

There was a strange quality which fettered every newborn ghost: he could only go in the direction into which he was pushed by the hand of some stranger power. If the guardian of a ghost struck it on one side, it would move off in the direction indicated by the blow or the push until spirit strength and experience came and he could go alone. The newcomer desired to join in these games and started to go, but the sister slapped him on the breast and drove him away. These were shadow games into which those who entered could never go back to the substantial things of life.

Then there was a large grass house inside which many ghosts were making merry. The visitor wanted to join this great company, but the sister knew that, if he once was engulfed by this crowd of spirits in this shadowland, her brother could never escape. The crowds of players would seize him like a whirlwind and he would be unable to know the way he came in or the way out. Ka-ilio-hae tried to slip away from his sister, but he could not turn readily. He was still a very awkward ghost, and his sister slapped him back in the way she wanted him to go.

An island which was supposed to float on the ocean as one of the homes of the aumakuas (the ghosts of the ancestors) had the same characteristics. The ghosts lived on the shadows of all that belonged to the earth life. It was said that a canoe with a party of young people landed on this island of dreams and for some time enjoyed the food and fruits and sports, but after returning to their homes could not receive the nourishment of the food of their former lives, and soon died. The legends taught that no ghost passing out of the body could return unless it made the life of the aumakuas kapu to itself.

Soon the sister led her brother to a great field, stone walled, in which were such fine grass houses as were built only for chiefs of the highest rank. There she pointed to a narrow passageway into which she told her brother he must enter by himself.

"This," she said, "is the home of Walia, the high chief

of the ghosts living in this place. You must go to him. Listen to all he says to you. Say little. Return quickly. There will be three watchmen guarding this passage. The first will ask you, 'What is the fruit (desire) of your heart?' You will answer, 'Walia.' Then he will let you enter the passage.

"Inside the walls of the narrow way will be the second watchman. He will ask why you come; again answer, 'Walia,' and pass by him.

"At the end of the entrance the third guardian stands holding a raised spear ready to strike. Call to him, 'Kamake-loa' (The Great Death). This is the name of his spear. Then he will ask what you want, and you must reply, 'To see the chief,' and he will let you pass.

"Then again, when you stand at the door of the great house, you will see two heads bending together in the way so that you cannot enter or see the king and his queen. If these heads can catch a spirit coming to see the king without knowing the proper incantations, they will throw that ghost into the Po-Milu (the dark spirit world). Watch therefore and remember all that is told you.

"When you see these heads, point your hands straight before you between them and open your arms, pushing these guards off on each side. Then the ala-nui (the great way) will be open for you — and you can enter.

"You will see kahilis (soft long feather fans) moving over the chiefs. The king will awake and call, 'Why does this traveller come?' You will reply quickly, 'He comes to see the Divine One.' When this is said no injury will come to you. Listen and remember and you will be alive again."

Ka-ilio-hae did as he was told with the three watchmen, and each one stepped back, saying, "Noa" (the tabu is lifted), and he pushed by. At the door he shoved the two heads to the side and entered the chief's house to the ka-ikuwai (the middle), falling on his hands and knees. The servants were waving the kahilis this way and that. There was motion, but no noise.

The chief awoke, looked at Ka-ilio-hae, and said:

"Aloha, stranger, come near. Who is the high chief of your land?"

Then Ka-ilio-hae gave the name of his king, and the genealogy from the ancient times of the chiefs dead and in the spirit world.

The queen of ghosts arose, and the kneeling spirit saw one more beautiful than any woman in all the island, and he fell on his face before her.

The king told him to go back and enter his body and tell his people about troubles near at hand.

While he was before the king, twice he heard messengers call to the people that the sports were all over. Anyone not heeding would be thrown into the darkest place of the home of the ghosts when the third call had been sounded.

The sister was troubled, for she knew that at the third call the stone walls around the king's houses would close and her brother would be held fast forever in the spirit land. She uttered her incantations and passed the guard. Softly she called. Her brother reluctantly came. She seized him and pushed him outside. Then they heard the third call, and met the multitude of ghosts coming inland from their sports in the sea, and other multitudes hastening homeward from their work and sports on the land.

They met a beautiful young woman who called to them to come to her home, and pointed to a point of rock where many birds were resting. The sister struck her brother and forced him down to the seaside where she had her home and her responsibility, for she was one of the guardians of the entrance to the spirit world.

She knew well what must be done to restore the spirit to the body. She told her brother they must at once obey the command of the king. But the brother had seen the delights of the life of the aumakuas and wanted to stay. He tried to slip away and hide, but his sister held him fast and compelled him to go along the beach to his old home and his waiting body.

When they came to the place where the body lay, she

140

found a hole in the corner of the house and pushed the spirit through. When he saw the body, he was very much afraid and tried to escape, but the sister caught him and pushed him inside the foot up to the knee. He did not like the smell of the body and tried to rush back, but she pushed him inside again and held the foot fast and shook him and made him go to the head.

The family heard a little sound in the mouth and saw breath moving the breast. Then they knew that he was alive again. They warmed the body and gave a little food. When strength returned, he told his family all about his wonderful journey into the land of ghosts.

Ke-ao-mele-mele, the Maid of the Golden Cloud

THE HAWAIIANS never found gold in their islands. The mountains being of recent volcanic origin do not show traces of the precious metals; but hovering over the mountaintops clustered the glorious golden clouds built up by damp winds from the seas. The Maiden of the Golden Cloud belonged to the cloud mountains and was named after their golden glow.

Her name in the Hawaiian tongue was Ke-ao-mele-mele (The Golden Cloud). She was said to be one of the first persons brought by the gods to find a home in the Paradise of the Pacific.

In the ancient times, the ancestors of the Hawaiians came from far-off ocean lands, for which they had different names, such as The Shining Heaven, The Floating Land of Kane, The Far-off White Land of Kahiki, and Kuai-he-lani. It was from Kuai-he-lani that the Maiden of the Golden Cloud was called to live in Hawaii.

In this legendary land lived Mo-o-inanea (Self-reliant

Dragon). She cared for the first children of the gods, one of whom was named Hina, later known in Polynesian mythology as the Moon Goddess.

Mo-o-inanea took her to Ku, one of the gods. They lived together many years and a family of children came to them.

Two of the great gods of Polynesia, Kane and Kanaloa, had found a beautiful place above Honolulu on Oahu, one of the Hawaiian Islands. Here they determined to build a home for the first-born child of Hina.

Thousands of eepa (gnome) people lived around this place, which was called Waolani. The gods had them build a temple which was also called Waolani (Divine Forest).

When the time came for the birth of the child, clouds and fogs crept over the land, thunder rolled and lightning flashed, red torrents poured down the hillsides, strong winds hurled the rain through bending trees, earthquakes shook the land, huge waves rolled inland from the sea. Then a beautiful boy was born. All these signs taken together signified the birth of a chief of the highest degree—even of the family of the gods.

Kane and Kanaloa sent their sister Anuenue (Rainbow) to get the child of Ku and Hina that they might care for it. All three should be the caretakers.

Anuenue went first to the place where Mo-o-inanea dwelt, to ask her if it would be right. Mo-o-inanea said she might go, but if they brought up that child he must not have a wife from any of the women of Hawaii-nui-akea (Great Wide Hawaii).

Anuenue said, "Suppose I get that child; who is to give it the proper name?"

Mo-o-inanea said: "You bring the child to our brothers and they will name this child. They have sent you, and the responsibility of the name rests on them."

Anuenue said goodby, and in the twinkling of an eye stood at the door of the house where Ku dwelt.

Ku looked outside and saw the bright glow of the rainbow but no cloud or rain. He called Hina. "Here is a strange thing! You must come and look at it. There is no rain and there are no clouds or mist, but there is a rainbow at our door."

They went out, but Anuenue had changed her rainbow body and stood before them as a very beautiful woman, wrapped only in the colors of the rainbow.

Ku and Hina began to shiver with a nameless terror as they looked at this strange maiden. They faltered out a welcome, asking her to enter their house.

As she came near to them Ku said, "From what place do you come?"

Anuenue said: "I am from the sky, a messenger sent by my brothers to get your child that they may bring it up. When grown, if the child wants its parents, we will bring it back. If it loves us it shall stay with us."

Hina bowed her head and Ku wailed, both thinking seriously for a little while. Then Ku said: "If Mo-o-inanea has sent you, she shall have the child. You may take this word to her."

Anuenue replied: "I have just come from her and the word I brought you is her word. If I go away I shall not come again."

Hina said to Ku: "We must give this child according to her word. It is not right to disobey Mo-o-inanea."

Anuenue took the child and studied the omens for its future. Then she said, "This child is of the very highest, the flower on the top of the tree."

She prepared to take the child away, and bade the parents farewell. She changed her body into the old rainbow colors shining out of a mist. Then she wrapped the child in the rainbow, bearing it away.

Ku and Hina went out, looking up and watching the cloud of rainbow colors floating in the sky. Strong, easy winds blew and carried this cloud out over the ocean. The navel string had not been cut off. Anuenue broke off part and threw it into the ocean, where it became the Hee-makoko, a blood-red squid. This is the legendary

143

origin of that kind of squid.

Anuenue passed over many islands, coming at last to Waolani, to the temple built by the gnomes under Kane and Kanaloa. They consecrated the child and cut off another part of the navel cord. Kanaloa took it to the Nuuanu pali back of Honolulu, to the place called Ka-ipu-o-Lono. Kane and Kanaloa consulted about servants to live with the boy, and decided that they must have only ugly ones, who would not be desired as wives by their boy. Therefore they gathered together the lame, crooked, deformed, and blind among the gnome people. There were hundreds of these living in different homes and performing different tasks. Anuenue was the ruler over all of them.

This child was named Kahanai-a-ke-Akua (The One Adopted by the Gods). He was given a very high kapu by Kane and Kanaloa. No one was allowed to stand before him and no person's shadow could fall upon him.

Hina again conceived. The signs of this child appeared in the heavens and were seen on Oahu. Kane wanted to send Lanihuli and Waipuhia, their daughters, living near the pali of Waolani and Nuuanu. The girls asked where they should go.

Kane said: "We send you to the land Kuai-he-lani, a land far distant from Hawaii, to get the child of Hina. If the parents ask you about your journey, tell them you have come for the child. Tell our names and refer to Mo-o-inanea. You must now look at the way by which to go to Kuai-he-lani."

They looked and saw a great bird — Iwa. They got on this bird and were carried far up in the heavens. By and by the bird called two or three times. The girls were frightened and looking down saw the bright shining land of Kuai-he-lani below them. The bird took them to the door of Ku's dwelling place.

Ku and Hina were caring for a beautiful girl-baby. They looked up and saw two fine women at their door. They invited them in and asked whence they came and why they traveled.

The girls told them they were sent by the gods Kane and Kanaloa. Suddenly a new voice was heard. Mo-o-inanea was by the house. She called to Ku and to Hina, telling them to give the child into the hands of the strangers, that they might take her to Waka, a great priestess, to be brought up by her in the ohia forests of the island of Hawaii. She named that girl Paliula, and explained to the parents that when Paliula should grow up, to be married, the boy of Waolani should be her husband. They were all carried by the bird, Iwa, far away in the sky to Waolani, where they told Kane and Kanaloa the message or prophecy of Mo-o-inanea.

The gods send Iwa with the child to Waka, on Hawaii, to her dwelling place in the districts of Hilo and Puna, where she was caring for all kinds of birds in the branches of the trees and among the flowers.

Waka commanded the birds to build a house for Paliula. This was quickly done. She commanded the bird Iwa to go to Nuumea-lani, a far-off land above Kuai-he-lani, the place where Mo-o-inanea was now living.

It was said that Waka, by her magic power, saw in that land two trees, well cared for by multitudes of servants. The name of one was "Makalei." This was a tree for fish. All kinds of fish would go to it. The second was "Kalala-ika-wai." This was the tree used for getting all kinds of food. Call this tree and food would appear.

Waka wanted Mo-o-inanea to send these trees to Hawaii.

Mo-o-inanea gave these trees to Iwa, who brought them to Hawaii and gave them to Waka. Waka rejoiced and took care of them. The bird went back to Waolani, telling Kane and Kanaloa all the journey from first to last.

The gods gave the girls resting places in the fruitful lands under the shadow of the beautiful Nuuanu precipices.

Waka watched over Paliula until she grew up, beautiful

like the moon of Mahea-lani (Full Moon).

The fish tree, Makalei, which made the fish of all that region tame, was planted by the side of running water, in very restful places spreading all along the riversides to the seashore. Fish came to every stream where the trees grew and filled the waters.

The other tree was planted and brought prepared food for Paliula. The hidden land where this place was has always been called Paliula, a beautiful green spot — a home for fruits and flowers and birds in a forest wilderness.

When Paliula had grown up, Waka went to Waolani to meet Kane, Kanaloa, and Anuenue. There she saw Kahanai-a-ke-Akua and desired him for Paliula's husband. There was no man so splendid and no woman so beautiful as these two. The caretakers decided that they must be man and wife.

Waka returned to the island of Hawaii to prepare for the coming of the people from Waolani.

Waka built new houses finer and better than the first, and covered them with the yellow feathers of the mamo bird, with the colors of the rainbow resting over. Anuenue had sent some of her own garments of rainbows.

Then Waka went again to Waolani to talk with Kane and Kanaloa and their sister Anuenue. They said to her: "You return, and Anuenue will take Kahanai and follow. When the night of their arrival comes, lightning will play over all the mountains above Waolani and through the atmosphere all around the temple, even to Hawaii. After a while, around your home the leaves of the trees will dance and sing and the ohia trees themselves bend back and forth, shaking their beautiful blossoms. Then you may know that the Rainbow Maiden and the boy are by your home on the island of Hawaii."

Waka returned to her home in the tangled forest above Hilo. There she met her adopted daughter and told her about the coming of her husband.

Soon the night of rolling thunder and flashing lightning came. The people of all the region around Hilo were filled with fear. Kane-hekili (Flashing Lightning) was a miraculous body which Kane had assumed. He had gone before the boy and the rainbow, flashing his way through the heavens.

The gods had commanded Kane-hekili to dwell in the heavens in all places wherever the gods desired him to be, so that he could go wherever commanded. He always obeyed without questioning.

The thunder and lightning played over ocean and land while the sun was setting beyond the islands in the west.

After a time the trees bent over, the leaves danced and chanted their songs. The flowers made a glorious halo as they swayed back and forth in their dances.

Kane told the Rainbow Maiden to take their adopted child to Hawaii-nui-akea.

When she was ready, she heard her brothers calling the names of trees which were to go with her on her journey. Some of the legends say that Laka, the hula god, was dancing before the two. The tree people stood before the Rainbow Maiden and the boy, ready to dance all the way to Hawaii. The tree people are always restless and in ceaseless motion. The gods told them to sing together and dance. Two of the tree people were women, Ohia and Lamakea. Lamakea is a native whitewood tree. There are large trees at Waialae in the mountains of the island Oahu. Ohia is a tree always full of fringed red blossoms. They were very beautiful in their wind bodies. They were kupuas, or wizards, and could be moving trees or dancing women as they chose.

The Rainbow Maiden took the boy in her arms up into the sky, and with the tree people went on her journey. She crossed over the islands to the mountains of the island of Hawaii, then went down to find Paliula.

She placed the tree people around the house to dance and sing with soft rustling noises.

Waka heard the chants of the tree people and opened the door of the glorious house, calling for Kahanai to come in. When Paliula saw him, her heart fluttered with trembling delight, for she knew this splendid youth was the husband selected by Waka, the prophetess. Waka called the two trees belonging to Paliula to bring plenty of fish and food.

Then Waka and Anuenue left their adopted children in the wonderful yellow feather house.

The two young people, when left together, talked about their birthplaces and their parents. Paliula first asked Kahanai about his land and his father and mother. He told her that he was the child of Ku and Hina from Kuai-he-lani, brought up by Kane and the other gods of Waolani.

The girl went out and asked Waka about her parents, and learned that this was her first-born brother, who was to be her husband because they had very high divine blood. Their descendants would be the chiefs of the people. This marriage was a command from parents and ancestors and Mo-o-inanea.

She went into the house, telling the brother who she was, and the wish of the gods.

After ten days they were married and lived together a long time.

At last, Kahanai desired to travel all around Hawaii. In this journey he met Poliahu, the white-mantle girl of Mauna Kea, the snow-covered mountain of the island of Hawaii.

Meanwhile, in Kuai-he-lani, Ku and Hina were living together. One day Mo-o-inanea called to Hina, telling her that she would be the mother of a more beautiful and wonderful child than her other two children. This child should live in the highest places of the heavens and should have a multitude of bodies which could be seen at night as well as in the day.

Mo-o-inanea went away to Nuumea-lani and built a a very wonderful house in Ke-alohi-lani (Shining Land), a house always turning around by day and by night like the ever moving clouds. Indeed, it was built of all kinds of clouds and covered with fogs. There she made a spring of flowing water and put it outside for the coming child to have as a bath. There she planted the seeds of magic flowers, Kanikawi and Kanikawa, legendary plants of old Hawaii. Then she went to Kuai-he-lani and found Ku and Hina asleep. She took a child out of the top of the head of Hina and carried it away to the new home, naming it Ke-ao-mele-mele (The Yellow Cloud), the Maiden of the Golden Cloud, a wonderfully beautiful girl.

No one with a human body was permitted to come to this land of Nuumea-lani. No kupuas were allowed to make trouble for the child.

The ao-opua (narrow-pointed clouds) were appointed watchmen serving Ke-ao-mele-mele, the Maiden of the Golden Cloud. All the other clouds were servants: the ao-opua-kakahiaka (morning clouds), ao-opua-ahiahi (evening clouds), ao-opua-aumoe (night clouds), ao-opua-kiei (peeking clouds), ao-opua-aha-lo (down-looking clouds), ao-opua-ku (image-shaped clouds rising at the top of the sea), opua-hele (morning-flower clouds), opua-noho-mai (resting clouds), opua-mele-mele (gold-colored clouds), opua-lani (clouds high up), ka-pae-opua (at surface of sea or clouds along the horizon), ka-lani-opua (clouds up above horizon), ka-maka-o-ka-lani (clouds in the eye of the sun), ka-wele-lau-opua (clouds highest in the sky).

All these clouds were caretakers watching out for the welfare of that girl. Mo-o-inanea gave them their laws for service.

She took Ku-ke-ao-loa (The Long Cloud of Ku) and put him at the door of the house of clouds, with great magic power. He was to be the messenger to all the cloud-lands of the parents and ancestors of this girl.

"The Eye of the Sun" was the cloud with magic power to see all things passing underneath, near or far.

Then there was the opua-alii, cloud-chief with the name of Ka-ao-opua-ola (The Sharp-pointed Living Cloud). This was the sorcerer and astronomer, never weary, never tired, knowing and watching over all things.

149

Mo-o-inanea gave her mana-nui, or great magic power, to Ke-ao-mele-mele—with divine kapus. She made this child the heir of all the divine islands. Therefore she was able to know what was being done everywhere. She understood how Kahanai had forsaken his sister to live with Poliahu. So she went to Hawaii to aid her sister Paliula.

When Mo-o-inanea had taken the child from the head of Hina, Ku and Hina were aroused. Ku went out and saw wonderful cloud images standing near the house, like men. Ku and Hina watched these clouds shining and changing colors in the light of the dawn, as the sun appeared. The light of the sun streamed over the skies. For three days these changing clouds were around them. Then in the midst of these clouds appeared a strange land of the skies surrounded by the ao-opua (the narrow-pointed clouds). In the night of the full moon, the akua (ghost) shadow of that land leaped up into the moon and became fixed there. This was the Alii-wahine-aka-malu (The Queen of Shadows), dwelling in the moon.

Ku and Hina did not understand the meaning of these signs or shadows. They went back into the house, falling into deep sleep.

Mo-o-inanea spoke to Hina in her dreams, saying that these clouds were signs of her daughter born from the head—a girl having great knowledge and miraculous power in sorcery, who would take care of them in their last days. They must learn all the customs of kilo-kilo, or sorcery.

Mo-o-inanea again sent Ku-ke-ao-loa to the house of Ku, that cloud appearing as a man at their door.

They asked who he was. He replied: "I am a messenger sent to teach you the sorcery or witcheries of cloud land. You must have this knowledge that you may know your cloud daughter. Let us begin our work at this time."

They all went outside the house and sat down on a stone at the side of the door.

Ku-ke-ao-loa looked up and called Mo-o-inanea by

name. His voice went to Ke-alohi-lani, and Mo-o-inanea called for all the clouds to come with their ruler, Ke-ao-mele-mele.

Arise, O yellow cloud,
Arise, O cloud — the eye of the sun,
Arise, O beautiful daughters of the skies,
Shine in the eyes of the sun, arise!

Ke-ao-mele-mele arose and put on her glorious white kapas like the snow on Mauna Kea. At this time the cloud watchmen over Kuai-he-lani were revealing their cloud forms to Hina and Ku. The Long Cloud told Hina and Ku to look sharply into the sky to see the meaning of all the cloud forms which were servants of the divine chiefess— their habits of meeting, moving, separating, their forms, their number, the stars appearing through them, the fixed stars and moving clouds, the moving stars and moving clouds, the course of the winds among the different clouds.

When he had taught Ku and Hina the sorcery of cloud land, he disappeared and returned to Ke-alohi-lani.

Some time afterward, Ku went out to the side of their land. He saw a cloud of very beautiful form, appearing like a woman. This was resting in the sky above his head. Hina woke up, missed Ku, looked out and saw Ku sitting on the beach watching the clouds above him. She went to him and by her power told him that he had the desire to travel and that he might go on his journey and find the woman of his vision.

A beautiful chiefess, Hiilei, was at that time living in one of the large islands of the heavens. Ku and Hina went to this place. Ku married Hiilei, and Hina found a chief named Olopana and married him. Ku and Hiilei had a redskinned child, a boy, whom they named Kau-mai-liula (Twilight Resting in the Sky). This child was taken by Mo-o-inanea to Ke-alohi-lani to live with Ke-ao-mele-mele. Olopana and Hina had a daughter whom they called Kau-lana-iki-pokii (Beautiful Daughter of Sunset), who was taken by Ku and Hiilei.

151

Hina then called to the messenger cloud to come and carry a request to Mo-o-inanea that Kau-mai-liula be given to her and Olopana. This was done. Thus they were all separated from each other, but in the end the children were taken to Hawaii.

Meanwhile Paliula was living above Hilo with her husband, Kahanai-a-ke-Akua (Adopted Son of the Gods). Kahanai became restless and determined to see other parts of the land, and started on a journey around the islands. He soon met a fine young man, Waiola (Water of Life).

Waiola had never seen anyone so glorious in appearance as the child of the gods. He fell down before him, saying: "I have never seen anyone so divine as you. You must have come from the skies. I will belong to you through the coming years."

The chief said, "I take you as my aikane (bosom friend) to the last days."

They went down to Waiakea, a village near Hilo, and met a number of girls covered with wreaths of flowers and leaves. Kahanai sent Waiola to sport with them. He himself was of too high rank. One girl told her brother Kanuku to urge the chief to come down, and sent him leis. He said he could not receive their gift, but must wear his own lei. He called for his divine caretaker to send his garlands, and immediately the most beautiful rainbows wrapped themselves around his neck and shoulders, falling down around his body.

Then he came down to Waiakea. The chief took Kanuku also as a follower and went on up the coast to Hamakua.

The chief looked up to Mauna Kea and there saw the mountain women, who lived in the white land above the trees. Poliahu stood above the precipices in her kupuaano (wizard character), revealing herself as a very beautiful woman wearing a white mantle.

When the chief and his friends came near the cold place where she was sitting, she invited them to her home, inland and mountainward. The chief asked his friends to go with him to the mountain house of the beauty of Mauna Kea.

They were well entertained. Poliahu called her sisters, Lilinoe and Ka-lau-a-kolea, beautiful girls, and gave them sweet-sounding shells to blow. All through the night they made music and chanted the stirring songs of the grand mountains. The chief delighted in Poliahu and lived many months on the mountain.

One morning Paliula in her home above Hilo awoke from a dream in which she saw Poliahu and the chief living together. She told Waka, asking if the dream were true. Waka, by her magic power, looked over the island and saw the three young men living with the three maidens of the snow mantle. She called with a penetrating voice for the chief to return to his own home. She went in the form of a great bird and brought him back.

But Poliahu followed, met the chief secretly, and took him up to Mauna Kea again, covering the mountain with snow so that Waka could not go to find them.

Waka and the bird friends of Paliula could not reach the mountaintop because of the cold. Waka went to Waolani and told Anuenue about Paliula's trouble.

Anuenue was afraid that Kane and Kanaloa might hear that the chief had forsaken his sister, and was much troubled. She asked Waka to go with her to see Mo-o-inanea at Ke-alohi-lani, but the gods Kane and Kanaloa could not be deceived. They understood that there was trouble, and came to meet them.

Kane told Waka to return and tell the girl to be patient; the chief should be punished for deserting her.

Waka returned and found that Paliula had gone away, wandering in the forest, picking lehua flowers on the way up toward the Lua Pele, the volcano pit of Pele, the goddess of fire. There she had found a beautiful girl and took her as an aikane (friend) to journey around Hawaii. They traveled by way of the districts of Puna, Kau, and Kona to Waipio, where she saw a fine-looking man standing above a precipice over which leaped the wonderful mist-falls of Hiilawe. This young chief married the beautiful girl friend of Paliula.

Poliahu by her kupua power recognized Paliula, and told the chief that she saw her with a new husband.

Paliula went on to her old home and rested many days. Waka then took her from island to island until they were near Oahu. When they came to the beach, Paliula leaped ashore and went up to Manoa Valley. There she rushed into the forest and climbed the ridges and precipices. She wandered through the rough places, her clothes torn and ragged.

Kane and Kanaloa saw her sitting on the mountainside. Kane sent servants to find her and bring her to live with them at Waolani. When she came to the home of the gods in Nuuanu Valley, she thought longingly of her husband and sang this mele:

Lo, at Waolani is my lei of the blood-red rain,
The lei of the misty rain gathered and put together,
Put together in my thought with tears.
Spoiled is the body by love,
Dear in the eyes of the lover.
My brother, the first-born,
Return, oh, return, my brother.

Paliula, chanting this, turned away from Waolani to Waianae and dwelt for a time with the chiefess Kalena.

While Paliula was living with the people of the cold winds of Waianae, she wore leis of mokihana berries and fragrant grass, and was greatly loved by the family. She went up the mountain to a great gulch. She lay down to sleep, but heard a sweet voice saying, "You cannot sleep on the edge of that gulch." She was frequently awakened by that voice. She went on up the mountain ridges above Waianae. At night when she rested she heard the voices again and again. This was the voice of Hii-lani-wai, who was teaching the hula dance to the girls of Waianae. Paliula wanted to see the one who had such a sweet voice. She went along the pali and came to a hula house, but the house was closed tight and she could not look in.

She sat down outside. Soon Hii-lani-wai opened the door and saw Paliula and asked her to come in. It was the first time Paliula had seen this kind of dancing. Her delight in the dance took control of her mind, and she forgot her husband and took Hii-lani-wai as her aikane, dwelling with her for a time.

One day they went out into the forest. Kane had sent the dancing trees from Waolani to meet them. While in the forest they heard the trees singing and dancing like human beings. Hii-lani-wai called this a very wonderful thing. Paliula told her that she had seen the trees do this before. The trees made her glad.

They went down to the seaside and visited some days. Paliula desired a boat to go to the island of Kauai. The people told them of the dangerous waters, but since the girls were stubborn, they were given a very small boat. Hii-lani-wai was steering, and Paliula was paddling and bailing out the water. The anger of the seas did not arise. On the way Paliula fell asleep, but the boat swiftly crossed the channel. Their boat was covered with all the colors of the rainbow. Some women on land at last saw them and beckoned with their hands for them to come ashore.

Malu-aka (Shadow of Peace) was the most beautiful of all the women on Kauai. She was kind and hospitable and took them to her house. The people came to see these wonderful strangers. Paliula told Malu-aka her story. She rested with the Kauai girls, then went with Malu-aka over the island and learned the dances of Kauai, becoming noted throughout the island for her wonderful grace and skill, dancing like the wind, feet not touching the ground. Her songs and the sounds of the whirling dance were lifted by the winds and carried into the dreams of Ke-ao-mele-mele.

Meanwhile, Ke-ao-mele-mele was living with her cloud watchmen and Mo-o-inanea at Ke-alohi-lani. She began to have dreams, hearing a sweet voice singing and seeing a glorious woman dancing, while winds were whispering in the forests. For five nights she heard the song and the sound of the dance. Then she told Mo-o-inanea, who explained her dream, saying: "That is the voice of Paliula, your sister, who is dancing and singing near the steep places of Kauai. Her brother-husband has forsaken her and she has had much trouble. He is living with Poliahu on Hawaii."

When Ke-ao-mele heard this, she thought she would go and live with her sister. Mo-o-inanea approved of the thought and gave her all kinds of kupua power. She told her to go and see the god Kane, who would tell her what to do.

At last she started her journey with her watching clouds. She went to see Hina and Olopana, and Ku and Hiilei. She saw Kau-mai-liula (Twilight Resting in the Sky), who was very beautiful, like the deep red flowers of the ohia in the shadows of the leaves of the tree. She determined to come back and marry him after her journey to Oahu.

When she left Kuai-he-lani with her followers, she flew like a bird over the waves of the sea. Soon she passed Niihau and came to Kauai to the place where Paliula was dancing, and as a cloud with her cloud friends spied out the land. The soft mists of her native land were scattered over the people by these clouds above them. Paliula was reminded of her birth land and the loved people of her home.

Ke-ao-mele-mele saw the beauty of the dance and understood the love expressed in the chant. She flew away from Kauai, crossed the channel, came to Waolani. There she met Kane and Kanaloa, and told them she had come to learn from them what was the right thing to do for the sister and the husband who had deserted her. When Kane suggested a visit to Hawaii to see Paliula and the chief, she flew over the islands to Hawaii. Then she went up the mountain with the ao-pii-kai (a cloud rising from the sea and climbing the mountain) until she saw Poliahu and her beautiful sisters.

156

Poliahu looked down the mountainside and saw a woman coming, but she looked again and the woman had disappeared. In a little while a golden cloud rested on the summit of the mountain. It was the maid in her cloud body, watching her brother and the girl of the white mountains. For more than twenty days she remained in that place. Then she returned to Waolani on Oahu.

Ke-ao-mele-mele determined to learn the hulas and the accompanying songs. Kane told her she ought to learn these things. There was a fine field for dancing at the foot of the mountain near Waolani, and Kane had planted a large kukui tree by its side to give it shade.

Kane and his sister Anuenue went to this field and sat down in their place. The daughters of Nuuanu Pali were there. Kane sent Ke-ao-mele-mele after the dancing goddess, Kapo, who lived at Mauna Loa. She was the sister of the poison gods and knew the art of sorcery. Ke-ao-mele-mele took gifts, went to Kapo, made offerings, and thus for the first time secured a goddess for the hula.

Kapo taught Ke-ao-mele-mele the chants and the movements of the different hulas until she was very skillful. She flew over the seas to Oahu and showed the gods her skill. Then she went to Kauai and danced on the surf and in the clouds and above the forests and in the whirlwinds. Each night she went to one of the other islands, danced in the skies and over the waters, and returned home. At last she went to Hawaii, to Mauna Kea, where she saw Kahanai, her brother. She persuaded him to leave the maiden of the snow mantle and return to Waolani.

Paliula and her friends had returned to the home with Waka, where she taught to the leaves of clinging vines and the flowers and leaves on the tender swinging branches of the forest trees new motions in their dances with the many kinds of winds.

One day Kahanai saw signs among the stars and in the clouds which made him anxious to travel. He asked Kane for a canoe. Kane called the eepa and the menehune people and told them to make canoes to carry Kahanai to his parents.

These boats were made in the forests of Waolani. When the menehunes finished their boat, they carried it down Nuuanu Valley to Puunui. There they rested, and many of the little folk came to help, taking the canoe down, step by step, to the mouth of the Nuuanu Stream, where they had the aid of the river to the ocean.

The menehunes left the boat floating in the water and went back to Waolani. Of the fairy people it was said: "No task is difficult. It is the work of one hand."

On the way down Nuuanu Valley, the menehunes came to Ka-opua-ua (Storm Cloud). They heard the shouting of other people and hurried along until they met the Namunawa people, the eepas, carrying a boat, pushing it down. When they told the eepas that the chief had already started on his journey with double canoes, the eepas left their boat there to slowly decay; but it is said that it lasted many centuries.

The people who made this boat were the second class of the little people living at Waolani, having the characters of human beings, yet having also the power of the fairy people. These were the men of the time of Kane and the gods.

Kahanai and his friends were in their boat when a strong wind swept down Nuuanu, carrying the dry leaves of the mountains and sweeping them into the sea. The waves were white as the boat was blown out into the ocean. Kahanai steered by magic power, and the boat like lightning swept away from the islands to the homes of Ku and Hina. The strong wind and the swift current were with the boat, and the voyage was through the waves like swift lightning flashing through clouds.

Ku and Hiilei saw the boat coming. Its signs were in the heavens. Ku came and asked the travelers, "What boat is this, and from what place has it come?"

Kahanai said, "This boat has come from Waolani, the

home of the gods Kane and Kanaloa and of Ke-ao-mele-
mele."

Then Ku asked again, "Whose child are you?"

He replied, "The son of Ku and Hina."

"How many other children in your family?"

He said: "There are three of us. I am the boy and there
are two sisters, Paliula and Ke-ao-mele-mele. I have been
sent by Ke-ao-mele-mele to get Kau-mai-liula and Kau-
lana-iki-pokii to go to Oahu."

Ku and his wife agreed to the call of the messenger for
their boy Kau-mai-liula. When Kahanai saw him, he
knew that there was no other one so fine as this young
man, who quickly consented to go to Oahu with his
servants.

Ku called for some beautiful red boats with red sails,
red paddles — everything red. Four good boatmen were
provided for each boat, men who came from the land of
Ulu-nui — the land of the yellow sea and the black sea of
Kane — and obeyed the call of Mo-o-inanea. They had
kupua power. They were relatives of Kane and Kanaloa.

The daughter of Hina and Olopana, Kau-lana-iki-
pokii, cried to go with her brother, but Mo-o-inanea
called for her dragon family to make a boat for her, and
ordered one of the sorcerer dragons to go with her and
guard her. They called the most beautiful shells of the
sea to become the boats for the girl and her attendants.
They followed the boats of Kahanai. With one stroke of
the paddles, the boats passed through the seas around
the home of the gods. With the second stroke, they broke
through all the boundaries of the great ocean, and with
the third dashed into the harbor of old Honolulu, then
known as Kou.

When the boats of Kahanai and Kau-mai-liula came to
the surf of Mamala, there was great shouting inland of
Kou, the voices of the eepas of Waolani. Mists and rainbows rested over Waolani. The menehunes gathered in
great multitudes at the call of Kane, who had seen the
boats approaching.

The menehune people ran down to lift up the boats belonging to the young chief. They made a line from Waolani to the sea. They lifted up the boats and passed them from hand to hand without any effort, shouting with joy.

While these chiefs were going up to Waolani, Ke-ao-mele-mele came from Hawaii in her cloud boats.

Kane had told the menehunes to prepare houses quickly for her. It was done like the motion of the eye. Ke-ao-mele-mele entered her house, rested, and after a time practiced the hula.

The chiefs also had houses prepared, which they entered.

The shell boats found difficulty in entering the bay because the other boats were in the way. They turned off to the eastern side of the harbor. Thus the ancient name of that side was given Ke-awa-lua (The Second Harbor, or the second landing place in the harbor). Here they landed very quietly. The shell boats became very small, and Kau-lana and her companions took them and hid them in their clothes. They went along the beach and saw some fish. The attendants took them for the girl. This gave the name Kau-lana-iki-pokii to that place to this day. As they went along, the dragon friend made the signs of a high chief appear over the girl. The red rain and arching bow were over her. The name was given to that place, Ka-ua-koko-ula (Blood Rain), which is the name to this day.

The dragon changed her body and carried the girl up Nuuanu Valley very swiftly to the house of Ke-ao-mele-mele (The Maiden of the Golden Cloud) without the knowledge of Kane and the others. They heard the hula of Ke-ao-mele-mele. Soon she felt that someone was outside, and looking saw the girl and her friend, with the signs of a chief over her.

So she called:

Is that you, O eye of the day?
O lightninglike eye from Kahiki,

The remembered one coming to me.
The strong winds have been blowing,
Trembling comes into my breast,
A stranger perhaps is outside,
A woman whose sign is the fog,
A stranger and yet my young sister,
The flower of the divine homeland,
The wonderful land of the setting sun
Going down into the deep blue sea.
You belong to the white ocean of Kane,
You are Kau-lana-iki-pokii,
The daughter of the sunset,
The woman coming in the mist,
In the thunder and the flash of lightning
Quivering in the sky above.
Light falls on the earth below.
The sign of the chiefess,
The woman high up in the heavens,
Kau-lana-iki-pokii,
Enter, enter, here am I.

Those outside heard the call and understood that Ke-ao-mele-mele knew who they were. They entered and saw her in all the beauty of her high divine blood.

They kissed. Kau-lana told how she had come. Ke-ao-mele-mele told the dragon to go and stay on the mountain by the broken pali at the head of Nuuanu Valley. She went to the precipice and became the watchman of that place. She was the first dragon on the islands. She watched with magic power. Later, Mo-o-inanea came with many dragons to watch over the islands. Ke-ao-mele-mele taught her young sister the different hulas and meles, so that they were both alike in their power.

When the young men heard hula voices in the other houses, they thought they would go and see the dancers. At the hour of twilight Waolani shook as if in an earthquake, and there was thunder and lightning.

The young men and Anuenue went to the house and saw the girls dancing, and wondered how Kau-lana had come from the far-off land.

Ke-ao-mele-mele foretold the future for the young people. She told Kau-lana that she would never marry, but should have magic medicine power for all coming days. Kahanai should have the power over all customs of priests and sorcerers and knowledge of sacrifices, and should be the bosom friend of the medicine goddess. She said that they would all go to Waipio, Hawaii. Kane, Kanaloa, and Anuenue approved of her commands.

Ke-ao-mele-mele sent Kau-lana to Hawaii to tell Paliula to come and live with them at Waipio and find Kahanai once more. Kau-lana hastened to Hawaii in her shell boat. She called, "O my red shell boat of the deep blue sea and the black sea, come up to me!"

The shell boat appeared on the surface of the sea, floating. The girl was carried swiftly to Hawaii. There she found Waka and Paliula and took them to Waipio. They lived for a time there, then all went to Waolani to complete the marriage of Ke-ao-mele-mele to Kau-mai-liula.

Kane sent Waka and Anuenue for Ku and Hiilei, Hina and Olopana with Mo-o-inanea to come to Oahu.

Mo-o-inanea prepared large ocean-going canoes for the two families, but she and her people went in their magic boats.

Mo-o-inanea told them they would never return to these lands, but should find their future home in Hawaii.

Waka went on Ku's boat; Anuenue was with Hina. Ku and his friends looked back, the land was almost lost. They soon saw nothing until the mountains of Oahu appeared before them.

They landed at Heeia on the northern side of the Nuuanu precipice, went over to Waolani, and met all the family who had come before.

Before Mo-o-inanea left her land, she changed it, shutting up all the places where her family had lived. She told all her kupua dragon family to come with her to the place where the gods had gone. Thus she made the old lands

162

entirely different from any other lands, so that no other persons but gods or ghosts could live in them.

Then she rose up to come away. The land was covered with rain clouds, heavy and black. The land disappeared and is now known as "The Hidden Land of Kane."

She landed on western Oahu, at Waialua, so that place became the home of the dragons, and it was filled with the dragons from Waialua to Ewa. This was the coming of dragons to the Hawaiian Islands.

At the time of the marriage of Ke-ao-mele-mele and Kau-mai-liula, the Beautiful Daughter of Sunset came from the island of Hawaii bringing the two trees Makalei and Makuukao, which prepared cooked food and fish. When she heard the call to the marriage, she came with the trees. Makalei brought great multitudes of fish from all the ocean to the Koo-lau-poko side of the island of Oahu. The ocean was red with the fish. Makuukao came to Nuuanu Valley with Kau-lana, entered Waolani, and provided plenty of food.

Then Makalei started to come up from the sea. Kau-lana-iki-pokii told the gods and people that there must not be any noise when that great tree came up from the sea. They must hear and remain silent.

When the tree began to come to the foot of the pali, the menehunes and eepas were astonished and began to shout with a great voice, for they thought this was a mighty kupua from Kahiki coming to destroy them.

When they shouted, Makalei fell down at the foot of the pali near Ka-wai-nui, and lies there to this day. So this tree never came to Waolani, and the fish were scattered around the island.

Kau-lana's wrath was very great, and he told Kane and the others to punish these noisy ones, to take them away from this wonderful valley of the gods. He said, "No family of these must dwell on Waolani." Thus the fairies and the gnomes were driven away and scattered over the islands.

For a long time The Maiden of the Golden Cloud and

her husband, Twilight Resting in the Sky, ruled over all the islands even to the mysterious lands of the ocean. When death came, they laid aside their human bodies and never made use of them again — but as aumakuas, or ghost-gods, they assumed their divine forms. In the skies and over the mountains and valleys, they have appeared for hundreds of years, watching over and cheering their descendants.

Puna and the Dragon

TWO IMAGES of goddesses wrere clothed in yellow kapa cloth and worshipped in the temples. One was Kiha-wahine, a noted dragon goddess, and the other was Haumea, who was also known as Papa, the wife of Wakea, a great ancestor god among the Polynesians.

Haumea is said to have taken as her husband Puna, a chief of Oahu. He and his people were going around the island. The surf was not very good, and they wanted to find a better place. At last they found a fine surfing place where a beautiful woman was floating on the sea.

She called to Puna, "This is not a good place for surfing." He asked, "Where is there a place?" She answered, "I know where there is one, far outside." She desired to get Puna. They swam way out in the sea until they were out of sight, nor could they see the sharp peaks of the mountains. They forgot everything else but each other. This woman was Kiha-wahine.

The people on the beach wailed, but did not take canoes to help them. They swam over to Molokai. Here they left their surfboards on the beach and went inland. They came to the cave house of the woman. They saw no man inside nor did they hear any voice; all was quiet.

Puna stayed there as a kind of prisoner and obeyed the

commands of the woman. She took care of him and prepared his food. They lived as husband and wife for a long time, and at last his real body began to change.

Once he went out of the cave. While standing there he heard voices, loud and confused. He wanted to see what was going on, but he could not go, because the woman had laid her law on him, that if he went away he would be killed.

He returned to the cave and asked the woman, "What is that noise I heard from the sea?" She said: "Surfriding, perhaps, or rolling the maika stone. Someone is winning and you heard the shouts." He said, "It would be fine for me to see the things you have mentioned." She said, "To-morrow will be a good time for you to go and see."

In the morning he went down to the sea to the place where the people were gathered together, and saw many sports.

While he was watching, one of the men, Hinole, the brother of his wife, saw him and was pleased. When the sports were through, he invited Puna to go to their house and eat and talk.

Hinole asked him, "Whence do you come, and what house do you live in?" He said, "I am from the mountains, and my house is a cave." Hinole meditated, for he had heard of the loss of Puna at Oahu. He loved his brother-in-law, and asked, "How did you come to this place?" Puna told him all the story. Then Hinole told him his wife was a goddess. "When you return and come near to the place, go very easily and softly, and you will see her in her real nature, as a mo-o, or dragon; but she knows all that you are doing and what we are saying.

"Now listen to a parable. Your first wife, Haumea, is the first born of all the other women. Think of the time when she was angry with you. She had been sporting with you and then she said in a tired way, 'I want the water.' You asked, 'What water do you want?' She said, 'The water from Poliahu of Mauna Kea.' You took a water jar and made a hole so that the water always leaked

165

out, and then you went to the pit of Pele. That woman Pele was very old and bleary-eyed, so that she could not see you well, and you returned to Haumea. She was that wife of yours. If you escape this mo-o wife, she will seek my life. It is my thought to save your life, so that you can look into the eyes of your first wife."

The beautiful dragon woman had told him to cry with a loud voice when he went back to the cave. But when Puna was going back he went slowly and softly, and saw his wife as a dragon, and understood the words of Hinole. He tried to hide, but was trembling and breathing hard.

His wife heard and quickly changed to a human body, and cursed him, saying: "You are an evil man coming quietly and hiding, but I heard your breath when you thought I would not know you. Perhaps I will eat your eyes. When you were talking with Hinole you learned how to come and see me."

The dragon goddess was very angry, but Puna did not say anything. She was so angry that the hair on her neck rose up, but it was like a whirlwind, soon quiet and the anger over. They dwelt together, and the woman trusted Puna, and they had peace.

One day Puna was breathing hard, for he was thirsty and wanted the water of the gods.

The woman heard his breathing, and asked, "Why do you breathe like this?" He said: "I want water. We have dwelt together a long time and now I need the water." "What water is this you want?" He said, "I must have the water of Poliahu of Mauna Kea, the snow-covered mountain of Hawaii."

She said, "Why do you want that water?" He said: "The water of that place is cold and heavy with ice. In my youth my good grandparents always brought water from that place for me. Wherever I went I carried that water with me, and when it was gone more would be brought to me, and so it has been up to the time that I came to dwell with you. You have water and I have been

166

drinking it, but it is not the same as the water mixed with ice, and heavy. But I would not send you after it, because I know it is far away and attended with toil unfit for you, a woman."

The woman bent her head down, then lifted her eyes, and said: "Your desire for water is not a hard thing to satisfy. I will go and get the water."

Before he had spoken of his desire he had made a little hole in the water jar, as Hinole had told him, that the woman might spend a long time and let him escape.

She arose and went away. He also arose and followed. He found a canoe and crossed to Maui. Then he found another boat going to Hawaii and at last landed at Kau.

He went up and stood at the edge of the pit of Pele. Those who were living in the crater saw him and cried out, "Here is a man, a husband for our sister." He quickly went down into the crater and dwelt with them. He told all about his journey.

Pele heard these words, and said: "Not very long from now, your wife will be here coming after you, and there will be a great battle. But we will not let you go or you will be killed, because she is very angry against you. She has held you, the husband of our sister Haūmea. She should find her own husband and not take what belongs to another. You stay with us and at the right time you can go back to your wife."

Kiha-wahine went to Poliahu, but could not fill the water jar. She poured the water in and filled the jar, but when the jar was lifted it became light. She looked back and saw the water lying on the ground, and her husband far beyond at the pit of Pele. Then she became angry and called all the dragons of Molokai, Lanai, Maui, Kahoolawe, and Hawaii.

When she had gathered all the dragons she went up to Kilauea and stood on the edge of the crater and called all the people below, telling them to give her the husband. They refused to give Puna up, crying out: "Where is your husband? This is the husband of our sister; he does not belong to you, O mischief maker."

Then the dragon goddess said, "If you do not give up this man, of a truth I will send quickly all my people and fill up this crater and capture all your fires." The dragons threw their drooling saliva in the pit, and almost destroyed the fire of the pit where Pele lived, leaving Kamoho-alii's place untouched.

Then the fire moved and began to rise with great strength, burning off all the saliva of the dragons. Kihawahine and the rest of the dragons could not stand the heat even a little while, for the fire caught them and killed a large part of them in that place. They tried to hide in the clefts of the rocks. The earthquakes opened the rocks and some of the dragons hid, but fire followed the earthquakes and the fleeing dragons. Kiha-wahine ran and leaped down the precipice into a fishpond called by the name of the shadow, or aka, of the dragon, Loko-aka (The Shadow Lake).

She was imprisoned in the pond, husbandless, scarcely escaping with her life. When she went back to Molokai she meant to kill Hinole, because she was very angry at his act in aiding Puna to escape. She wanted to punish him; but Hinole saw the trouble coming from his sister and arose and leaped into the sea, becoming a fish in the ocean.

When he dove into the sea, Kiha-wahine went down after him and tried to find him in the small and large coral caves, but could not catch him. He became the hinalea, a fish dearly loved by the fishermen of the islands.

The dragon goddess continued seeking, swimming swiftly from place to place. Ounauna saw her passing back and forth, and said, "What are you seeking, O Kihawahine?" She said, "I want Hinole." Ounauna said: "Unless you listen to me you cannot get him, just as when you went to Hawaii you could not get your husband from Pele. You go and get the vine inalua, and come back and make a basket and put it down in the sea. After a while dive down and you will find that man has come

168

inside. Then catch him."

The woman took the vine, made the basket and came down and put it in the sea. She left it there a little while, then dove down. There was no Hinole in the basket, but she saw him swimming along outside of the basket. She went up, waited awhile, came down again and saw him still swimming outside. This she did again and again, until her eyes were red because she could not catch him. Then she was angry, and went to Ounauna and said: "O slave, I will kill you today. Perhaps you told the truth, but I have been deceived, and will chase you until you die."

Ounauna said: "Perhaps we should talk before I die. I want you to tell me just what you have done, then I will know whether you followed directions. Tell me in a few words. Perhaps I forgot something."

The dragon said, "I am tired of your words and I will kill you." Then Ounauna said, "Suppose I die, what will you do to correct any mistakes you have made?"

Then she told how she had taken vines and made a basket and used it. Ounauna said: "I forgot to tell you that you must get some sea eggs and crabs, pound and mix them together, and put them inside the basket. Put the mouth of the basket down. Leave it for a little while, then dive down and find your brother inside. He will not come out, and you can catch him." This is the way the hinalea is caught to this day.

After she had caught her brother she took him to the shore to kill him, but he persuaded her to set him free. This she did, compelling him ever after to retain the form of the fish hinalea.

Kiha-wahine then went to the island of Maui and dwelt in a deep pool near the old royal town of Lahaina.

After Pele had her battle with the dragons, and Puna had escaped according to the directions of Hinole, he returned to Oahu and saw his wife, Haumea, a woman with many names, as if she were the embodiment of many goddesses.

After Puna disappeared, Kou became the new chief of

Oahu. Puna went to live in the mountains above Kalihi-uka. One day Haumea went out fishing for crabs at Heeia, below the precipice of Koolau, where she was accustomed to go. Puna came to a banana plantation, ate, and lay down to rest. He fell fast asleep and the watchmen of the new chief found him. They took his loincloth and tied his hands behind his back, bringing him thus to Kou, who killed him and hung the body in the branches of a breadfruit tree. It is said that this was at Wai-kahalulu, just below the steep diving rocks of the Nuuanu Stream.

When Haumea returned from gathering moss and fish to her home in Kalihi-uka, she heard of the death of her husband. She had taken an akala vine, made a pa-u, or skirt, of it, and tied it around her when she went fishing. But she forgot all about it and, as she hurried down to see the body of her husband, all the people turned to look at her and shouted out, "This is the wife of the dead man."

She found Puna hanging on the branches. Then she made that breadfruit tree open. Leaving her pa-u on the ground where she stood, she stepped inside the tree and bade it close about her and appear the same as before. The akala, of which the pa-u had been made, lay where it was left, took root, and grew into a large vine.

The fat of the body of Puna fell down through the branches and the dogs ate it below the tree. One of these dogs belonged to the chief Kou. It came back to the house, played with the chief, then leaped, caught him by the throat, and killed him.

IV. Myths and Legends
of Old Oahu

Legendary Places in Honolulu

HO-NO-LU-LU is a name made by the union of two words: "Hono" and "lulu." Some say it means "Sheltered Hollow." The old Hawaiians say that "Hono" means "abundance" and "lulu" means "calm," or "peace," or "abundance of peace." The navigator who gave the definition "Fair Haven" was out of the way, inasmuch as the name does not belong to a harbor, but to a district having "abundant calm," or "a pleasant slope of restful land."

"Honolulu" was probably a name given to a very rich district of farm land near what is now known as the junction of Liliha and School Streets, because its chief was Honolulu, one of the high chiefs of the time of Kakuhihewa, according to the legends. Kamakau, the Hawaiian historian, describes this farm district thus: "Honolulu was a small district, a pleasant land looking toward the west — a fat land, with flowing streams and springs of water, abundant water for taro patches. Mists resting inland breathed softly on the flowers of the hala tree."

Kakuhihewa was a king of Oahu in the long, long ago, and was so noted that for centuries the island of Oahu has been named after him "The Oahu of Kakuhihewa." He divided the island among his favorite chiefs and officers, who gave their names to the places received by them from the king. Thus what is now known as Honolulu was, until the time of Kamehameha I about the year 1800, almost always mentioned as Kou, after the chief of Kou, who was an ilamuku (marshal) under King Kakuhihewa. Kou appears to have been a small district or, rather, a chief's group of houses and grounds, loosely defined as lying between Hotel Street and the sea and between Nuuanu Avenue and Alakea Street.

Ke-kai-o-Mamala was the name of the surf which came in the outer entrance of the harbor of Kou. It was named after Mamala, a chiefess who loved to play ko-

173

nane (Hawaiian checkers), drink awa, and ride the surf. Her first husband was the shark man Ouha, who later became a shark god, living as a great shark outside the reefs of Waikiki and Koko Head. Her second husband was the chief Hono-kau-pu, to whom the king gave the land east of Kou, which afterward bore the name of its chief. In this section of Kou now called Honolulu were several very interesting places.

Kewalo was the place where the kauwa, a very low class of servants, were drowned by holding their heads under the water. The custom was known as "ke-kai-hee-hee," "kai" meaning "sea" and "hee" "sliding along," hence the sliding of the servants under the waves of the sea. Kewalo was also the nesting ground of the owl who was the cause of a battle between the owls and the king Kakuhihewa, where the owls from Kauai to Hawaii gathered together and defeated the forces of the king.

Toward the mountains above Kewalo lies Makiki plain, the place where rats abounded, living in a dense growth of small trees and shrubs. This was a famous place for hunting rats with bows and arrows.

Ula-kua, the place where idols were made, was near the lumberyards at the foot of the present Richards Street.

Ka-wai-a-hao (The Water belonging to Hao), the site of the noted old native church, was the location of a fine fountain of water belonging to a chief named Hao.

Ke-kau-kukui was close to Ula-kua, and was the place where small konane (checker) boards were laid. These were flat stones with rows of little holes in which a game was played with black and white stones. Here Mamala and Ouha drank awa and played konane, and Kekua-naoa, father of Kamehameha V, built his home.

Kou was probably the most noted place for konane on Oahu. There was a famous stone almost opposite the site of the temple. Here the chiefs gathered for many a game. Property and even lives were freely gambled away. The Spreckels Building covers the site of this well-known gambling resort.

In Hono-kau-pu was one of the noted places for rolling the flat-sided stone disc known as the "maika stone." This was not far from Richards and Queen Streets, although the great "Ulu-maika" place for the gathering of the chiefs was in Kou. This was a hard, smooth track about twelve feet wide, extending from the corner of Merchant and Fort Streets, along the seaward side of Merchant Street to the place beyond Nuuanu Avenue known as the old iron works at Ula-ko-heo. Kamehameha I is recorded as having used this maika track.

Ka-ua-nono-ula (Rain-with-the-Red-Rainbow) was the place in this district for the wai-lua, or ghosts, to gather for their nightly games and sports. Under the shadows of the trees, near the present junction of Alakea and Merchant Streets, these ghosts made night a source of dread to all the people. Another place in Honolulu for the gathering of ghosts was at the corner of King Street and Nuuanu Avenue.

Puu-o-wai-na, or Punchbowl, was a "hill of sacrifice," or "offering," according to the meaning of the native words, and not "Wine-hill," as many persons have said. Kamakau, a native historian of nearly fifty years ago, says: "Formerly there was an imu ahi, a fire oven, for burning men on this hill. Chiefs and common people were burned as sacrifices in that noted place. Men were brought for sacrifice from Kauai, Oahu, and Maui, but not from Hawaii. People could be burned in this place for violating the kapus of the kapu divine chiefs. The great stone on the top of Punchbowl Hill was the place for burning men."

Part of an ancient chant concerning Punchbowl reads as follows:

O the raging kapu fire of Keaka,
O the high ascending fire of the sacrifice!
Kapu fire, scattered ashes,
Kapu fire, spreading heat.

Nuuanu Valley is full of interesting legendary places. The most interesting, however, is the little valley made by

175

a mountain spur pushing its way out from the Kalihi foothills into the larger valley and bearing the name of "Waolani," the wilderness home of the gods, and now the home of the Honolulu Country Club. This region belonged to the eepa people. These were almost the same as the ill-shaped, deformed, or injured gnomes of European fairy tales.

In this beautiful little valley which opened into Nuuanu Valley was the heiau Waolani built for Ka-hanai-a-ke-Akua (The Chief Brought Up by the Gods), long before the days of Kakuhihewa. It was said that the two divine caretakers of this chief were Kahano and Newa, and that Kahano was the god who laid down on the ocean, stretching out his hands until one rested on Kahiki (Tahiti or some other foreign land) and the other rested on Oahu. They came to be servants for this young chief, who was in the cave of the gods. They built fishponds and temples. They lived in Manoa Valley and on Punchbowl Hill. Ku-leo-nui (Ku-With-the-Loud-Voice) was their master. He could call them any evening. His voice was heard over all the island. They came at once and almost invariably finished each task before the rays of the rising sun drove them to their hidden resorts in forest or wilderness.

Waolani heiau was the place where the noted legendary musical shell "Kiha-pu" had its first home—from which it was stolen by Kapuni and carried to its historic home in Waipio Valley, Hawaii. Below Waolani Heights, the menehunes built the temple of Ka-he-iki for the "child-nourished-by-the-gods," and here the priest and prophet lived who founded the priest clan called "Mo-o-kahuna," one of the most sacred clans of the ancient Hawaiians. Not far from this temple was the scene of the dramatic plea of an owl for her eggs when taken from Kewalo by a man who had found her nest. It forms part of the story of the battle of the owls and the king.

Nearer the banks of the Nuuanu Stream was the great

breadfruit tree into which a woman thrust her husband by magic power when he was about to be slain and offered as a sacrifice to the gods. This tree became one of the most powerful wooden gods of the Hawaiians, being preserved, it is said, even to the times of Kamehameha I.

At the foot of Nuuanu Valley is Pu-iwa, a place by the side of the Nuuanu Stream. Here a father, Maikoha, told his daughters to bury his body, that from it might spring the wauke tree, used for making kapa ever since. From this place, the legend says, the wauke tree spread all over the islands.

In the bed of the Nuuanu Valley is the legendary stone called "The Canoe of the Dragon." This lies among the boulders in the stream not far from the old Kaumakapili Church premises.

In Nuuanu Valley was the fierce conflict between Kawelo, the strong man from Kauai, assisted by two friends, and a band of robbers. In this battle torn-up trees figured as mighty war clubs.

These are legendary places which border Kou, the ancient Honolulu. Besides these are many more spots of great interest, as in Waikiki and Manoa Valley, but these lie beyond the boundaries of Kou and ancient Honolulu. In Kou itself was the noted Pakaka Temple. This temple was standing on the western side of the foot of Fort Street long after the fort was built from which the street was named. It was just below the fort. Pakaka was owned by Kinau, the mother of Kamehameha V. It was a heiau, or temple, built before the time of Kakuhihewa. In this temple, the school of the priests of Oahu had its headquarters for centuries. The walls of the temple were adorned with heads of men offered in sacrifice.

Enormous quantities of stone were used in the construction of all these heiaus, often passed by hand from quarries at great distances, so that the work of erection was one consuming much time and energy.

According to the latest investigations there were one hundred and eight heiaus on the island of Oahu, some evidences of which may still be traced, showing the far-reaching influence of kings and priests over these primitive people.

The God of Pakaka Temple

PAKAKA was a heiau, or temple, at the foot of Fort Street. There are several legends connected with this heiau. One of the most interesting is that which tells how the god of the temple came into being.

The story of the god of this temple is a story of voyages and vicissitudes. Olopana had sailed away from Waipio, Hawaii, for the islands of distant seas. Somewhere in all that great number of islands which were grouped under the general name of "Kahiki," Olopana found a home. Here his daughter Mu-lei-ula (Mu-With-the-Red-Garland) was experiencing great trouble being near to childbirth. For some reason Haumea, one of the divine Polynesian ancestors, had stopped for a time to visit the people of that land. When the friends were afraid that Mu-lei-ula would die, Haumea came to help, saying: "In our land the mother lives. The mother and child both live."

The people said, "If you give us aid, how can we render payment or give you a reward?"

Haumea said: "There is a beautiful tree with two strange but glorious flowers, which I like very much. It is 'the tree of changing leaves' with two flowers, one kind singing sharply, and the other singing from time to time. For this tree I will save the life of the chief's daughter and her child."

Gladly the sick girl and her friends promised to give this beautiful tree to Haumea. It was a tree dearly loved by the princess.

Haumea commenced the prayers and incantations which accompanied her treatment of the sick, and the chiefess rapidly grew stronger. This had come so quickly and easily that she repented the gift of the tree with the beautiful flowers, and cried out, "I will not give the tree!"

Immediately she began to lose strength, and called to Haumea that she would give the tree if she could be forgiven and healed. However, as strength came to her once more she again felt sorry for her tree and refused to let it go. Again the incantations were broken off and the divine aid withdrawn.

Olopana in agony cried to his daughter: "Give up your tree. Of what use will it be with its flowers if you die?" Then Haumea, with the most powerful incantations, gave her the final strength, and mother and child both lived and became well and strong.

Haumea took the tree and traveled over the far seas to distant Hawaii. On that larger island she found no place to plant the tree. She crossed over to the island of Maui and came to the "four rivers." There she found the awa of the gods and prepared it for drinking, but needed fresh water to mix with it.

She laid her tree on the ground at Puu-kume by the Wai-hee Stream and went down after water. When she returned the tree had rooted. While she looked it began to stand up and send forth branches. She built a stone wall around it, to protect it from the winds. When it blossomed, Haumea returned to her divine home in Nuu-mealani, the land of mists and shadows where the gods dwelt.

By and by a man took his stone axe and went out to cut a tree, perhaps to make a god. He saw a new tree, short and beautiful, and after hours of labor cut it down. The night was coming on, so he left it as it fell and went home.

That night a fierce and mighty storm came down from the mountains. Blood-red were the streams of water pouring down into the valleys. During twenty nights and twenty days the angry rain punished the land above

179

and around Waihee. The river was more than a rushing torrent. It built up hills and dug ravines. It hurled its mighty waves against the wall inside which the tree stood. It crushed the wall, scattered the stones, and bore the tree down one of the deep ravines. The branches were broken off and carried with the trunk of the tree far out into the ocean.

For six months the waves tossed this burden from one place to another, and at last threw the largest branch on the reef near the beach of Kailua, on the island of Hawaii. The people saw a very wonderful thing. Where this branch lay stranded in the water, fish of many kinds gathered leaping around it. The chiefs took this wonderful branch inland and made the god Makalei, which was a god of Hawaii for generations.

Another branch came into the possession of some of the Maui chiefs and was used as a stick for hanging bundles upon. It became a god for the chiefs of Maui, with the name of Ku-ke-olo-ewa.

The body of the tree rolled back and forth along the beach near the four waters, and was wrapped in the refuse of the sea. A chief and his wife had not yet found a god for their home. In a dream they were told to get a god. For three days they consulted priests, repeated prayers and incantations and offered sacrifices to the great gods, while they made search for wood from which to cut out their god. On the third night the omens led them down to the beach and they saw this trunk of a tree rolling back and forth. A dim haze was playing over it in the moonlight. They took that tree, cut out their god, and called it Ku-hoo-nee-nuu. They built a heiau, or temple, for this god, and named that heiau Waihau and made it kapu, or a sacred place to which the priests and high chiefs alone were admitted freely.

The mana, or divine power, of this god was very great, and it was a noted god from Hawaii to Kauai. Favor and prosperity rested upon this chief who had found the tree, made it a god, and built a temple for it.

The king who was living on the island of Oahu heard about this tree, and sent servants to the island of Maui to find out whether or no the reports were true. If true they should bring that god to Oahu.

They found the god and told the chief that the king wanted to establish it at Kou, and would build a temple for it there. The chief readily gave up his god and it was carried over to its new home. The temple, or heiau, was built at Kou and the god Ku-hoo-nee-nuu placed in it. This temple was Pakaka, the most noted temple on the island of Oahu, while its god, the log of the tree from a foreign land, became the god of the chiefs of Oahu.

Legend of the Breadfruit Tree

THE WONDERFUL breadfruit tree was a great tree growing on the eastern bank of the rippling brook of Puehuehu, near the Nuuanu Street Bridge. It was a kapu tree, set apart for the high chief from Kou and the chiefs from Honolulu to rest under while on their way to bathe in the celebrated diving pool of Wai-kaha-lulu. That tree became a god, and this is the story of its transformation:

Papa and Wakea were the ancestors of the great scattered sea-going and sea-loving people living in all the islands now known as Polynesia. They had their home in every group of islands where their descendants could find room to multiply.

They came to the island of Oahu and, according to almost all the legends, were the first residents. The story of the magic breadfruit tree, however, says that Papa sailed from Kahiki (a far-off land) with her husband Wakea, landing on Oahu and finding a home in the mountain upland near the precipice of Kilohana.

Papa was a kupua — a woman having many wonderful

181

and miraculous powers. She had also several names. Sometimes she was called Haumea, but at last she left her power and a new name, Ka-meha-i-kana, in the magic breadfruit tree.

Papa was a beautiful woman, whose skin shone like polished dark ivory through the flowers and vines and leaves which were the only clothes she knew. Where she and her husband had settled down they found a fruitful country, with bananas and sugar cane and taro. They built a house on the mountain ridge and feasted on the abundance of food around them. Here they rested, well protected when the rains were falling or the hot sun was shining.

Papa day by day looked over the seacoast which stretches away in miles of marvelous beauty below the precipices of the northern mountain range of the island of Oahu. Clear, deep pools, well filled with most delicate fish, lay restfully among moss-covered projections of the bordering coral reef. The restless murmur of surf waves beating in and out through the broken lines of the reef called to her. Catching up some long leaves of the hala tree, she made a light basket and hurried down to the sea. In a little while she had gathered sea moss and caught all the crabs she wished to take home.

She turned toward the mountain range and carried her burden to Hoakola, where there was a spring of beautiful clear, cold, fresh water. She laid down her moss and crabs to wash them clean.

She looked up, and on the mountainside discerned there something strange. She saw her husband in the hands of men who had captured and bound him and were compelling him to walk down the opposite side of the range. Her heart leaped with fear and anguish. She forgot her crabs and moss and ran up the steep way to her home. The moss rooted itself by the spring, but the crabs escaped to the sea.

On the Honolulu side of the mountains were many chiefs and their people. Living among them was Lele-hoo-mao, the ruler, whose fields were often despoiled by Papa and her husband. It was his servants who, while searching the country around these fields, had found and captured Wakea. They were forcing him to the temple Pakaka to be there offered in sacrifice. They were shouting, "We have found the mischief-maker and have tied him."

Papa threw around her some of the vines which she had fashioned into a skirt, and ran over the hills to the edge of Nuuanu Valley. Peering down the valley, she saw her husband and his captors, and cautiously she descended. She found a man by the side of the stream of Puehuehu, who said to her: "A man has been carried by, who is to be baked in an oven this day. The fire is burning in the valley below."

Papa said, "Give me water to drink."

The man said, "I have none."

Then Papa took a stone and smashed it against the ground. It broke through into a pool of water. She drank and hastened on to the breadfruit tree at Nini, where she overtook her husband and the men who guarded him. He was alive, his hands bound behind him and his leaf clothing torn from his body. Wailing and crying that she must kiss him, she rushed to him and began pushing and pulling him, whirling him around and around.

Suddenly the great breadfruit tree opened and she leaped with him through the doorway into the heart of the tree. The opening closed in a moment.

Papa, by her miraculous power, opened the tree on the other side. They passed through and went rapidly up the mountainside to their home, which was near the head of Kalihi Valley.

As they ran Papa threw off her vine pa-u, or skirt. The vine became the beautiful morning-glory, delicate in blossom and powerful in medicinal qualities. The astonished men had lost their captive. According to the ancient Hawaiian proverb, "Their fence was around the field of nothingness." They pushed against the tree, but the opening was tightly closed. They ran around under the heavy-leaved branches and found nothing. They believed that the great tree held their captive in its magic power.

Quickly ran the messenger to their high chief, Lele-hoo-mao, to tell him about the trouble at the kapu bread-fruit tree at Nini and that the sacrifice for which the oven was being heated was lost.

The chiefs consulted together and decided to cut down that tree and take the captive out of his hiding place. They sent tree cutters with their stone axes.

The leader of the tree cutters struck the tree with his stone axe. A chip leaped from the tree, struck him, and he fell dead. Another caught the axe. Again chips flew and the workman fell dead. Then all the cutters struck and gashed the tree. Whenever a chip hit anyone he died, and the sap of the tree flowed out and was spattered under the blows of the stone axes. Whenever a drop touched a workman or a bystander, he fell dead.

The people were filled with fear and cried to their priest for help.

Wohi, the priest, came to the tree, bowed before it, and remained in silent thought a long time. Then he raised his head and said: "It was not a woman who went into that tree. It was Papa from Kahiki. She is a goddess and has a multitude of bodies. If we treat her well we shall not be destroyed."

Wohi commanded the people to offer sacrifices at the foot of the tree. This was done with prayers and incantations. A black pig, black awa, and red fish were offered to Papa. Then Wohi commanded the woodcutters to rub themselves bountifully with coconut oil and go fearlessly to their work. Chips struck them and the sap of the tree was spattered over them, but they toiled on unhurt until the great tree fell.

Out of this magic breadfruit tree a great goddess was made. Papa gave it one of her names, Ka-meha-i-kana, and endowed it with power so that it was noted from

Kauai to Hawaii. It became one of the great gods of Oahu, but was taken to Maui, where Kamehameha secured it as his god to aid in establishing his rule over all the islands.

The peculiar divine gift supposed to reside in this image made from the wonderful breadfruit tree was the ability to aid worshippers in winning land and power from other people and wisely employing the best means of firmly establishing their own government, thus protecting and preserving the kingdom.

Papa dwelt above the Kalihi Valley and looked down over the plains of Honolulu and Ewa covered with well-watered growing plants which gave food or shade to the multiplying people.

It is said that after a time she had a daughter, Kapo, who also had kupua, or magic power. Kapo had many names, such as Kapo-ula-Kinau and Laka. She was a high tabu goddess of the ancient Hawaiian hulas, or dances. She had also the power of assuming many bodies at will and could appear in any form from the mo-o, or lizard, to a human being.

Kapo is the name of a place and of a wonderful stone with a "front like the front of a house and a back like the tail of a fish." The legends of sixty years ago say that Kapo still stood in that place as one of the guardians of Kalihi Valley.

Kapo was born from the eyes of Haumea, or Papa.

Papa looked away from Kapo and there was born from her head a sharp pali, or precipice, often mist-covered; this was Ka-moho-alii. Then Pele was born. She was the one who had mighty battles with Kamapuaa, the pig man, who almost destroyed the volcano of Kilauea. It was Ka-moho-alii who rubbed sticks and rekindled the volcanic fires for his sister Pele, thus driving Kamapuaa down the sides of Kilauea into the ocean.

These three, according to the Honolulu legends, were the highest-born children of Papa and Wakea.

Down the Kalihi stream below Papa's home were two

stones to which the Hawaiians gave eepa, or gnomelike, power. If any traveler passes these stones on his way up to Papa's resting place, that wayfarer stops by these stones, gathers leaves and makes leis, or garlands, and places them on these stones, that there may be no trouble in all that day's wanderings.

Sometimes mischievous people dip branches from lehua trees in water and sprinkle the eepa rocks; then woe to the traveler, for piercing rains are supposed to fall. From this comes the proverb belonging to the residents of Kalihi Valley, "Here is the sharp-headed rain of Kalihi" (Ka ua poo lipilipi o Kalihi).

The Water of Life of Kane

THE HAWAIIANS of long ago shared in the belief that somewhere along the deep sea beyond the horizon around their islands, or somewhere in the cloud land above the heavens which rested on their mountains, there was a land known as "The land of the water of life of the gods." In this land was a lake of living water in which always rested the power of restoration to life. This water was called in the Hawaiian language Ka-wai-ola-a-Kane, literally "The water of life of Kane."

Kane was one of the four greatest gods of the Polynesians. In his hands was placed the care of the water of life. If any person secured this water, the power of the god went with it. A sick person drinking it would recover health, and a dead person sprinkled with it would be restored to life.

In the misty past of the Hawaiian Islands a king was very, very ill. All his friends thought that he was going to die. The family came together in the enclosure around the house where the sick man lay. Three sons were wailing sorely because of their heavy grief.

An old man, a stranger passing by, asked them the cause of the trouble. One of the young men replied, "Our father lies in that house very near death."

The old man looked over the wall upon the young men and said slowly: "I have heard of something which would make your father well. He must drink of the water of life of Kane. But this is very hard to find and difficult to get."

The old man disappeared, but the eldest son said, "I shall not fail to find this water of life, and I shall be my father's favorite and shall have the kingdom." He ran to his father for permission to go and find this water of life.

The old king said: "No, there are many difficulties and even death in the way. It is better to die here." The prince urged his father to let him try, and at last received permission.

The prince, taking his water calabash, hastened away. As he went along a path through the forest, suddenly an ugly little man, a dwarf (an a-a), appeared in his path and called out, "Where are you going that you are in such a hurry?" The prince answered roughly: "Is this your business? I have nothing to say to you." He pushed the little man aside and ran on.

The dwarf was very angry and determined to punish the rough speaker. He made the path twist and turn and grow narrow before the traveler. The further the prince ran, the more bewildered he was, and the more narrow became the way. Thicker and thicker were the trees and vines and ferns through which the path wound. At last he fell to the earth, crawling and fighting against the tangled masses of ferns and the clinging tendrils of the vines of the land of fairies and gnomes. They twined themselves around him and tied him tight with living coils, and finally he lay like one who was dead.

For a long time the family waited and at last came to the conclusion that he had been overcome by some difficulty. The second son said that he would go and find the water of life. Taking his water calabash, he ran swiftly along the path which his brother had taken. His thought was also a selfish one, that he might succeed where his brother had failed and so win the kingdom.

As he ran along he met the same little man, who was the king of the fairies although he appeared as a dwarf. The little man called out, "Where are you going in such a hurry?"

The prince spoke roughly, pushed him out of the way, and rushed on. Soon he also was caught in the tangled woods and held fast like one who was dead.

Then the last, the youngest son, took his calabash and went away thinking that he might be able to rescue his brothers as well as get the water of life for his father. He met the same little man, who asked him where he was going. He told the dwarf about the king's illness and the report of the "water of life of Kane," and asked the dwarf if he could aid in any way. "For," said the prince, "my father is near death, and this living water will heal him and I do not know the way."

The little man said: "Because you have spoken gently and have asked my help and have not been rough and rude as were your brothers, I will tell you where to go and will give you aid. The path will open before you at the bidding of this strong staff which I give you. By and by you will come to the palace of a king who is a sorcerer. In his house is the fountain of that water of life. You cannot get into that house unless you take three bundles of food which I will give you. Take the food in one hand and your strong staff in the other. Strike the door of that king's house three times with your staff and an opening will be made. Then you will see two dragons with open mouths ready to devour you. Quickly throw food in their mouths and they will become quiet. Fill your calabash with the living water and hurry away. At midnight the doors will be shut, and you cannot escape."

The prince thanked the little man, took the presents, and went his way rejoicing. After a long time he came to the strange land and the sorcerer's house. Three times he struck until he broke the wall and made a door for himself. He saw the dragons and threw the food into their mouths, making them his friends. He went in and saw some young chiefs, who welcomed him and gave him a war club and a bundle of food. He went on to another room, where he met a beautiful maiden whom he loved at once with all his heart. She told him as she looked in his eyes that after a time they would meet again and live as husband and wife. Then she showed him where he could get the water of life, and warned him to be in haste. He dipped his calabash in the spring and leaped through the door just at the stroke of midnight.

With great joy he hastened from land to land and from sea to sea watching for the little man, the a-a, who had aided him so much. As if his wish were known, soon the little man appeared and asked him how he fared on his journey. The prince told him about the long way and his success and then offered to pay as best he could for all the aid so kindly given.

The dwarf refused all reward. Then the prince said he would be so bold as to ask one favor more. The little man said, "You have been so thoughtful in dealing with me as one highly honored by you, ask and perhaps I can give you what you wish."

The prince said, "I do not want to return home without my brothers; can you help me find them?"

"They are dead in the forest," said the dwarf. "If you find them they will only do you harm. Let them rest in their beds of vines and ferns. They have evil hearts."

But the young chief pressed his kindly thought and the dwarf showed him the tangled path through the forest. With his magic staff he opened the way and found his brothers. He sprinkled a little of the water of life over them and strength returned to them. He told them how he had found the "living water of Kane," and had received gifts and also the promise of a beautiful young bride. The brothers forgot their long deathlike sleep and were jealous and angry at the success of their younger brother.

They journeyed far before they reached home. They passed a strange land where the high chief was resisting a large body of rebels. The land was lying desolate and the people were starving. The young prince pitied the high chief and his people and gave them a part of the bundle of food from the house of the god Kane. They ate and became very strong. Then he let the chief have his war club. Quickly the rebels were destroyed and the land had quiet and peace.

He aided another chief in his wars, and still another in his difficulties, and at last came with his brothers to the seacoast of his own land. There they lay down to sleep. But the wicked brothers felt that there were no more troubles in which they would need the magic aid of their brother. They first planned to kill him, but the magic war club seemed to defend him. Then they took his calabash of the water of life and poured the water into their water jars, filling his calabash again with salt, sickish seawater.

They went on home the next morning. The young prince pressed forward with his calabash, and gave it to his father, telling him to drink and recover life. The king drank deeply of the salt water and was made more seriously sick, almost to death. Then the older brothers came, charging the young prince with an attempt to poison his father. They gave him the real water of life and he immediately became storng as in the days of his youth.

The king was very angry with the youngest son and sent him away with an officer who was skilled in the forest. The officer was a friend of the young prince and helped him to find a safe hiding place, where he lived for a long time.

By and by the three great kings came from distant lands with many presents for the prince who had given them peace and great prosperity. They told the father what a wonderful son he had, and wanted to give him their thanks. The father called the officer whom he had sent away with the young man and acknowledged the wrong he had done. The officer told him the prince was not dead, and the king sent messengers to find him.

Meanwhile, one of the most beautiful princesses of all the world had sent word everywhere that she would be seated in her house and any prince who could walk straight to her along a line drawn in the air by her sorcerers, without turning to either side, should be her husband. There was a day set for the contest.

The messengers sent out by the king to find the prince knew all about this contest. They made all things known to their young chief when they found him. He went with his swift steps of love to the land of the beautiful girl. His brothers had both failed in their most careful endeavors, but the young prince followed his heart's desire and went straight to a door which opened of its own accord. Out leaped the maiden of the palace of the land of Kane. Into his arms she rushed and sent her servants everywhere to proclaim that her lord had been found.

The brothers ran away to distant lands and never returned. The prince and the princess became king and queen and lived in great peace and happiness, administering the affairs of their kingdom for the welfare of their subjects.

Mamala, the Surfrider

"KOU" WAS a noted place for games and sports among the chiefs of long ago. A little to the east of Kou was a pond with a beautiful grove of coconut trees belonging to a chief, Hono-kau-pu, and afterward known by his name. Straight out toward the ocean was the narrow entrance to the harbor, through which rolled the finest surf waves of old Honolulu. The surf bore the name of "Ke-kai-o-Mamala" (The Sea of Mamala). When the surf rose high it was called "Ka-nuku-o-Mamala" (The Nose of Mamala).

Mamala was a chiefess of kupua character. This meant that she was a mo-o, or gigantic lizard or crocodile, as well as a beautiful woman, and could assume whichever shape she most desired. One of the legends says that she was a shark and woman, and had for her husband the shark man Ouha, afterward a shark god having his home in the ocean near Koko Head. Mamala and Ouha drank awa together and played konane on the large smooth stone at Kou.

Mamala was a wonderful surfrider. Very skillfully she danced on the roughest waves. The surf in which she most delighted rose far out in the rough sea, where the winds blew strong and whitecaps were on waves which rolled in rough disorder into the bay of Kou. The people on the beach, watching her, filled the air with resounding applause, clapping their hands over her extraordinary athletic feats.

When the chief, Hono-kau-pu, chose to take Mamala as his wife, she left Ouha and lived with her new husband. Ouha was angry and tried at first to injure Hono and Mamala, but he was driven away. He fled to the lake Ka-ihi-Kapu toward Waikiki. There he appeared as a man with a basketful of shrimps and fresh fish, which he offered to the women of that place, saying, "Here is life (a living thing) for the children." He opened his basket, but the shrimps and the fish leaped out and escaped into the water.

The women ridiculed the god-man. As the ancient legendary characters of all Polynesia could not endure anything that brought shame or disgrace upon them in the eyes of others, Ouha fled from the taunts of the women, casting off his human form and dissolving his connection with humanity. Thus he became the great shark god of the coast between Waikiki and Koko Head.

The surfrider was remembered in the beautiful mele, or chant, coming from ancient times and called the mele of Hono-kau-pu:

The surf rises at Koolau,

Blowing the waves into mist,
Into little drops,
Spray falling along the hidden harbor.
There is my dear husband Ouha,
There is the shaking sea, the running sea of Kou,
The crablike moving sea of Kou.
Prepare the awa to drink, the crab to eat.
The small konane board is at Hono-kau-pu.
My friend on the highest point of the surf.
This is a good surf for us.
My love has gone away.
Smooth is the floor of Kou,
Fine is the breeze from the mountains.
I wait for you to return,
The games are prepared,
Pa-poko, pa-loa, pa-lele.
Leap away to Tahiti
By the path to Nuumealani (home of the gods).
Will that lover (Ouha) return?
I belong to Hono-kuu-pu,
From the top of the tossing surf waves.
The eyes of the day and the night are forgotten.
Kou has the large konane board.
This is the day, and tonight
The eyes meet at Kou.

A Shark Punished at Waikiki

AMONG THE legendary characters of the early Hawaiians was Ka-ehu—the little yellow shark of Pearl Harbor. He had been given magic power and great wisdom by his ancestor Ka-moho-alii, the shark god, brother of the fire goddess Pele.

Part of his life had been spent with his parents, who

guarded the sea precipices of the coast of Puna in the southern part of the island of Hawaii. While at Pearl Harbor he became homesick for the beauty of Puna, and chanted:

O my land of rustling lehua trees!
Rain is treading on your budding flowers,
It carries them to the sea.
They meet the fish in the sea.
This is the day when love meets love.
My longings are stirring within me
For the spirit friends of my land.
They call me back to my home.
I must return.

Ka-ehu called his shark friends and started along the Oahu shores on his way to Hawaii. At Waikiki they met Pehu, a shark visitor from Maui, who lived in the sea belonging to Hono-ka-hau. Pehu was a man-eating shark and was swimming back and forth at Kalehua-wike, near the Moana Hotel. He was waiting for some surfrider to go out far enough to be caught.

Ka-ehu asked him what he was doing there. He replied, "I am catching a crab for my breakfast."

Ka-ehu said, "We will help you catch your crab."

He told Pehu to go near the coral reef while he and his large retinue of sharks would go seaward. When a number of surfriders were far out, he and his sharks would appear and drive them shoreward in a tumultuous rush; then Pehu could easily catch the crab. This pleased the shark from Maui. He went close to the reef and hid himself in its shadows.

Ka-ehu said to his friends: "We must kill this man-eating shark who is destroying our people. This will be a part of our pay to them for honoring us at Puu-loa (Pearl Harbor). We will all go and push Pehu into the shallow water."

A number of surfriders poised on the waves, and Pehu called for the other sharks to come, but Ka-ehu told him to wait for a better chance. Soon two men started on a

194

wave from the distant dark blue sea where the high surf begins.

Ka-ehu gave a signal for an attack. He told his friends to rush in under the great wave and, as it passed over the waiting Pehu, crowd the men and their surfboards to one side and push the leaping Pehu so that he would be upset. Then while he was floundering in the surf they must hurl him over the reef.

As Pehu leaped to catch one of the coming surfriders, he was astonished to see the man shoved to one side. Then as he rose almost straight up in the water he was caught by the other sharks and tossed over and over until he plunged head first into a deep hole in the coral. There he thrashed his great tail about, but only forced himself farther in so that he could not escape.

The surfriders were greatly frightened when they saw the company of sharks swimming swiftly outside the coral reef. But they were not afraid of Pehu. They went out to the hole and killed him and cut his body in pieces. Inside the body they found hair and bones, showing that this shark had been destroying some of their people.

They took the pieces of the body of that great fish to Pele-ula, where they made a great oven and burned the pieces.

Ka-ehu passed on toward Hawaii as a knight-errant, meeting many adventures and punishing evil-minded residents of the great sea.

The Creation of Man

The sky is established.
The earth is established.
Fastened and fastened,
Always holding together,
Entangled in obscurity,
Near each other a group of islands
Spreads out like a flock of birds.
Leaping up are the divided places.
Lifted far up are the heavens.
Polished by striking,
Lamps rest in the sky.
Presently the clouds move,
The great sun rises in splendor,
Mankind arises to pleasure,
The moving sky is above.

KU, KANE, Lono, and Kanaloa were the first gods made.

The gods had come from far off, unknown lands. They brought with them the mysterious people who live in precipices and trees and rocks. These were the invisible spirits of the air.

The earth was a calabash. The gods threw the calabash cover upward and it became the sky. Part of the thick "flesh" became the sun. Another part was the moon. The stars came from the seeds.

The gods went over to a small island called Mokapu, and thought they would make man to be chief over all other things. Mololani was the crater hill which forms the little island. On the sunrise side of this hill, near the sea, was the place where red dirt lay mixed with dark blue and black soil. Here Kane scratched the dirt together and made the form of a man.

Kanaloa ridiculed the mass of dirt and made a better form, but it did not have life. Kane said, "You have made

196

a dirt image; let it become stone."

Then Kane ordered Ku and Lono to carefully obey his directions. They were afraid he would kill them. At once they caught one of the spirits of the air and pushed it into the image Kane had made.

When the spirit had been pushed into the body, Kane stood by the image and called, "Hiki au-E-ola! E-ola!" (I come, live! live!)

Ku and Lono responded, "Live! live!" Then Kane called again, "I come, awake! awake!" and the other two responded, "Awake! awake!" and the image became a living man.

Then Kane cried, "I come, arise! arise!" The other gods repeated, "Arise! arise!" and the image stood up — a man with a living spirit. They named him Wela-ahi-lani-nui, or "The Great Heaven Burning Hot."

They chanted, giving the divine signs attending the birth of a chief:

The stars were burning.
Hot were the months.
Land rises in islands,
High surf is like mountains.
Pele throws out her body (of lava).
Broken masses of rain from the sky.
The land is shaken by earthquakes.
Ikuwa (the showery month) reverberates with thunder.

The gods took this man to their home and nourished him. When he became strong, he went out to walk around the home of the gods. Soon he noticed a shadow going around with his body. It walked when he walked, and rested when he rested. He wondered what this thing was, and called it "aka," or "shadow."

When he slept, Ku, Kane and Lono tore open his body, and Kane took out a woman, leaving Ku and Lono to heal the body. Then they put the woman by the side of the man and they were alike.

Wela-ahi-lani-nui awoke and found a beautiful one lying by him, and thought: "This is that thing which has been by my side, my aka. The gods have changed it into this beautiful one." So he gave her the name "Ke-aka-huli-lani" (The-Heaven-Changed-Shadow). These were the ancestors of the Hawaiians and all the peoples of the islands of the great ocean.

It must be remembered that there are many other Hawaiian legends which mention other first men and women as ancestors of the Hawaiian people.

The Chief with the Wonderful Servants

A CERTAIN chief who lived on the island of Oahu in the very misty memory of long, long ago thought he would travel over his lands and see their condition. So pleased was he that he boasted of his wide domain when he met a fellow traveler. The man said, "I can see the lands of Wakea and Papa and they are larger and fairer than these fine places of yours." Then they decided to go together to find that wonderful land of the gods.

Soon they passed a man standing by the wayside. The chief asked him what he was doing. The man replied: "I am Mama-loa (The Very Swift). I am waiting for the sun to rise, that I may run and catch him." They all waited until the sun appeared and started to rise above the island. The man ran very fast and caught it, tied it, and held it as a prisoner for a time.

Then the three traveled together—the chief, whose name was Ikaika-loa (The Very Strong); the man who could see clearly a long distance, whose name was Ike-loa (The Farsighted); and Mama-loa. In a little while they saw two men sleeping by the path. One was shivering with cold; his name was Kanaka-make-anu (Man Who Dies in the Cold). The other was burning as if over a fire; his name was Kanaka-make-wela (Man Who Dies in the Fire). They warmed one and cooled the other, and all went on together.

198

They came to a field for rat shooting, and found a man standing with bow and arrow, shooting very skillfully. His name was Pana-pololei (The Straight Shooter). They asked him to go to the lands of Wakea and Papa, and he journeyed with them. By and by they found a man lying by the path with his ear to the ground. The chief asked him, "What are you doing?" He looked up and said, "I have been listening to the quarrel between Papa and Wakea." The man who was listening to their harsh words was Hoo-lohe-loa (The Man Who Could Hear Afaroff). They all journeyed on until they entered a land [around Nuuanu Valley] more beautiful than any they had ever seen before.

The watchmen of that country saw six fine-looking men coming, and with them a seventh man, superior in every way. The report of the coming of these strangers was quickly sent to the chiefess who ruled the land under Wakea and Papa. She commanded her chief to take his warriors and meet these strangers and bring them to her house. There they were entertained. While they slept, the chiefess gathered her people together until the enclosure around the houses was filled with people.

In the morning Ikaika-loa, the chief, said to the chiefess: "I have heard that you propound hard riddles. If I guess your riddles you shall become my wife." The chiefess agreed, took him out of the house, and said, "The man who is now my husband is standing by the door of the house of Wakea and Papa; where is the door of that house?" The chief turned to Ike-loa and secretly asked if he could see the door of Papa's house. He looked all around and at last said: "The door of that house is where the trunk of that great tree is. If you are strong and can break that tree you can find the door, because it is in one of the roots of that tree."

Then the chief went out to that tree and lifted and twisted the bark and tore away the wood, opening the door.

After this the chiefess said: "There are three dogs.

199

One belongs to our high chief, Wakea; one to his wife, Papa; and one is mine. Can you point out the dog belonging to each of us?"

The chief whispered to his servant Hoo-lohe-loa, "Listen and learn the names of the dogs." So the man who could hear clearly put his ear to the ground and heard Papa telling her servants: "This black dog of Papa's shall go out first, then the red dog of Wakea. The white dog belonging to the chiefess shall go last." Thus the chief learned how to name the dogs.

When the black dog leaped through the door the chief cried out, "There is the black dog belonging to Papa."

When the red dog followed, he said, "That is the red dog of Wakea."

Then came the white dog, and the chief cried out, "That white dog belongs to you, O chiefess."

After this, they prepared for a feast. The chiefess said: 'Very far is the sweet water we wish. You send one of my women each with a calabash for water. If your man comes back first while we eat, we will marry."

The chief gave a calabash to Mama-loa and he made ready to go — a woman with her calabash standing by his side. At the word they started on their race. The man ran swiftly, thinking there was no one among all men so swift as he, but the woman passed him and was leaving him far behind.

The chief called Pana-pololei, the straight shooter, and told him they needed his skill. He took his bow and arrows and shot. Far, far the arrow sped and whizzed just back of the head of the woman. She was so startled that she stumbled and fell to the ground and the man passed by.

After a time the chief said to Ike-loa, the farsighted, "How are they running now?"

The servant said, "The woman is again winning."

The chief said to his rat hunter, "Perhaps you have another arrow?" and again an arrow sped after the swift runners. It grazed the back of the woman and she fell.

Mama-loa passed her, rushed to the spring, filled his calabash and started back. But the woman was very swift and, quickly dipping her calabash, turned and soon passed the man. An arrow sped touching the head of the woman, and she fell forward breaking the calabash and spilling the water. But she leaped up and saved a little water and hastened after the man who had sped past her.

"Ah, how she runs! She flies by the man as they are almost at the end of their race," exclaimed Ike-loa.

Then the chief called to his bowman: "O Pana-pololei! Perhaps you have another arrow?" The bowman shot a blunt arrow, striking the woman's breast, and she fell, out of breath, losing all the water from her broken calabash.

The chief took the calabash from his man, poured water into a coconut cup, and gave to the chiefess to drink.

When the woman came the chiefess asked why she had failed. The woman replied: "I passed that man, but something struck me and I fell down. This came to me again and again, but I could not see anything. At last I fell and the calabash was broken and all the water lost, and this man won the race."

Meanwhile Mama-loa was being ridiculed by the other servants of the chief. He asked: "Why do you laugh at me? Did you not see my victory?"

They laughed the more, and said: "Ka! If we had not aided you, you would have been defeated." Then they told him how he had been watched by the farsighted one and aided by the arrows of his friend.

The chiefess told the chief that she had one more test before the marriage could take place.

She said: "In this land there are two places, one very hot and one very cold. If you can send men to live in these two places we will marry."

Then the chief said to Kanaka-make-anu, "You die in the cold, but perhaps you can go to the very hot place for the chiefess." And Kanaka-make-wela, who suffered from heat, was asked to go into the cold. The two servants said: "We go, but will never return. These are our natural dwelling places."

There were no more riddles to solve. The chief and chiefess married and lived royally in that beautiful land of the gods.

The Great Dog Ku

KU, THE dog man, decided to come down from the clouds and visit mankind. He assumed the form of a little dog and went around almost unnoticed.

Ku saw a group of three rainbows, moving from place to place or resting for a long time above the home of a high chief. Sometimes the rainbows went up to the forests of ohia and kukui trees on the mountainside. Sometimes they rested over the deep pools made by the waterfalls of the swiftly descending mountain streams. More frequently the beautiful colors were arched over a small grove of trees around a bathing pool protected on two sides by steep ledges of rock over which diverging streams poured their cool waters, which rose from the shadows and rippled away through the little valley toward the sea. On the remaining side of this sequestered nook was a sunny beach of black sand, back of which the trees opened their promise of refreshing shade.

Here Na-pihe-nui, the daughter of the high chief, came daily with her company of maidens to bathe and sport in the water and then let the afternoon hours pass in rest and pleasant conversation.

One day while diving into the pool from a shelf on the rocky ledge, one of the girls saw something moving on the shore. She called to her companions and with them hastened to the place where their clothes had been thrown down. Here they found a little white dog lying on the kapa mantle of the princess.

For a time they played with the little stranger and were very much delighted with his unusual intelligence. He gamboled around them in great delight, obeying the call of one after the other, but showing very marked preference for the princess. When the maidens returned home they took the little dog with them and cared for him.

The high chief, Polihale, was interested in the peculiar powers possessed by this strange dog. Perhaps he thought it was under the control of some spirit. His suspicions were in some way aroused and the dog was watched. Soon the chief learned that this was a man of marvellous ability, who could appear as a dog or a man at his own pleasure. Then the chief called his retainers and ordered them to kill this dog. They gathered stones and clubs and tried to surround it, but it dashed into the woods and made its escape. It was the great dog Ku, who had seen the three rainbows and followed them to the bathing pool and then, having seen the princess, had determined to find an opportunity to carry her away as his wife. This premature discovery drove him away before he could accomplish his purpose.

Then Ku changed himself into a man of fine appearance and came boldly to the high chief's home, demanding the princess in marriage. But the chief, warned by the omens as studied by his soothsayers, refused.

Ku was in great anger. He threatened to kill the chief's people and to destroy the protectors of the princess; but the high chief drove him away.

A dream came to the high chief, in which he saw a strange man coming as a great dog. The next morning as he looked toward the mountains he saw this same large dog stretching itself out of a cave on the mountainside. He knew that this dog with magical powers would be a very difficult enemy to overcome.

The chief soon learned that Ku was catching his people one by one and devouring them. He decided to take final issue with his enemy.

Selecting a cave, he hid all the women of his family in it, placing the princess in their care. They took provisions with them and prepared for a long siege. Water could be found in the cave itself. Stones were placed before the opening so that the enemy would find it hard to enter.

Then the high chief and his followers waged war against Ku, the dog man. But Ku was very strong and overthrew his pursurers when they closed in around him. Many times he killed some of the chief's people and carried their bodies away to feast upon them. He was also very swift in his motion, rapidly passing from place to place. Sometimes he fell like a flash of lightning upon a group of his foes, and then in an incredibly short time he would make an attack in a far distant place.

The high chief became desperate and offered sacrifices to his gods and secured charms from his priests. Incantations and prayers were prepared against Ku.

At last a terrific battle was fought and Ku was overpowered and beaten to the ground. Still he fought fiercely, but the hard wooden spears pierced him and the heavy clubs broke his bones, until he lay a crushed and bleeding mass at the feet of his conquerors. Then they cut his body in two pieces, throwing one piece to one side and the other to a place some distance away. Then the power of the priests was invoked and the two parts of the body of Ku-ilio-loa became two great stones, which have been objects of veneration among the Hawaiians for many years.

Ku stretches his form along the mountains and sometimes reveals himself as the great dog among the myriad shapes which the changing clouds are ever assuming. Sometimes he is seen in the clouds of Oahu, and then again his form is in the skies of other islands.

The Cannibal Dog Man

KA-HANAI-A-KE-AKUA (The Adopted Child of the Gods) was the chief whose followers fought with the dragon god Kuna, for a canoe in Nuuanu Valley. He was a friend of the fairies — the menehune people. When he had grown into young manhood and was going to have a temple of his own, with his own gods to worship, the menehunes heard about the plan for the walls and altars, and determined to build that temple for the chief.

As soon as the night shadows had fallen over the mountains back of Honolulu, the menehunes were called together by their luna, or leader. The stones necessary for the heiau (temple) walls were pointed out. Flat-sided stones were selected for raised places and altars; smooth stones were called for from the seashore to be laid down as the temple floor. Bamboo and ohia sticks were to be brought with which to build platforms for sacrifices, such as the bodies of human victims. All parts of the temple building, even to the thatched houses for the priests and chiefs, were portioned among the little people.

In one night the work was finished, a feast was eaten, and the menehunes had scattered in the shadows of the forest thickets.

Kahanai took possession of his temple and dedicated it with the kapu service and ceremonies. This meant that a kapu of silence or a kapu forbidding work of any kind would be announced, and all the people of the district, or place in which the temple was located, would obey that kapu until the dedication ceremonies were all over and the words "Noa, ua noa" were used, meaning that the kapu was over and everything could be freely done as before.

The name given to this temple was Ka-he-iki.

In this temple the chief placed his friend and guardian, Kahilona, who had cared for him from his babyhood, as his priest and teacher. Kahilona was the priest of this temple. Kahilona prepared this chant for the temple building.

> Gone is the little house,
>   The little house.
> Gone is the large house,
>   The large house.
> Gone is the short house,
>   The short house.
> Gone is the little house,
> From Maiuu to Maaa-e.
> Let this be commenced.

> Build, with the soft beat of the drum,
> With the murmur of the voice of the gods,
> With the low whine of the dog,
> With the low grunt of the pig,
> And the soft whispers of men.
>   Here am I, Kahilona,
>   The teacher of prayer,
>   Proclaimed by Kahilona.

A kupua who was a dog man overthrew the government of Kahanai and became the ruling power between Nuuanu Valley and the sea. His own house and heiau were at Lihue, a place toward the Waianae Mountains. This kupua never attacked or injured any members of the family of the very high chief or king of the island of Oahu; but he was a cannibal, and many of the people were killed and eaten by him. He could appear at will either as a man or a dog.

His name was Kaupe. After he had eaten some of the people of Oahu, he went over the water to eat the men of Maui. He then went on to Hawaii, where he captured the son of one of the high chiefs and carried him back to Oahu, putting him in the temple at Lihue to keep him there until the time came for a human sacrifice. Then the boy was to be killed and laid on a platform before the gods.

The father of that boy left Hawaii to follow him to Oahu, thinking there might be some way of saving his son. If he failed he could at least die with him. When the father came to Oahu, he very quietly landed and looked for someone to give him aid. After a time he met Kahilona, the caretaker of the temple of the menehunes, and told him all his trouble.

The priest taught the father the proper incantations by which he could get his boy away from the magic power of Kaupe, and save both himself and his boy. Then he also taught the father a prayer which he was to use if Kaupe should learn of their escape and pursue them.

At night he approached the temple at Lihue, repeating the chant which Kahilona had taught him. He watched for the signs which the priest had told him would indicate the place where the boy was kept, and followed them carefully. He continually repeated his chant until he came inside the walls and found the dog asleep, guarding the boy. The father slipped in, cautiously aroused the boy, and unfastened the cords which bound him. Then they quietly passed the dog, guarded by the incantation:

O Ku! O Lono! O Kane! O Kanaloa!
Save us two! Save us two!

Thus they passed out of the temple and fled toward the temple of Ka-he-iki.

While they were running, a great noise was heard far behind them. The dog had been awakened, and had discovered the escape of his prisoner. Then, rushing like a whirlwind around the temple, he found the direction in which they had fled. This was the path naturally taken by those leaving Oahu to escape to Hawaii. The great dog, only waiting to learn the course taken, pursued them on the wings of the wind.

The two chiefs fled, but saw that it was impossible to outrun the dog. Then the father uttered the prayer which the priest had said would save them if Kaupe followed. They ran with increased strength and swiftness, but the dog would soon be upon them. Again the father repeated the prayer:

O Ku! O Lono! O Kane! O Kanaloa!
By the power of the gods,
By the strength of this prayer,
Save us two! Save us two!

Then they found a great stone at Moanalua under which they were able to hide.

The dog had only one thought, which was that the father and son would return to Hawaii as speedily as possible aided by their gods. He rushed to the beach, leaped into the air, and flew to Hawaii.

The chiefs went to the temple Ka-he-iki, and were gladly welcomed by the priest, Kahilona, who taught them the prayers by which they could overcome and destroy the dog man.

After they were fully instructed they returned to their home on Hawaii and waged war against their enemy. They obeyed the directions of the priest and finally killed Kaupe.

But the ghost of Kaupe was not killed. He returned as a ghost-god to the highest part of Nuuanu Valley, where in his shadow body he can sometimes be seen in the clouds which gather around the mountaintops or come down the valley. Sometimes his cloud form is that of a large dog, and sometimes he is very small; but there his ghost rests and watches over the lands which at one time he filled with terror.

Kahilona, the priest of the temple Ka-he-iki, became the ancestor of one of the greatest of the priestly clans of the islands — the Mo-o-kahuna (The Priests of the Dragon) class of Oahu, noted for their ability to read the signs of sky and sea and land.

The Canoe of the Dragon

KOA TREES, out of which the finest and most enduring calabashes of the old Hawaiians were made, grew near the ocean's sandy shore, but the koa trees from which canoes were carved and burned were, according to some wise plan of providence, placed on rough, precipitous mountainsides or on the ridges above.

The fierce winds of the mountains and the habit of bracing themselves against difficulties made the koa trees cross-grained and slow in growth. The koa was the best tree of the Hawaiian Islands for the curled, twisted, and hard-grained wood needed in canoes, which were beaten by overwhelming surf waves, rolled over sandy beaches, or smashed against coral or lava reefs.

From the time the canoe was cut in the mountains and was dragged and rolled over lava beds or sent crashing down steep mountainsides to the time it lay worn out and conquered by the decay of old age, it was always ready to meet the roughest kind of life into which its maker and owner could force it to go.

The calabash used in the plains and in the mountains came from a tree grown in beautiful lines by the sea. The canoe came from the hard mountain koa, far from its final workshop. There were gods, sacrifices, ceremonies, priests, and even birds in the rites and superstitions of the canoemakers.

Kupulupulu was the god of the koa forest. Any wanderer in the woods was in the domain of that god. It was supposed that every rustling footstep was heard by most acute ears, and every motion of the hand was watched by the sharpest eyes. Dread of the unseen and unheard made every forest rover tremble until he had made some proper offering and uttered some effective incantation.

The ceremony and the wages of the priest who went up the mountain to select a koa tree for canoe cutting

were like this: First he found a fine-appearing tree which
he thought would make the kind of canoe desired. Then
he took out his fire sticks and rubbed rapidly until he had
sparks of fire in the wood dust of his lower stick. He
caught the fire and made a burning oven (imu), heated
some stones, cooked a black pig and a chicken, and prepared food for a feast, and then prayed:

> O Kupulupulu — *the god!*
> *Here is the pig,*
> *Here is the chicken,*
> *Here is food.*

> O Kupulupulu!
> O Kulana wao!
> O Ku-ohia laka!
> O Ku waha ilo!
> *Here is food for the gods.*

The aumakuas, or spirits of ancestors, were supposed
to join with the gods of the prayer in partaking of the
shadow of the feast, leaving the substance for the canoe
makers.

After the offering and prayer, the priests ate and then
lay down to sleep until the next day. In the morning after
another feast they began to cut the tree.

David Malo, in his *Hawaiian Antiquities*, said that the
priest took his stone axe and called upon the female deities of the canoe cutters thus:

> O Lea and Ka-pua-o-alakai!
> *Listen now to the axe.*
> *This is the axe which is to cut the tree for the canoe.*

Another account says that when the canoe priest
began to cut the tree, and also as long as they were chopping it down, they were talking to the gods thus:

> O Ku Akua! O Paapaaina!
> *Take care while the tree is falling,*
> *Do not break our boat,*
> *Do not let the tree smash and crack.*

When the tree began to tremble and its leaves and

branches rustle, a kapu of silence was enjoined upon the workmen, that the tree itself might be the only one heard by the watching gods.

When the tree had fallen, a careful watch was made for Lea, the wife of Moku-halii, the chief god of the canoe carvers — those who hollowed out the canoe.

It was supposed that Lea had a double body. Sometimes she was a human being and sometimes she appeared as a bird.

Her bird body was that of the elepaio, a little bird covered with speckled feathers, red and black on the wings, the woodpecker of the Hawaiians.

"When she calls she gives her name 'E-le-pai-o, E-le-pai-o, E-le-pai-o!' very sweetly."

If she calls while the tree is being cut down and then flies gently down to the fallen tree and runs up and down from end to end, and does not touch the tree, nor bend the head over, striking the wood, then that tree is sound and good for a canoe.

But if the goddess strikes the tree here and there, it is rotten and of no use, and is left lying on the ground.

David Malo says: "When the tree had fallen, the head priest mounted the trunk, axe in hand, and called out in a loud voice, 'Smite with the axe, and hollow the canoe! Give me my malo!'"

The priest's wife would hand him a white ceremonial malo with which he girded himself. He then walked along the tree a few steps and called out in a loud voice, "Strike with the axe, and hollow it! Grant us a canoe!"

Then he struck a blow on the tree with the axe. This was repeated until he reached the point where the head of the tree was to be cut off. Here he wreathed the tree with the ieie vine, repeated a prayer, commanded silence, and cut off the top of the tree.

This done, the priest declared the ceremony performed and the kapu lifted.

Then the priests took their stone adzes, hollowed out the canoe on the inside, and shaped it on the outside

211

until in its rough shape it was ready to be dragged by the people down to the beach and finished and polished for its work in the sea.

Ka-hanai-a-ke-Akua was a chief residing near Kou. He lived in the time when gods and men mingled freely with each other and every kapu chief was more or less of a god because of his high birth.

His priests went up Nuuanu Valley to a place on the side where forests covered a small valley running into the side hills of the larger and more open valley. Great koa trees fit for canoe making were found in this forest. However, this part of the valley belonged to the eepa people—the deformed or ill-shaped gnomes of woodland or plain. Sometimes they seemed to be crippled and warped in mind as well as in body. They could be kind and helpful, but they were often vindictive and quarrelsome. There were also ferocious mo-o, or dragon gods, watching for prey. Travelers were destroyed by them. They sometimes appeared as human beings, but were always ready to become mo-os.

One of these gods came down to the place where the priests were cutting the koa canoe for the high chief. He watched the ceremonies and listened to the incantations while the tree was being cut down. He tried to throw obstacles in the way of the men who were steadily breaking chips from the tree trunk. He directed the force of the wind sweeping down the valley against them. He sent black clouds burdened with heavy, driving rain. He made discouraging omens and sent signs of failure, but the priests persevered.

At last the tree fell and was accepted. It was speedily trimmed of its branches, cut roughly to the required shape, and partly hollowed out. Then coconut ropes and vines were fastened around it, and the people began to pull it down the valley to the harbor of Kou.

As they started to drag the log over rough lava ridges outcropping along the valley side, they found their first effort checked. The log did not move down into the valley. Rather, it seemed to go up the hillside. The god caught one end and pulled back. Another mighty effort was put forth and the canoe and the god slipped over the stones and partly down the hillside. But the dragon god braced himself again and made the canoe very heavy. He could not hold it fast and it came down to the men. It was very difficult to drag it through the forest of the valley side or the thickets of the valley, and the men pulled it down into the rough, rocky bed of the little stream known as Nuuanu. It was thought that the flowing water would help the men and the slippery stones would hinder the god.

Down they went, pulling against each other. The god seemed to feel that the struggle under such conditions was hopeless. He let go of the canoe and turned to the flowing water.

Beautiful waterfalls and cascades abound all along the course of this mountain stream. It is fed by springs and feathery waterfalls which throw the rainfall from the tops of the mountains far down into the valley.

The god hastened along this water-course, stopped up the springs, and turned aside the tributary streams, leaving the bed of the stream dry. Then he went down once more, caught the canoe, and pulled back. It was weary, discouraging work, and the chief's people became very tired of their struggle. The night fell when they were still some distance from the sea.

They had come to a place known as Ka-ho-o-kane, in the heart of modern Honolulu. In this place there were sharp turns, steep banks, and great stones. Here the dragon god fought most earnestly and wedged the log fast in the rocks.

The task had become so difficult and it was so dark that the high chief allowed his priests to call the people away, leaving the log in the place where the last struggle was made. It was a gift to the mo-o, the dragon, and was known as "The Canoe of the Dragon God." It is said that it lies there still, changed into a stone, stuck fast along

with the other huge stones among which the water from
the mountain finds its way, laughing at the defeat of the
canoe makers.

The Wonderful Shell

NEAR NIOLAPA, on the eastern side of Nuuanu Valley,
is the stone where Kapuni rested when he came after the
shell known as the Kiha-pu. Kapuni was a child of Kau-
hola, who was said to have been a chief, who was born,
was walking and had grown up, had become a father, a
grandfather, and had died, all in one day. Kapuni was
born in Waipio Valley, was placed in the temple of Pakaa-
luna, and was made a god.

Two gods came from Puna. They were Kaaku and
Kaohuwalu. They waited above Hakalaoa, looking down
in Waipio. There they saw Kapuni leaping. He touched a
branch of a kukui tree and fell down. He leaped again and
touched the short top branches of the kukui and fell
down.

Kaakau said to Kaohuwalu, "Suppose we get Kapuni
to go with us as our traveling companion, one with us
in fierce storms or in the cold, heavy dews of night."

Kaohuwalu assented, and they arose and went down.
They called to Kapuni, asking him to leap up. He tried
again and again and always fell back.

Kaakau caught him as he fell and cut off part of his
body because he was too heavy. Then he could fly to the
sky and return again.

Kaakau asked him how he was succeeding. He replied,
"Very well indeed; I am swift in flight." Then Kaakau
said, "Will you go with us on a journey?" Kapuni said,
"Yes."

They went away to the lands of Kahiki and returned to
Kauai. From there they heard the wonderful voice of a
shell sounding from the temple of Waolani in Nuuanu
Valley.

Kapuni said, "What is that thing which makes such a sound?"

Kaakau said, "That is a shell which belongs to the eepas (gnomes), the people of Waolani, Oahu."

"I want that shell very much," said Kapuni. Kaakau told him that the task would be very difficult and danger-ous, for the shell was guarded by watchmen from hill to hill, from the sea to the summit of the valley, and along all the pathways to the neighboring villages.

The gods, however, crossed the channel to Oahu, and rested at night above Kahakea. Here was a temple, Pa-kaaluna, upon a hill above Waolani. In it was a noted drum. Kapuni told his friends to stay there waiting for him. If he did not return before the red dust of the dawn was in the sky, they would know he was dead. If he re-turned he would have the shell.

Then he approached the prison enclosure outside the temple. Here he waited by a rock for all the watchmen on the high places around the temple to fall asleep. When the stars arose in the heavens above Nuuanu and all were sound asleep, he entered the temple and took the shell. He flew away and found his companions.

They made a great jump and leaped to Kalaau Point. As they flew over the water to Molokai, the shell touched the top of a wave and sang with a clear voice.

The god of Waolani Temple heard the shell singing, looked, and found that it had been stolen. He rushed from the temple, flew over the Nuuanu precipice, and went out into the channel from which he had heard the sound.

Kapuni hid among the waves; the shell ceased its song. The god of Waolani went back and forth over the water but could find nothing.

After the god gave up the search, Kapuni went on to Molokai and then to Maui and Hawaii. As it flew across the channel between Maui and Hawaii, the shell struck a high wave and broke off a corner.

When they were on the hills of Hawaii they found the

temple built at Hainoa. There the gods of Hawaii were gathered together.

Kiha was high chief of Hawaii at that time, and had been dwelling in Waipio Valley, cultivating his plant, planting awa, and building a temple for his gods.

When that temple was finished and the tabu of silence lifted from all the surrounding country, he went to Kawaihae and built another temple, establishing another altar for his gods. He placed the usual kapu upon all the land around Kawaihae.

But the kapu was broken by the sound of that shell blown by the gods of Hainoa Temple. He was very much troubled, but the gods were too strong for him. At last help came to him from Puapualenalena (The Yellow Flower), a dog belonging to a master who had left his home in Niihau some time before. Puapualenalena was seeking his master, and found him on the uplands of Hawaii.

The dog excelled in his skill as a thief, stealing pigs, chickens, kapa cloth, and all kinds of other property for his master.

The master told that dog to get the kapu awa roots of the king, which were growing on the hillsides of Waipio Valley. When that place was stripped, he sent the dog to the precipices of Waimanu, and he took nearly all that was there.

Then the king commanded his people to watch the awa fields and catch the one who was stealing his growing awa.

They began their watch. When the night was almost over and the dawn was touching the sky, they found the thief. These men followed the dog and caught his master in a cave, all wrinkled from drinking much awa.

They took the master and the dog to King Kiha as prisoners, and the king planned to have them steal that shell which troubled him. If they failed they should be put to death. This was the sentence of the king upon his prisoners.

The master talked with his dog, and told him all the word of the king. They planned to pay for the theft of the awa, but not by the death of their bodies.

The dog went out to win the shell from the gods under cover of the night, when the darkness was great and all kinds of shell voices were mingling with other voices of the woodland and wilderness.

Then came the softly resonant voice of that shell blown by the gods. According to an ancient chant, "The song of Kiha-pu calls Kauai," meaning the song is listened to from far distant Kauai.

The dog ran swiftly while the sound of the shell was great, and hid in a corner of a stone wall of the heiau. He waited and waited a long time. The dawn was almost at hand. Then the watchers fell into deep sleep.

The dog crept softly inside, seized the shell, and slipped it away from its place. Then he leaped over six walls of the heiau, but touched the seventh and outside wall. Then the shell sang out loud and clear.

The gods were aroused. They followed, but the dog leaped into a pool of water and concealed himself and the shell while the gods dashed by. They searched the road towards Waipio, then rushed toward the Kona district.

The dog flew from the pond down the precipice of Waipio Valley and laid the shell at the feet of Kiha, the king of Hawaii. The dog and his master were given a high place in the affections of the king.

The shell was renowned for its wonderful sound, and could call the warriors of the king from any distance when the king caused it to be blown. It was known as Kiha's shell, the Kiha-pu.

This shell was carefully preserved by the chiefs of Hawaii from that ancient time. Generation after generation it was cared for. In the time of Kamehameha III it was kept in his palace. It was among the treasures of King Kalakaua, and now has its resting place in the hands of ex-Queen Liliuokalani in Honolulu.

When Kapuni died his bones, worshipped as those of a

217

god, were kept at Kaawaloa until the kapu and the temples were overthrown.

The Ghost Dance on Punchbowl

PUNCHBOWL (Pu-o-waina) lies back of Honolulu. It is an extinct volcano. Inside the crater rim is a basin whose sides are grass-covered, with groups of trees here and there. The little houses and small gardens of squatters show that there is no longer any fear of subterranean activity. A large part of the city of Honolulu is built on what were once the brown, desolate sides of the volcano sloping down to the sea.

Punchbowl is one of the last attempts of the goddess of fire to retain her hold on the island of Oahu. The great ridge of mountains which forms the backbone of the island is a gigantic remnant of volcanic action. But the craters out of which this vast mass of lava was poured died centuries before the foothill craters threw out the last black sand of Punchbowl or uplifted the coral and the white sand and shells of Leahi or Diamond Head.

In the indefinite long ago, Kakei was the moi, or high ruling chief, of Oahu. He was enterprising and brave. He not only perfected himself in the use of the spear, the war club, and the sling stone, but he rallied around him the restless young chiefs of the districts which acknowledged his supremacy. His court was filled with men who gave and received blows, who won and lost in the many games, who were penniless today and rich tomorrow, and yet took all that came as a matter of course.

Kakei called these younger chiefs together and told them to return to their districts for a time and make preparations for a voyage and a battle. They must see that many new canoes were made and the best of the old ones repaired and repolished. They must select the bravest and best of their retainers and have them well armed

218

and well provisioned. He hinted that it might be a long journey. Therefore they had better provide strong mat sails for all the canoes. It might be many days. Therefore the provisions should be such as would last. At once the young men with great joy hastened to their homes to obey the will of their chief.

It was impossible to keep the people from talking about the expedition. Excitement predominated. The shrill voices of the women shouted the news from valley to valley. The hum of unwonted industry was heard over all the island. Imagination was keenly intent to discover the point threatened by the proposed excursion. Night after night the people discussed the various enemies of their king, and his prospects for successful battle with them; or they talked of the enlargement of his kingdom by the acquisition of Molokai or the increase of riches by a foray along the coasts of Hawaii. They prophesied great victories and much spoil.

Months passed by and all the preparations were complete. A splendid body of warriors were gathered around their high chief. The large flotilla of canoes was launched, the sails set, and the colored pennants placed at the end of each mast. The young chiefs were brilliant in their bright yellow and red war capes and hideous with the war masks which many of them proudly wore as they leaped into their canoes and shouted "Aloha" to the friends whom they were leaving.

As soon as the boats had left the shore, the chief turned to the north rather than to the south, as all had been led to believe would be the course. Sails and paddles were both used freely. The winds of the seas and the strong arms of the oarsmen vied with each other in hastening the fleet toward the island of Kauai. Night crept over the waters, but the bright stars were unclouded and the path over the waters was as straight by night as it had been by day.

The morning star was shining and the dawn was painting the clear sky with wonderful tints of pearl when

Kakei and his army of warriors, already on the land, raised their war cry and assaulted the people of the village of Waimea.

Catching war club and spear, the chief of Waimea rushed out of his house, raising his war cry. His men, half awake, confused and dazed by the sudden attack, attempted to aid him in resisting the invaders. But the battle was short and decisive. In a very little while, many people were killed. The thatched houses were set on fire and a great destruction wrought.

Kakei had ordered his warriors to seize the canoes, the women and children, and whatever plunder in calabashes, mats, kapa cloth, stone implements, and feather cloaks could be had, and gather all together on the beach.

The captured canoes and their own great fleet were filled and the return safely made to Oahu. Kakei and his warriors sailed around the island to Honolulu Harbor. There the beach was covered with the new riches and the captive women and children. The king ordered a great feast to be prepared on the slopes of Punchbowl. Fish in abundance were caught, pigs and chickens were slaughtered, many ovens with red-hot stones were made ready, and huge calabashes of awa prepared.

Kakei and his victorious warriors gathered around the poi bowl, while the hula girls danced most joyously before them.

Suddenly the earth shook under them, the poi bowls rocked as if tossed on the waters of the sea, the feast which had been spread before them moved from place to place as if made of things of life. The rocky cliffs of Punchbowl began to separate and come crashing down the hillside in great masses. The people fled in every direction, leaving a part of their number crushed under the falling stones.

Then came another mighty earthquake. The side of Punchbowl opened and a flood of lava poured out, mixed with clouds of steam and foul gases. Down over the place where the feast was spread on the luau mats poured the fire. The feast became the food of the fire goddess.

Then a wonderful thing appeared above the flowing lava, in the midst of the clouds hovering over the crater. A number of the aumakua of Kauai were seen in a solemn and stately dance. Back and forth they moved to the rhythm of steady peals of erupting gases. The clouds swayed to and fro, while the ghosts moved back and forth among them. The spirits of the ancestors had come to protect the women and children of the households whose friendly deities they were. It was the ceremonial, sacred dance of the spirits, to be followed by swift punishment of those who had brought such great injury to Kauai.

But while the ghosts continued their awful dance, the terrified king and his warriors hastily prepared a propitiation. The captured women and children were called to the beach. All the plunder brought from Waimea was hastily collected and placed in the hands of the captives. The kahunas, the priests of the king, were sent to the slope above Punchbowl Hill to cry out to the aumakuas that all the reparation possible would be made at once.

The warriors placed the captives and their goods in canoes, and started back to Kauai. As the canoes passed out of sight, the earthquakes ceased. No longer was there the thunder of imprisoned gases leaping to liberty. The fires died away, and the flood of lava cooled. The aumakuas had accepted the offered repentance of the king and his warriors.

It is said that the fire never again returned to that crater or to the island of Oahu.

The Bird Man of Nuuanu Valley

NAMAKA WAS a noted man of the time of Kalaniopuu. He was born on Kauai, but journeyed forth to find someone he would like to call his lord. He was skilled in managing land (kalai-aina), an orator (kakaolelo), and could recite genealogies (kuauhau). He excelled in spear throwing (lonomakaihe); boxing or breaking the back of his opponent (lua); leaping or flying (lele); and astronomy (kilo). All this he had learned on Kauai.

Sailing from Kauai, he landed on Oahu. In Nuuanu Valley he met Pakuanui, a very skillful man, a fine orator and boxer. He was the father of Ka-ele-o-waipio, a noted man of the time of Kamehameha, the maker of a chant for the missionaries at Kailua.

Toward the upper end of Nuuanu Valley, in a place named Ka-hau-komo, where spreading hau trees cluster on both sides of the road, Namaka and Pakuanui had a contest. They prepared themselves for boxing and wrestling, and then faced each other to show their skill and agility.

This man from Kauai appeared like a rainbow bending over the hau trees, arched in the red rain, or in the mist cloud over the Pali, as he circled around Pakuanui. He was like the ragged clouds of Lanihuli, or the wind rushing along the top of the Pali. His hands were like the rain striking the leaves of the bushes of Malailua. He was so swift and strong that he could catch Pakuanui in any part of his body.

The man of Oahu could not hold Namaka. That Kauai man was as slippery as an eel, and as hard to hold as certain kinds of smooth, slimy fish, always escaping the hands of Pakuanui. But he could strike any place. The hill of the forehead he struck, the ridge of the nose also. There was no place he could not touch. He rushed like a whirlwind around the man. However, he did not try to kill Pakuanui. He wis

Pakuanui was very n
he could not do anything display his skill.
kill him when they should red and angry because
Nuuanu Valley), to which the ka, and planned to
ing contest. ali (the precipice of
When they came to Kapili at th ng after the box-
narrow place, Pakuanui said to Nam he Pali, a very
fore me." u may go be-
Namaka passed by on the outside an
him a kick, knocking him over the Pali, ex nui gave
be dashed to pieces on the rocks at the foot g him to
pice. e preci-

But Namaka flew away from the edge of the Pali. The people who were watching said: "He went off. He flew off from the Pali like an io bird, leaping into the air of Lanihuli, spreading out his arms like wings. When the strong wind twisted and whirled, Namaka was lifted like a kite by the wind, and hung among the kukui branches below a little waterfall which is on the western side of the precipice where a rivulet starts on its way to the ocean." Then he leaped to the ground and went away to Maui. At Pohakuloa, on Maui, Namaka leaped down some precipices, showing his strength and skill.

When Namaka came to Hawaii, Kalaniopuu was king. He liked him very much and hoped to have him as his lord.

However, another man from Kauai was a favorite with the king. He knew Namaka, and was afraid that he might be supplanted when the king should learn about Namaka's wonderful powers. He gave no welcome to Namaka, but turned him away.

Namaka went to Waimea and found Hinai, the high chief of that place, a near relative to Kalaniopuu. He told Hinai what he could do, and was made a favorite of the high chief.

He taught Hinai how to be very skillful in all his arts, and especially in leaping from precipices. He hoped that

Hinai's skill wou... ...abroad, and the king would
hear and wish t... ...eacher come to live with him.
Hinai becam... ...ficient, and even wonderful, in
standing on ... ...g of high precipices and leaping
down unhur... ...places have been pointed out to the
young peop... ...eir parents.
When th... ...ite of Kalaniopuu heard that there was
a very sk... ...an from Kauai stopping with the high
chief of ... ...ea, he told the king that an enemy from
Kauai y... ...Waimea.
The... ...listened to this man, and then he charged
Nama... ...with trying to make his relative Hinai so skillful j... ...leaping down high places that he could always
escape any attempt to injure him.

The favorite said: "This man, Namaka, can fly over mountains and streams and precipices and plains and not be killed. He is a rebel against your kingdom."

Kalaniopuu commanded some men to go and kill this stranger from Kauai, telling them to begin war upon Hinai if he opposed their attempt to take the stranger.

Namaka had prepared himself for escape by digging in the ground and making a pit under his house, with a tunnel and an opening some distance away.

The warriors from Kalaniopuu surrounded the house, thinking he was inside. They consulted about the best method of killing him, and decided to burn him up. They set fire to the house and destroyed it and went away, believing this stranger had been burned to death.

Namaka easily escaped from Hawaii and crossed over to Maui, where he remained some time. But he found no one whom he wished to take as his lord. Then he went to Oahu, and at last returned to his home on Kauai.

There, prophesying about the chiefs of Hawaii, whom he had considered superior to those on Maui and Oahu, but not equal to the royal family of Kauai, he spoke thus: "There is no ruling chief in Hawaii who can step his foot on the kapu sand of Kahamaluihi (Kauai). There is no war canoe or divine chief who can come to Kauai unless a treaty has been made between the two ruling chiefs."

The natives call this a prophecy of the skilled chief who could fly from Nuuanu Pali, and think it was fulfilled because Kamehameha never conquered Kauai, but secured it by concession from its king.

The Owls of Honolulu

PUEO

THERE ARE three celebrated "owl" localities in the suburbs of Honolulu—one in Manoa Valley, the second near the foot of Punchbowl Hill, and one at Waikiki. In Manoa the owl god lived, and at Waikiki the famous "battle of the owls" was fought.

Manoa Valley is one of the most beautiful rainbow valleys in the world. Some of the highest peaks of Oahu lie near its head. The winds which blow down the Pacific Ocean from the northeast strike the mountaintops. Each cool breeze leaves its burden of moisture in a fleecy cloud to fall down the mountainside into the valley. Cloud follows cloud, descending the slopes of the foothills in gentle rain.

Almost all day long the valley is open to the sun, which, looking on the luxuriant verdure and clinging mist, sends its abundant blessing of penetrating light. Rainbows upon rainbows are painted on the steep precipices at the head of the valley. There are arches and double arches of exquisite beauty, smashed fragments of scattered color, broad pillars of glorious fire blazing around green branches of ghostlike trees, great bands of opal hues lying in magnificent masses on the hillside, and lunar rainbows almost circular, outlined in soft prismatic shades in the time of the full moon.

When showers creep down the valley one by one,

rainbows also chase each other in matchless symmetry of quiet, graceful motion. Sometimes the mist in the doorway of the valley has become so ethereal that splendid arches hang in the apparently clear sky without cloud support.

It is no wonder that from time immemorial the Hawaiians have made the valley the home of royal chiefs, with the rainbow maiden as their daughter. The story of this child of the skies is told in the legend of Ka-hala-o-Puna (The Sweet-scented Hala Flower of Puna). Woven into this legend is also the legend of the owl god of the family to which this maiden belonged, for his home as well as hers was in Manoa Valley.

Almost in the middle of the valley is a hill on which, many years ago, a temple was built and dedicated as the home of the owl god Pueo. The hill now bears the name of "Puu-pueo," or "The Hill of the Owl."

It was from this temple that the owl god rescued the rainbow maiden three times when she had been thrice killed and buried by her faithless suitor, a chief of Waikiki.

Ka-hala (The Hala Flower) had followed this chief almost to the lower end of the valley, but she became weary. The angry chief struck her with a bunch of hala nuts, killed her, and buried her under a mass of leaves and dirt near the spot called Aihualama. Pueo, the owl god, had carefully watched the journey of this one of his people. When he saw her struck down, he hastened to the spot swiftly, dashed aside the dirt, pulled out the body, and carried it in his claws back to the head of the valley, where by charms and incantations he healed her wounded head and restored her to life. Soon her beauty came back to her and surrounded her so that she walked as if encompassed with rainbows.

Again the Waikiki chief, to whom she had been affianced by her parents, came after her. Again he became angry because she grew weary in the new way by which he led over a high ridge dividing Manoa from a neighboring valley. A second time he seized a bunch of hala nuts swinging on their long stems, and with this as a club struck her on the head, killing her. He covered the body with ferns and vines and went away. The watching owl god took the body tenderly, cared for it and restored it to life. Once more the radiance of a divine chiefess rested in rainbows around the girl and her Manoa Valley home.

The third time the chief called for her, she obeyed with trembling and followed him up the almost precipitous sides of Manoa Valley, over ridges, and across valleys and turbulent streams until they came to the ridge by the Waolani Temple in Nuuanu Valley. There he killed her and buried her. But Pueo scratched away the leaves and dirt, and again gave her life.

At the head of Manoa Valley are many waterfalls pouring down the precipices. The longer and most feathery of these falls are said to be the tears of Ka-hala as she suffered from the attacks of the faithless chief of Waikiki.

Pueo, the owl god, was also Pueo-alii, or "King of Owls." He had kahunas (priests) who consulted him by signs, and the aumakuas, or ghost-gods, who dealt sometimes in oracles. He was thought to be a chief leading his army of ghosts along the hillside below the Puu-honua Temple, now the site of the Castle estate.

From his own residence on Owl's Hill, he governed all the valley, apparently with much wisdom. It was said that one of the dwellers in the valley displeased him. He captured the man and at once ordered the death penalty, calling him a rebel. The man secured the attention of the owl god for a moment, and presented the plea that he ought to be permitted to say something for himself before he was punished. This seemed reasonable. The execution was delayed and the man proved that he was innocent of the charge against him. The owl god established a law that a person must be proved guilty before he could be condemned and punished. This came to be a custom among the Hawaiians as the years passed by.

The legends say that the fairy people, the menehunes, built a temple and a fort a little farther up the valley above Puu-pueo, at a place called Kukaoo, where even now a spreading hau tree shelters under its branches the remaining walls and scattered stones of the Kuakoo Temple. It is a very ancient and very noted temple site. Some people say that the owl god and the fairies became enemies and waged bitter war against each other. At last the owl god beat the drum of the owl clan and called the owl gods from Kauai to give him aid. They flew across the channel in a great cloud and reinforced the owl god. Then came a fierce struggle between the owls and the little people. The fort and the temple were captured and the menehunes driven out of the valley.

KAPOI

The second legendary owl locality is found near the foot of Punchbowl Hill.

Honolulu as the name of even a village was not known at that time. Apparently there were very few people living along the watercourse coming down Nuuanu Valley. It may have been that even Kou (the ancient name for Honolulu) had not been heard. At any rate, the sea-coast was a place of growing rushes and nesting birds. A dry, heated plain, almost entirely destitute of trees, extended up to the foothills. Taro patches and little groves of various trees bordered each watercourse. The population was small and widely scattered. There was a legend of a band of robbers which infested this region. It was almost a "desolate place."

Down Pauoa Valley dashes a stream of beautiful clear water. This passes along the eastern edge of the small extinct crater known as Punchbowl Hill, whose ancient name was Pu-o-waina. The water from this stream was easily diverted into choice taro-patch land. Here not far from the upper end of Fort Street at Kahehuna lived a man by the name of Kapoi.

His grass house was decaying. The thatch was falling to pieces. It was becoming a poor shelter from the storms which so frequently swept down the valley. Kapoi went to the Kewalo marsh near the beach, where tall pili grass was growing, to get a bundle of the grass to use for thatching. He found a nest of owl's eggs. He took up his bundle of grass and nest of eggs and returned home.

In the evening he prepared to cook the eggs. With his fire sticks he had made a fire in his small imu, or oven. An owl flew down and sat on the wall by the gate. Kapoi had almost finished wrapping the eggs in ti leaves and was about to lay them on the hot stones when the owl called to him: "O Kapoi! Give me my eggs."

Kapoi said, "How many eggs belong to you?"

The owl replied, "I have seven eggs."

Then Kapoi said, "I am cooking these eggs for I have no fish."

The owl pleaded once more: "O Kapoi! Give me back my eggs."

"But," said Kapoi, "I am already wrapping them for cooking."

Then the owl said: "O Kapoi! You are heartless, and you have no sorrow for me if you do not give back my eggs."

Kapoi was touched, and said, "Come and get your eggs."

Because of this kindness the owl became Kapoi's god, who commanded him to build a heiau (temple) and make a raised place and an altar for sacrifice. The name of the place where he was to build his temple was Manoa. Here he built his temple. He laid a sacrifice and some bananas on the altar, and established the day for the kapu to begin and the day also when the kapu should be lifted.

This was talked about by the people. By and by the high chief heard that a man had built a temple for his god, had made it kapu, and had lifted the kapu.

Kakuhihewa was living at Waikiki. He was the king after whom the island of Oahu was named Oahu-a-

Kakuhihewa. This was the especial name of Oahu for centuries. Kakuhihewa encouraged sports and games, as well as agriculture and fishing. His house was so large that its dimensions have come down in the legends, about two hundred and fifty by one hundred feet. Kakuhihewa was kind, and yet this offense of Kapoi was serious in the eyes of the people in view of their ancient customs and ideas. Kakuhihewa had made a law for his temple which he was building at Waikiki. He had established his kapu over all the people and had made the decree that, if any chief or man should build a temple with a kapu on it and should lift that kapu before the kapu on the king's temple should be over, that chief or man should pay the penalty of death as a rebel.

This king sent out his servants and captured Kapoi. They brought him to Waikiki and placed him in the king's heiau of Kapalaha. He was to be killed and offered in sacrifice to the offended god of the king's temple.

KUKAEUNAHIO

The third legendary locality for the owl gods was the scene of the "battle of the owls." This was at Waikiki. Kapoi was held prisoner in the Waikiki heiau. Usually there was a small, foursquare, stone-walled enclosure in which sacrifices were kept until the time came when they should be killed and placed on the altar. In some such place Kapoi was placed and guarded.

His owl god was grateful for the return of the eggs, and determined to reward him for his kindness and protect him as a worshipper. In some way there must be a rescue. This owl god was a "family god," belonging only to this man and his immediate household. According to the Hawaiian custom, any individual could select anything he wished as the god for himself and family.

Kapoi's owl god secured the aid of the king of owls who lived in Manoa Valley on Owl's Hill. The king of owls sent out a call for the owls of all the islands to come and make war against the king of Oahu and his warriors.

Kauai legends say that the sound of the drum of the owl king was so penetrating that it could be heard across all the channels by the owls on the different islands. In one day the owls of Hawaii, Lanai, Maui, and Molokai had gathered at Kalapueo, east of Diamond Head. The owls of Koolau and Kahikiku, Oahu, gathered together in Kanoniakapueo, in Nuuanu Valley. The owls of Kauani and Niihau gathered in the place toward the sunset — Pueo-hulu-nui, near Moanalua.

Kakuhihewa had set apart the day of Kane — the day dedicated to the god Kane and given his name — as the day when Kapoi should be sacrificed. This day was the twenty-seventh of the lunar month. In the morning of that day the priests were to slay Kapoi and place him on the altar of the temple in the presence of the king and his warriors.

At daybreak the owls rallied around that temple. As the sun rose, its light was obscured. The owls were clouds covering the heavens. Warriors and chiefs and priests tried to drive the birds away. The owls flew down and tore the eyes and faces of the men of Kakuhihewa. They scratched dirt over them and befouled them. Such an attack was irresistible. Kakuhihewa's men fled, and Kapoi was set free.

Kakuhihewa said to Kapoi: "Your god has mana (miraculous power) greater than my god. Your god is a true god."

Kapoi was saved. The owl was worshipped as a god. The place of that battle was Kukaeunahio-ka-pueo. (The Confused Noise of Owls Rising in Masses).

The Two Fish from Tahiti

STRANGERS to Hawaiian history should know that, to the Hawaiians, Tahiti meant any faraway or foreign land. Tahiti belongs to the Society Islands. Centuries ago it was one of the points visited by the Vikings of the Pacific, the Polynesian searovers, among whom certain chiefs of the Hawaiian Islands were not the least noted. They sailed to Tahiti and Samoa and other islands of the great ocean and returned after many months, celebrating their voyages in personal chants.

Thus the names of places many hundreds of miles distant from the Hawaiian group were recorded in the chants and legends of the most famous families of Hawaiian chiefs and kings. Some of the names brought back by the wanderers appear to have been given to places in their own homeland. A large district on the island of Maui where, it is said, the friends of a Viking would gather for feasting and farewell dancing, was named Kahiki-nui (The Great Tahiti). A point of land not far from this district was called Keala-i-kahiki (The Way to Tahiti). These names are not of recent origin, but are found in the scenes described by roving ancestors noted in genealogies of long ago. Probably, about the same time that the Vikings of Scandinavia were roaming along the Atlantic coasts, the Pacific seamen were passing from group to group among the Pacific Islands.

After many voyages and several years, probably the people who never wandered became careless concerning the specific name of the place to which some of their friends had sailed, and included the whole outside world in the comprehensive declaration, "Gone to Kahiki." At any rate, this has been the usage for some centuries among the Hawaiians.

The story I am about to tell you came to me as a marvelous, mysterious, miraculous myth of the long ago,

232

when strange powers dwelt in both animals and me.
and when cannibalism might have been carried on, to be
reported later under the guise of eating the flesh of
beast or fish.

In the long ago there were two "fish" crossing the
trackless waters of the Pacific Ocean. Their home was in
one of the faraway lands, known as Tahiti. These "fish"
were great canoes filled with men. They decided that
they would like to visit some of the lands about which
they had heard in the legends related by their fathers.
They knew that certain stars were always in certain
places in the sky during a part of every year. By sailing
according to these stars at night and the sun by day, they
felt confident that they could find the wonderful fire
land of Hawaii, about which they had been taught in the
stories of returned travelers. So the two "fish"—the
two boats—after weary days and nights of storm and
calm, of soft breeze and strong, continuous winds, found
the northeast side of the island of Oahu, with its rugged
front of steep, precipitous rocks.

The travelers landed first on a point of land extending
far out into the sea, terminating in a small volcano. Here
they made examination of the unfriendly coast and decided to journey entirely around the island, one fish or
boat going toward the north and the other toward the
south. They were apparently intending to pass around
the island and find an appropriate location for a settle-
ment. Possibly they planned to make a permanent home,
or hoped to meet some good community into which they
might be absorbed. The point of land which marked the
separation of the two companies is called Makapuu. The
boat which sailed toward the north found no good resting place until it came to the fishing village of Hauula.

The stories told by the old people of the present time
do not give any details of the meeting between the
strangers and the people residing in the village. Evidently there was dissension and at last a battle. The whole
story is summed up by the Hawaiian legend in the say-

ig: "The fish from Tahiti was caught by the fishermen of Hauula. They killed it and cut it up into pieces for food." Thus the visitors found death instead of friendship, and cannibalism was thereby veiled by calling the victims "fish" and the victory a "catch."

The custom of hiding hints of cannibalistic feasts and more definite human sacrifices under the name of "fish" continued through the centuries even after the discovery of the islands by Captain Cook and the advent of white men. David Malo, a native writer who, about the year 1840, wrote a concise sketch of Hawaiian history and customs, described the capture of human sacrifices by the priests when needed for temple worship. He says: "The priest conducted a ceremony called Ka-papa-ulua. It was in this way: The priest accompanied by a number of others went out to sea to fish for ulua with hook and line, using squid for bait. If they were unsuccessful and got no ulua, they returned to land and went from one house to another, shouting out to the people within and telling them some lie or other and asking them to come outside. If anyone did come out, him they killed and, thrusting a hook in his mouth, carried him away to the heiau (temple)." This sacrifice was called ulua, and was placed before the god of the temple as if it were a fish. Sometimes a part of the body, usually an eye, was eaten during the ceremonies of consecrating the offering to the idol. This custom has passed the test of centuries, and probably was the last remnant of cannibalism in the Hawaiian Islands. It endured even to the time of the abolition of the temples and their idols.

The second fish from Tahiti had gone on southward in its journey around the island of Oahu. It passed the rough and desolate craters of Koko Head on the eastern end of the island. It swam by Diamond Head and the beautiful Waikiki Beach. Either the number of the inhabitants was so large that they were afraid to make any stay or else they preferred to make the complete circuit of the island before locating, for they evidently made

234

only a very short stay wherever they landed and then hurried on their journey.

By the time they reached Kaena, the northwestern cape of Oahu, they were evidently anxious concerning their missing companions. Not a boat was seen on the miles of water between Kaena and Kahuku, the most northerly point on the island. The legend says that the fish changed itself into a man and went inland to search the coast for its friend, but the search was unsuccessful. It was now a weary journey from point to point, watching the sea and exploring all the spots on the beach where it seemed as if there was any prospect of finding a trace of their expected friends. Where a break in the coral reef permitted their boat to approach the land, they forced their way to shore. Then when the thorough search failed again, the boat was pushed out over the line of white inrolling breakers to the great sea, until at last the Tahitians came to Kahuku.

Now they appeared no longer as "fish," but went to the village at Kahuku as men. They made themselves at home among the people and were invited to a great feast. They heard the story of a battle with a great fish at Hauula and the capture of the monster. They heard how it had been cut up and its fragments widely distributed among the villages on the northwest coast. Evidently provision had been made for several great feasts. The people of Kahuku, although several miles distant from Hauula, had received their portion. The friendly strangers must share this great gift with them.

But the men from Tahiti with heavy hearts recognized the fragments as a part of their companion. They could not partake of the feast, but by kindliness and strategy they managed not only to decline the invitation but also to secure some portions of the flesh to carry down to the sea. These were thrown into the water, and immediately came to life. They had the color of blood as a reminder of the death from which they had been reclaimed. Ever after they bore the name of "Hilu-ula," or "The Red Hilu."

Then the "fish" from Tahiti went on around to Hauula. They went up to the kapu land back of Hauula. They pulled up the kapu flags. Then they dammed up the waters of the valley above the village until there was sufficient for a mighty flood. The storms from the heavy clouds drove the people into their homes. Then the Tahitians opened the floodgates of their mountain reservoir and let the irresistible waters down upon the village. The houses and their inhabitants were swept into the sea and destroyed. Thus vengeance came upon the cannibals.

The Tahitians were "fish." Therefore they went back into the ocean to swim around the islands. Sometimes they came near enough to the haunts of fishermen to be taken for food. They bear the name "hilu." But there are two varieties. The red hilu is cooked and eaten, but never eaten without having felt the power of fire. The trace of the cannibal feast is always over its flesh. Therefore it has to be removed by purification of the flames over which it is prepared for food. The blue hilu, the natives say, is salted and eaten uncooked. Thus the legend says the two fish came from Tahiti, and thus they became the origin of some of the beautiful fish whose colors flash like the rainbow through the clear waters of Hawaii.

Another legend somewhat similar to this is told by the natives of Hauula. There is a valley near this village called Kaipapau (The Valley of the Shallow Sea). Here lived an old kahuna, or priest, who always worshipped the two great gods Kane and Kanaloa. These gods had their home in the place where the old man continually worshipped them, but they loved to go away from time to time for a trip around the island.

Once the gods came to their sister's home and received from her dried fish for food. This they carried to the sea and threw into the waters, where it became alive again and swam along the coast while the gods journeyed inland. By and by they came to the little river on which the old man had his home. The gods went inland along the bank of the river, and the fish turned also, forcing their way over the sandbank which marked the mouth of tl little stream. Then they went up the river to a pool before the place where the gods had stopped. Ever since, when high water has made the river accessible, these fish, named ulua, have come to the place where the gods were worshipped by the kahuna and where they rested and drank awa with him. When the gods had taken enough of the awa of the priest they turned away with the warning that, when he heard a great noise on the shore, he must not go down to see what the people were doing, but ask what the excitement was about. If it was a shark or a great fish, he was to remain at home. He must not go to that place.

A few days later a big wave came up from the sea and swept over the beach. When the water flowed back there was left a great whale, the tail on the shore and the head out in the sea. The people came to see the whale. They thought that it was dead. They played on its back and leaped in the deep waters from its head. Their shouts of joy and loud laughter reached the ears of the priest, who was living inland. Then the people came to the riverside to gather vines and flowers with which to make wreaths. Probably it was the intention of the villagers to cut the great fish into pieces and have a feast.

The old priest was very anxious to see the marvelous fish. He forgot the warning of the gods and went to the seaside. The people shouted for the old man to come quickly. The old priest stood by the tail of the great fish. As if to welcome him the tail moved. He climbed on the back and ran to the head and leaped into the sea. The people cheered the priest as he returned to the beach and a second time approached the whale. Again there was the motion of the tail, and again the priest ran along the back, but as he leaped the whale caught him and carried him away to Tahiti. Therefore a name was given to a point of land not far from this place — the name of "Ka-loe-o-ka-palaoa" (The Cape of the Whale).

Iwa, the Notable Thief of Oahu

IN ANCIENT Hawaii, thieving was an honorable profession. It required cultivation as well as natural ability. Even as late as the days of Captain Cook and his discovery of the Hawaiian Islands, there is the record of a chief whose business was to steal successfully. When Captain Cook discovered the island of Kauai, a chief by the name of Kapu-puu (The Kapu Hill) was one of the first to go out to the ships. He went saying, "There is plenty of iron (hao). I will 'hao' (steal) the 'hao,' for to 'hao' (to plunder) is my livelihood." As one historian expressed this saying: "To plunder is with me house and land." The chief, however, was detected in the act and was shot and killed. The natives never seemed to blame Captain Cook for the death of that chief. The thief was unsuccessful. Really, the sin of stealing consisted in being detected.

The story of Iwa, the successful thief, goes back to the days when Umi was king of Hawaii, fourteen generations of kings before Kamehameha the First. The king Umi was well known in Hawaiian historical legends, and many important events are dated with his reign as the reference point.

In Puna, Hawaii, while Umi was king, there lived a fisherman by the name of Keaau. He was widely known for his skill in fishing with a wonderful shell. It was one of the leho shells, and was used in catching squid. Its name was Kalo-kuna. Keaau always returned from fishing with his canoe full. After a time he was talked about all around the island, and Umi heard about the magic leho of the fisherman.

At that time Umi dwelt in Kona, where he was fishing after the custom of those days. He sent a messenger commanding the fisherman to bring his shell to Kona, where he could show its power and skill. Then the king, who had the right to take all the property of any of his

238

subjects, took the shell from the fisherman.

Keaau's heart became very sore for the loss of his shell. He went to a man on Hawaii who was skilled in theft and asked him to secretly steal the leho and return it to him. He brought his canoe filled with his property—a pig, some fruit and awa, and black-and-white spotted sheets —to give to the thief who could get back his shell. But neither this thief nor any others on the islands of Hawaii, Maui, or Molokai was sufficiently skillful to give him any aid.

Then he passed on to Oahu, where he met a man fishing who, according to the custom of the people, invited him to land and accept hospitality. When the feast was over, they asked him the object of his journey. He told the story of the loss of his leho, and said that he was traveling to find "a thief able to steal back the shell taken by the strong hand of the chief of Hawaii."

Then the Oahu people told him about Iwa and his marvelous skill in plundering. They directed him to row his canoe around by Mokapu and then land, and he would find a boy without a malo (loincloth). He must give him the offering—the good things brought in the canoe. He found the boy and placed before him the gifts. They killed the pig and cooked it over hot stones. Then they had a feast, and the boy thief asked the traveler why he had come to him. The fisherman told all his trouble and asked Iwa to go with him to recover the shell. To this Iwa consented, and after a night's rest prepared to go to Hawaii.

When the time came for the journey, he placed Keaau in front and took his place to steer and paddle. The name of his paddle was Kapahi, which means "Scatter the Water." Iwa told the fisherman to look sharp at the land before them; then he talked to his paddle, saying, "Let the ocean meet the sea of Iwa." He struck his paddle once into the sea and the canoe rushed by the little islands along the coast and passed to Niihau. From Niihau in four paddle strokes the canoe lay before the coast of Havaii, where Umi and his chiefs were fishing. One of the canoes had a palm-branch house built over it to shade the fisherman. Iwa asked if that was the royal canoe and, learning that it was, quickly backed his canoe around a headland and prepared to dive, saying to his friend, "I will go and steal that leho."

He leaped into the water and sank to the bottom of the ocean. He walked along under the sea aided by his magic power until he came to the place where the king's canoes were floating. Over the side of the king's boat hung the cord to which the shell was fastened. Iwa rose quietly under the canoe and caught the leho, slowly drew it down to the bottom, broke the cord and fastened it to sharp rocks, and then went back to the place where Keaau was waiting for him. All along the way, the giant squid and devilfish fought him and tried to take the shell from his hands, but by incantations and the power of his gods he escaped to the canoe. Leaping in, he gave the leho to the fisherman and paddled away to Puna. There he dwelt with Keaau for a little while.

When the boy thief took the cord of Umi, the king thought that a very great squid had seized the shell and let the line run, afraid lest it might break and the shell be lost. But when he tried to pull he found it fast below. He sent to the land for all the people who could dive, but none of them could go to the bottom. Ten days and ten nights he waited in his canoe. Then he sent over all the island of Hawaii for those who knew how to dive in deep water, but all the noted divers failed.

The messenger came to the place where Iwa was staying. Keaau was away fishing. Iwa took the messenger to the place where the fisherman dried squid and showed him a great many already caught. Then Iwa said, "Go back and tell your king that the leho is not on the line, but a rock is holding it fast."

The messenger returned to the king and reported the saying of Iwa. Then the king sent swift men to run and bring Iwa to him. The boy agreed to go to Umi, and sped

240

more swiftly than the runners sent for him. When
stood before Umi, he told the king all his story and leap
into the sea, diving down, breaking the rock and bring
ing up the piece to which the line had been tied.

Umi then wanted Iwa to return to Puna and steal that
Leho for him. Iwa went back to the fisherman's house,
and that night stole the shell for the king.

When Umi received the shell he rejoiced greatly at the
skill of this thief. Then he thought about his kapu stone
axe in Waipio Valley, and wished to test this boy thief
again.

This sacred stone axe really belonged to Umi, the son
of Liloa, but it had been kept in the kapu heiau (sacred
temple) of Pakaalana in Waipio Valley. Two old women
were guardians of this kapu axe. It was tied fast in the
middle of a line. One end of that cord was fastened around
the neck of one old woman, and one end around the neck
of the other. Thus they wore the cord as a lei (wreath) of
that sacred stone axe of Umi.

When Umi asked the thief if he would steal this axe,
Iwa said he would try. But he waited until the sun was almost down. Then he ran swiftly to Waipio Valley as if he
were a messenger of the king, calling to the people and
establishing a kapu over the land:

> Sleep—sleep for the sacred stone axe of Umi.
> Kapu—let no man go forth from his house.
> Kapu—let no dog bark.
> Kapu—let no rooster crow.
> Kapu—let no pig make a noise.
> Sleep—sleep till the kapu is raised.

Five times he called the kapu, beginning at Puukapu
near Waimea, as he went on the guarded path to Waipio.
When he had established this kapu, he traveled down
to the place where the old women guarded the axe. He
called again, "Has sleep come to you two?" And they
answered, "Here we are; we are not asleep." He called
again: "Where are you? I would touch that sacred axe of
Umi and return and report that this hand has held the

red stone axe of the king."

He came near and took the axe and pulled the ends of the string tight around the necks of the old women, choking them and throwing them over. Then he broke the string and ran swiftly up the path over the precipice. The old women disentangled themselves and began to cry out, "Stolen is the kapu axe of Umi, and the thief has gone up toward Waimea!" The people followed Iwa from place to place, but could not overtake him and soon lost him.

Iwa went on to the king's place and lay down to sleep. As morning drew near, the king's people found him asleep and told the king he had not been away, but when Iwa was awake he was called to the king, who said, "Here, you have not got the stone axe."

"Perhaps not," said the boy, "but here is an axe which I found last night. Will you look at it?"

The king saw that it was his kapu axe, and wondered at the magic power of the thief, for he thought it was impossible to go to Waipio and return in the one night, and he knew how difficult it would be to get the axe and escape from the people.

He determined to give Iwa another trial—a contest with the best thieves of his kingdom. He asked if Iwa would consent to a death contest. The one surpassing in theft should receive a reward. The defeated should be put to death. This plan seemed right to the thief from Oahu. It would be a great battle—one against six.

The king called his clan of six thieves and Iwa, and told them that he would set apart two houses in which they could put their plunder. That night they were to go out and steal, and the one whose house contained the most property should be the victor. The report of the contest spread all through the village, and the people prepared to hide their property.

Iwa lay down to sleep while the six men quietly and swiftly passed among the people, stealing whatever they could. When they saw Iwa asleep they pitied him for his

certain death. Toward morning their house was almos
full, and still Iwa slept. The six thieves were very tired
and hungry. They prepared a feast and awa. They ate and
drank until overcome with drunkenness. A little before
dawn they also fell asleep.

Iwa arose, hastened to the house filled by the six
thieves, and hastily removed all their plunder to his own
house. Then he went quietly to Umi's sleeping house.
Showing his great skill, he removed the kapa sheets from
the bed in which the king was sleeping and piled them on
the other things in his house. Then he lay down again as
if asleep.

The morning cold fell on the king. He was chilled and
awoke, feeling for the sheets, but could not find them.
He remembered the contest, and as the daylight rested
upon the people, he called them together.

They went to the house of the six thieves and opened it
to look for their plunder, and not one thing was there.
It was entirely empty. After this they went to Iwa's
house. When the door was open, they saw the king's
kapa sheets on all the other plunder. The six thieves
were put to death, and Iwa was honored for some years
as the very dear friend of the king and the most adroit
thief in the kingdom.

After a time he longed for the place of his birth, and he
asked Umi to send him back to his parents. Umi filled a
double canoe with good things and let him go back to the
green-sided pali (precipice) of the district of Koolau, on
the island of Oahu.

Pikoi, the Rat Killer

LONG, LONG ago in the Hawaiian Islands, part of the children of a chief's family might be born real boys and girls, while others would be "gods" in the form of some one of the various kinds of animals known to the Hawaiians. These "gods" in the family could appear as human beings or as animals. They were guardians of the family or, perhaps it should be said, they watched carefully over some especial brother or sister, doing all sorts of marvelous things such as witches and fairies like to do for those whom they love.

In a family on Kauai, six girl gods were born and only one real girl and one real boy. These "gods" were all rats and were named "Kikoo," which was the name of the bow used with an arrow for rat shooting. They were "Bow of the Heaven," "Bow of the Earth," "Bow of the Mountain," "Bow of the Ocean," "Bow of the Night," and "Bow of the Day."

These rat-sister-gods seemed to have charge of their brother and his sports. His incantations and chants were made in their names. The real sister was named "Ka-ui-o-Manoa" (The Beauty of Manoa). She was a very beautiful woman, who came to Oahu to meet Pawaa, the chief of Manoa Valley, and marry him. He was an aikane (bosom friend) to Kakuhihewa, the king of Oahu. They made their home at Kahaloa in Manoa Valley. They also had Kahoiwai in the upper end of the valley.

The boy's name was Pikoi-a-ka-Alala (Pikoi, the Son of Alala). In his time the chief sport seemed to be hunting rats with bows and arrows. Pikoi as a child became very skillful. He was very clear and farsighted, and surpassed all the men of Kauai in his ability to kill hidden and far off rats. The legends say this was greatly due to the aid given by his rat-sisters. At that same time there was on Kauai a very wonderful dog, Puapualenalena (Pupua, the Yellow). That dog was very intelligent and very swift.

One day it ran into the deep forest and saw a small boy who was successfully shooting rats. The dog joined him. The dog caught ten rats while Pikoi shot ten.

Some days later the two friends went into a wilderness. In that day's contest the dog caught forty and the boy shot forty. Again and again they tried, but the boy could not win from the dog, nor could the dog beat the boy.

After a while they became noted throughout Kauai. The story of the skill of Pikoi was related on Oahu and repeated even on Hawaii. His name was widely known, although few had seen him.

One day his father Alala told Pikoi that he wanted to see his daughter in Manoa Valley. They launched their canoe and sailed across the channel, leaving the marvelous dog behind.

Midway in the channel Pikoi cried out: "Look! There is a great squid!" It was the squid Kakahee, who was a god. Pikoi took his bow and fitted an arrow to it, for he saw the huge creature hiding in a pit deep in the coral. The squid rose up from its cave and followed the boat, stretching out its long arms and trying to seize them. The boy shot the monster, using the bow and arrow belonging to the ocean. The enemy died in a very little while. This was near the cape of Kaena. The name of the land at that place is Kakahee. These monsters of the ocean were called kupuas. It was believed that they were evil gods, always hoping to inflict some injury on man.

Pikoi and his father landed and went up to Manoa Valley. There they met Ka-ui-o-Manoa and wept from great joy as they embraced each other. A feast was prepared, and all rested for a time.

Pikoi wandered away down the valley and out toward the lands overlooking the harbor of Kou (Honolulu). On the plain called Kula-o-ka-hua he saw a chiefess with some of her people. This plain was the comparatively level ground below Makiki Valley. Apparently it was ɔvered at that time with a small shrub, or dwarflike ɹee, called aweoweo. Rats were hiding under the shelter of the thick leaves and branches.

Pikoi went to the place where the people were gathered. The chiefess was Kahamaluihi, the wife of the king, Kakuhihewa. With her was her famous arrow-shooting chiefess, Ke-pana-kahu, who was shooting against Mainele, the noted rat-shooting chief of her husband. The queen had been betting with Mainele and had lost because he was a better shot that day than her friend. She was standing inside kapu lines under a shaded place, but Pikoi went in and stood by her. She was angry for a moment, and asked why he was there. He made a pleasant answer about wishing to see the sport.

She asked if he could shoot. He replied that he had been taught a little of the art. She offered him the use of a bow and arrow, and at that he said, "This arrow and this bow are not good for this kind of shooting."

She laughed at him. "You are only a boy; what can you know about rat hunting?"

He was a little nettled, and broke the bow and arrow, saying, "These things are of no use whatever."

The chiefess was really angry and cried out, "What do you mean by breaking my things, you deceitful child?"

Meanwhile Pikoi's father had missed him and had learned from his daughter that the high chiefess was having a rat-shooting contest. He took Pikoi's bow and arrows wrapped in kapa and went down with the bundle on his back.

Pikoi took a bow and arrow from the bundle and persuaded the high chiefess to make a new wager with Mainele. The queen, in kindly mood, placed treasure against treasure.

Mainele prepared to shoot first, agreeing with Pikoi to make fifteen the number of shots for the first trial.

Pikoi pointed out rat after rat among the shrubs until Mainele had killed fourteen. Then the boy cried: "There is only one shot more. Shoot that rat whose whiskers are by a leaf of that aweoweo tree. The body is concealed, but I can see the whiskers. Shoot that rat, O Mainele!"

Mainele looked the shrubs all over carefully, but could not see the least sign of a rat. The people went near and thrust arrows among the leaves, but could see nothing.

Then Mainele said: "There is no rat in that place. I have looked where you said. You are a lying child when you say that you see the whiskers of a rat."

Pikoi insisted that the rat was there. Mainele was vexed, and said: "Behold all the treasure I have won from the chiefess and the treasure which we are now betting. You shall have it all if you shoot and strike the whiskers of any rat in that small tree. If you do not strike a rat I will simply claim the present bet."

Then Pikoi took out of the bundle held by his father a bow and an arrow. He carefully strung his bow and fixed the arrow, pointing the eye of that arrow toward the place pointed out before.

The queen said, "That is a splendid bow." Her caretaker, however, was watching the beautiful eyes of the boy and his general appearance.

Pikoi was softly chanting to himself. This was his incantation or prayer to his sister-gods:

There he is, there he is, O Pikoi!
Alala is the father,
Koukou is the mother.
The divine sisters were born.
O Bent bow of Heaven!
O Bent bow of Earth!
O Bent bow of the Mountain!
O Bent bow of the Ocean!
O Bent bow of the Night!
O Bent bow of the Day!
O Wonderful Ones!
O Silent Ones!
Silent.
There is that rat—

That rat in the leaves of the aweoweo,
By the fruit of the aweoweo,
By the trunk of the aweoweo,
Large eyes have you, O Mainele;
But you did not see that rat.
If you had shot, O Mainele,
You would have hit the whiskers of that rat —
You would have had two rats — two.
Another comes — three rats — three!

Then Mainele said: "You are a lying child. I, Mainele, am a skillful shooter. I have struck my rat in the mouth or the foot or any part of the body, but no one has ever pierced the whiskers. You are trying to deceive."

Pikoi raised his bow, felt his arrow, and said to his father, "What arrow is this?"

His father replied, "That is the arrow Mahu, which eats the flower of the lehua tree."

Pikoi said: "This will not do. Hand me another." Then his father gave him Laukona (The Arrow which Strikes the Strong Leaf); but the boy said: "This arrow has killed only sixty rats and its eye is smooth. Give me one more."

His father handed him Huhui (The Bunched-together), an arrow having three or four sharp notches in the point.

Pikoi took it, saying, "This arrow wins the treasure," and went toward the tree, secretly repeating his chant.

Then he let the arrow go twisting and whirling around, striking and entangling the whiskers of three rats.

Mainele saw this wonderful shooting, and delivered all the treasures he had wagered. But Pikoi said he had not really won until he had killed fourteen more rats. He shot again a very long arrow among the thick leaves of the shrubs, and the arrow was full of rats strung on it from end to end, hanging on it by forties.

The people stood with open mouths in silent astonishment, and then broke out in wildest enthusiasm.

While they were excited, the boy and his father secretly went away to their home in Manoa Valley and remained there with Ka-ui-o-Manoa a long time, not visiting Waikiki or the noted places of the island of Oahu

Kakuhihewa, the king, heard about this strange contest and tried to find the wonderful boy. But he had entirely disappeared. The caretaker of the high chiefess was the only one who had carefully observed his eyes and his general appearance, but she had no knowledge of his home or how he had disappeared.

She suggested that all the men of Oahu be called, district by district, to bring offerings to the king. Two months were allowed each district, lest there should be a surplus of gifts and the people impoverished and reduced to a state of famine.

Five years passed. In the sixth year the valley of Manoa was called upon to bring its gifts.

Pikoi had grown into manhood and had changed very much in his general appearance. His hair was very long, falling far down his body. He asked his sister to cut his hair, and persuaded her to take her husband's sharktooth knives. She refused at first, saying, "These knives are kapu because they belong to the chief." At last she took the teeth—one above, or outside of the hair, and one inside—and tried to cut the hair. But it was so thick and stout that the handles broke and she gave up, saying, "Your hair is the hair of a god." However, that night while he slept his rat-sister-gods came and gnawed off his hair, some eating one place and some another. It was not even. From this the ancient saying arose: "Look at his hair. It was cut by rats."

Pawaa, the chief, came home and found his wife greatly troubled. She told him all that she had done, and he said: "Broken were the handles, not the teeth of the shark. If the teeth had broken, that would have been bad."

Pikoi's face had been discolored by the sister-gods, so that when he appeared with ragged hair no one knew him—not even his father and sister. He put on some beautiful garlands of lehua flowers and went with the Manoa people to Waikiki to appear before the king.

The people were feasting, surfriding, and enjoying all kinds of sports before they should be called to make obeisance to their king.

Pikoi wandered down to the beach at Ulu-kou, where the queen and her retinue were surfriding. While he stood near the water, the queen came in on a great wave which brought her before him. He asked for her papa (surfboard), but she said it was kapu to any one but herself. Any other taking that surfboard would be killed by the servants.

Then the chiefess, who was with the queen when Pikoi shot the rats of Makiki, came to the shore. The queen said, "Here is a surfboard you can use." The chiefess gave him her board and did not know him. He went out into the sea at Waikiki where the people were sporting. The surf was good only in one place, and that was kapu to the queen. Pikoi allowed a wave to carry him across to the high combers upon which she was riding. She waited for him, because she was pleased with his great beauty, although he had tried to disguise himself.

She asked him for one of his beautiful leis of lehua flowers, but he said he must refuse because she was kapu. "No! No!" she replied. "Nothing is kapu for me to receive. It will be kapu after I have worn it." He gave her the garland of flowers. That part of the surf is named Kalehua-wike (The Loosened Lehua).

Then he asked her to launch her board on the first wave and let him come in on the second. She did not go, but caught the second wave as he swept by. He saw her, and tried to cut across from his wave to the next. She followed him, and very skillfully caught that wave and swept to the beach with him.

A great cry came from the people. "That boy has broken the kapu!" "There is death for the boy!"

The king, Kakuhihewa, heard the shout and looked toward the sea. He saw the kapu queen and that boy on the same surf wave.

He called to his officers: "Go quickly and seize that

young chief who has broken the kapu of the queen. F.
shall not live."

The officers ran to him, seized him, tossed him around,
tore off his malo, struck him with clubs, and began to kill
him.

Pikoi cried: 'Stop! Wait until I have had word with the
king."

They led him to the place where the king waited. Some
of the people insulted him, and threw dirt and stones
upon him as he passed.

The king was in a kindly mood and listened to his ex-
planation instead of ordering him to be killed at once.

While he was speaking before the king, the queen and
the other women came. One of them looked carefully at
him and recognized some peculiar marks on his side. She
exclaimed, "There is the wonderful child who won the
victory from Mainele. He is the skillful rat shooter."

The king said to the woman, "You see that this is a
fine-looking young man, and you are trying to save him."

The woman was vexed, and insisted that this was truly
the rat shooter.

Then the king said: "Perhaps we should try him against
Mainele. They may shoot here in this house." This was
the house called the Hale-noa (Free for All the Family).
The king gave the rules of the contest. "You may each
shoot like the arrows on your hands (the ten fingers) and
five more — fifteen in all."

Pikoi was afraid of this contest. Mainele had his own
weapons, whereas Pikoi had nothing. But he looked
around and saw his father, Alala, who now knew him.
The father had the kapa bundle of bows and arrows. The
woman recognized him and called, "Behold the man who
has the bow and arrow for this boy!"

Pikoi told Mainele to shoot at some rats under the
doorway. He pointed them out one after the other until
twelve had been killed.

Pikoi said: "There is one more. His body cannot be
seen, but his whiskers are by the edge of the stone step."

Mainele denied that any rat was there, and refused to shoot.

The king commanded Pikoi not to shoot at any rat under the door, but to kill real rats, as Mainele had done.

Pikoi took his bow, bent it, and drew it out until it stretched from one side of the house to the other. The arrow was very long. He called to his opponent to point out rats.

Mainele could not point out any. Nor could the king see one around the house.

Pikoi shot an arrow at the doorstep and killed a rat which had been hiding underneath.

Then Pikoi shot a bent-over, old-man rat in one corner; then pointed to the ridgepole and chanted his usual chant, ending this time:

Straight the arrow strikes,
Hitting the mouth of the rat.
From the eye of the arrow to the end
Four hundred — Four hundred!

The king said: "Shoot your 'four hundred — four hundred.' Mainele shall pick them up, but if the eye of your arrow fails to find rats, you die."

Pikoi shot his arrow, which glanced along the ridgepole under the thatch, striking rat after rat until the arrow was full from end to end — hundreds and hundreds.

The high chief Pawaa knew his brother-in-law, embraced him, and wailed over his trouble. Then, grasping his war club, he stepped out of the house to find the men who had struck Pikoi and torn off his malo. He struck them one after the other on the back of the neck, killing twenty men. The king asked his friend why he had done this. Pawaa replied, "Because they evilly handled my brother-in-law — the only brother of my wife, 'The Beauty of Manoa.'"

The king said, "That is right."

The people who insulted Pikoi and thrown dirt upon him began to run away and try to hide. They fled in different directions.

Pikoi caught his bow and fixed an arrow and aga.
chanted to his rat-sister-gods, ending with an incanta·
tion against those who were in flight:
"*Strike! Behold there are the rats—the men!*
    The small man,
    The large man,
    The tall man,
    The short man,
    The panting coward.
Fly, arrow! and strike!
    Return at last!"
The arrow pierced one of the fleeing men, leaped aside
to strike another, passed from side to side around those
who had pitied him, striking only those who had been at
fault, searching out men as if it had eyes, at last returning to its place in the kapa bundle. The arrow was given
the name Ka-pua-akamai-loa (The Very Wise Arrow).
Very many were punished by this wise arrow.

Wondering and confused was the great assemblage of
chiefs, and they said to each other, "We have no warrior
who can stand before this very skillful young man."

The king gave Pikoi an honorable place among his
chiefs, making him his personal great rat hunter. The
queen adopted him as her own child.

No one had heard Pikoi's name during all these wonderful experiences. When he chanted his prayer in which
he gave his name, he had sung so softly that no one could
hear what he was saying. Therefore the people called
him Ka-pana-kahu-ahi (The Fire Building Shooter), because his arrow was like fire in its destruction.

Pikoi returned to Manoa Valley with Pawaa and his
father and sister. There he dwelt for some time in a
great grass house, the gift of the king.

Kakuhihewa planned to give him his daughter in marriage, but opportunity for new experiences in Hawaii
came to Pikoi, and he went to that island, where he became a noted bird shooter as well as a rat hunter, and
had his final contest with Mainele.

Mainele was very much ashamed when the king commanded him to gather up not only the dead bodies of all the people who were slain by that very wise arrow, but the bodies of the rats also. He was compelled to make the ground clean from the blood of the dead. He ran away and hid himself in a village with people of the low class until an opportunity came to go to the island of Hawaii to attempt a new record for himself with his bow and arrow.

V. A Longer Tale

The Bride from the Underworld

KU, one of the most widely known gods of the Pacific Ocean, was thought by the Hawaiians to have dwelt as a mortal for some time on the western side of the island of Hawaii. Here he chose a chiefess by the name of Hina as his wife, and to them were born two children. When he withdrew from his residence among men, he left a son on the uplands of the district of North Kona and a daughter on the seashore of the same district. The son, Hiku-i-kana-hele (Hiku of the Forest), lived with his mother. The daughter, Kewalu, dwelt under the care of guardian chiefs and priests by a temple, the ruined walls of which are standing even to the present day. Here she was carefully protected and perfected in all arts pertaining to the very high chiefs.

Hiku-of-the-Forest was not accustomed to go to the sea. His life was developed among the forests along the western slopes of the great mountains of Hawaii. Here he learned the wisdom of his mother and of the chiefs and priests under whose care he was placed. To him were given many of the supernatural powers of his father. His mother guarded him from the knowledge that he had a sister and kept him from going to the temple by the side of which she had her home.

Hiku was proficient in all the feats of manly strength and skill upon which chiefs of the highest rank prided themselves. None of the chiefs of the inland districts could compare with him in symmetry of form, beauty of countenance, and skill in manly sports.

The young chief noted the sounds of the forest and the rushing winds along the sides of the mountains. Sometimes, like storm voices, he heard from far off the beat of the surf along the coral reef. One day he heard a noise like the flapping of the wings of many birds. He looked toward the mountain, but no multitude of his

...athered friends could be found. Again the same sound awakened his curiosity. He now learned that it came from the distant seashore far below his home on the mountainside.

Hiku-of-the-Forest called his mother and together they listened as again the strange sound from the beach rose along the mountain gulches and was echoed among the cliffs.

"E Hiku," said the mother, "that is the clapping of the hands of a large number of men and women. The people who live by the sea are very much pleased and are expressing their great delight in some wonderful deed of a great chief."

Day after day the rejoicing of the people was heard by the young chief. At last he sent a trusty retainer to learn the cause of the tumult. The messenger reported that he had found certain kapu surf waters of the Kona beach and had seen a very high chiefess who alone played with her surfboard on the incoming waves. Her beauty surpassed that of any other among all the people, and her skill in riding the surf was wonderful, exceeding that of anyone whom the people had ever seen. Therefore the multitude gathered from near and far to watch the marvelous deeds of the beautiful woman. Their pleasure was so great that when they clapped their hands the sound was like the voices of many thunderstorms.

The young chief said he must go down and see this beautiful maiden. The mother knew that this chiefess of such great beauty must be Kewalu, the sister of Hiku. She feared that trouble would come to Kewalu if her more powerful brother shoud find her and take her in marriage, as was the custom among the people. The omens which had been watched concerning the children in their infancy had predicted many serious troubles. But the young man could not be restrained. He was determined to see the wonderful woman.

He sent his people to gather the nuts of the kukui, or

candlenut tree, crush out the oil, and prepare it f[c]
anointing his body. He had never used a surfboard, bu[t]
he commanded his servants to prepare the best one that
could be made. Down to the seashore Hiku went with his
retainers, down to the kapu place of the beautiful
Kewalu.

He anointed his body with the kukui oil until it glistened like the polished leaves of trees; then, taking his
surfboard, he went boldly to the kapu surf waters of
his sister. The people stood in amazed silence, expecting
to see speedy punishment meted out to the daring stranger. But the gods of the sea favored Hiku. Hiku had
never been to the seaside and had never learned the
arts of those who were skillful in the waters. Nevertheless, as he entered the water he carried the surfboard
more royally than any chief the people had ever known.
The sunlight shone in splendor upon his polished body
when he stood on the board and rode to the shore on the
crests of the highest surf waves, performing wonderful
feats by his magic power. The joy of the multitude was
unbounded, and a mighty storm of noise was made by
the clapping of their hands.

Kewalu and her maidens had left the beach before the
coming of Hiku and were resting in their grass houses
in a grove of coconut trees near the heiau. When the
great noise made by the people aroused her, she sent one
of her friends to learn the cause of such rejoicing. When
she learned that an exceedingly handsome chief of the
highest rank was sporting among her kapu waters she
determined to see him.

So, calling her maidens, she went down to the seashore and first saw Hiku on the highest crest of the
rolling surf. She decided at once that she had never seen
a man so comely, and Hiku, surfriding to the shore, felt
that he had never dreamed of such grace and beauty as
marked the maiden who was coming to welcome him.

When Kewalu came near, she took the wreath of
rare and fragrant flowers which she wore and coming

lose to him threw it around his shoulders as a token to all the people that she had taken him to be her husband.

Then the joy of the people surpassed all the pleasure of all the days before, for they looked upon the two most beautiful beings they had ever seen and believed that these two would make glad each others' lives.

Thus Hiku married his sister, Kewalu, according to the custom of that time, because she was the only one of all the people equal to him in rank and beauty, and he alone was fitted to stand in her presence.

For a long time they lived together, sometimes sporting among the highest white crests of storm-tossed surf waves, sometimes enjoying the guessing and gambling games in which the Hawaiians of all times have been very expert, sometimes chanting meles and genealogies and telling marvelous stories of sea and forest, and sometimes feasting and resting under the trees surrounding their grass houses.

Hiku at last grew weary of the life by the sea. He wanted the forest on the mountain and the cold, stimulating air of the uplands. But he did not wish to take his sister-wife with him. Perhaps the omens of their childhood had revealed danger to Kewalu if she left her home by the sea. Whenever he tried to steal away from her she would rush to him and cling to him, persuading him to wait for new sports and joys.

One night Hiku rose up very quietly and passed out into the darkness. As he began to climb toward the uplands the leaves of the trees rustled loudly in welcome. The night birds circled around him and hastened him on his way, but Kewalu was awakened. She called for Hiku. Again and again she called, but Hiku had gone. She heard his footsteps as his eager tread shook the ground. She heard the branches breaking as he forced his way through the forests. Then she hastened after him and her plaintive cry was louder and clearer than the voices of the night birds.

E Hiku, return! E Hiku, return!
O my love, wait for Kewalu!
Hiku goes up to the hills;
Very hard is this hill, O Hiku!
O Hiku, my beloved!

But Hiku by his magic power sent thick fogs and mists around her. She was blinded and chilled, but she heard the crashing of the branches and ferns as Hiku forced his way through them, and she pressed on, still calling:

E Hiku, beloved, return to Kewalu.

Then the young chief threw the long flexible vines of the ieie down into the path. They twined around her feet and made her stumble as she tried to follow him. The rain was falling all around her, and the way was very rough and hard. She slipped and fell again and again.

The ancient chant connected with the legend says:

Hiku is climbing up the hill.
Branches and vines are in the way.
And Kewalu is begging him to stop.
Raindrops are walking on the leaves.
The flowers are beaten to the ground.
Hopeless the quest, but Kewalu is calling:
"E Hiku, beloved! Let us go back together."

Her tears, mingled with the rain, streamed down her cheeks. The storm wet and destroyed the kapa mantle which she had thrown around her as she hurried from her home after Hiku. In rags she tried to force her way through the tangled undergrowth of the uplands, but as she crept forward step by step she stumbled and fell again into the cold, wet mass of ferns and grasses. Then the vines crept up around her legs and her arms and held her, but she tore them loose and forced her way upward, still calling. She was bleeding where the rough limbs of the trees had torn her delicate flesh. She was so bruised and sore from the blows of the bending branches that she could scarcely creep along.

At last she could no longer hear the retreating footsteps of Hiku. Then, chilled and desolate and deserted, she gave up in despair and crept back to the village. There she crawled into the grass house where she had been so happy with her brother Hiku, intending to put an end to her life.

The ieie vines held her arms and legs, but she partially disentangled herself and wound them around her head and neck. Soon the tendrils grew tight and slowly but surely choked the beautiful chiefess to death. This was the first suicide in the records of Hawaiian mythology.

As the body gradually became lifeless the spirit crept upward to the lua-uhane, the door by which it passed out of the body into the spirit world. This "spirit door" is the little hole in the corner of the eye. Out of it the spirit is thought to creep slowly as the body becomes cold in death. The spirit left the cold body a prisoner to the tangled vines, and slowly and sadly journeyed to Milu, the underworld home of the ghosts of the departed.

The lust of the forest had taken possession of Hiku. He felt the freedom of the swift birds who had been his companions in many an excursion into the heavily shaded depths of the forest jungles. He plunged with abandon into the whirl and rush of the storm winds which he had called to his aid to check Kewalu. He was drunken with the atmosphere which he had breathed throughout his childhood and young manhood. When he thought of Kewalu he was sure that he had driven her back to her home by the temple, where he could find her when once more he should seek the seashore.

He had only purposed to stay a while on the uplands, and then return to his sister-wife.

His father, the god Ku, had been watching him and had also seen the suicide of the beautiful Kewalu. He saw the spirit pass down to the kingdom of Milu, the home of the ghosts. Then he called Hiku and told him how heedless and thoughtless he had been in his treatment of Kewalu, and how in despair she had taken her life, the spirit going to the underworld.

Hiku, the child of the forest, was overcome with grief.

He was ready to do anything to atone for the suffering he had caused Kewalu, and repair the injury.

Ku told him that only by the most daring effort could he hope to regain his beloved bride. He could go to the underworld, meet the ghosts, and bring his sister back; but this could only be done at very great risk to himself, for if the ghosts discovered and captured him they would punish him with severest torments and destroy all hope of returning to the upperworld.

Hiku was determined to search the land of Milu and find his bride and bring her back to his Kona home by the sea. Ku agreed to aid him with the mighty power which he had as a god. Nevertheless, it was absolutely necessary that Hiku should descend alone and by his own wit and skill secure the ghost of Kewalu.

Hiku prepared a coconut shell full of oil made from decayed kukui nuts. This was very vile and foul-smelling. Then he made a long stout rope of ieie vines.

Ku knew where the door to the underworld was, through which human beings could go down. This was a hole near the seashore in the valley of Waipio on the eastern coast of the island.

Ku and Hiku went to Waipio, descended the precipitous walls of the valley, and found the door to the pit of Milu. Milu was the ruler of the underworld.

Hiku rubbed his body all over with the rancid kukui oil and then gave the ieie vine into the keeping of his father to hold fast while he made his descent into the world of the spirits of the dead. Slowly Ku let the vine down until at last Hiku stood in the strange land of Milu.

No one noticed his coming and so for a little while he watched the ghosts, studying his best method of finding Kewalu. Some of the ghosts were sleeping; some were gambling and playing the same games they had loved so well while living in the upperworld; others were feasting and visiting around the poi bowl as they had formerly been accustomed to do.

Hiku knew that the strong odor of the rotten oil would

263

be his best protection, for none of the spirits would want to touch him and so would not discover that he was flesh and blood. Therefore he rubbed his body once more thoroughly with oil and disfigured himself with dirt. As he passed from place to place searching for Kewalu, the ghosts said, "What a bad-smelling spirit!" So they turned away from him as if he was one of the most unworthy ghosts dwelling in Milu.

In the realm of Milu he saw the people in the game of rolling coconut shells to hit a post. Kulioe, one of the spirits, had been playing the kilu and had lost all his property to the daughter of Milu and one of her friends. He saw Hiku and said, "If you are a skillful man perhaps you should play with these two girls." Hiku said: "I have nothing. I have only come this day and I am alone." Kulioe bet his bones against some of the property he had lost. The first girl threw her cup at the kilu post. Hiku chanted:

> Are you known by Papa and Wakea,
> O eyelashes or rays of the sun?
> Mine is the cup of kilu.

Her cup did not touch the kilu post before Hiku. She threw again, but did not touch, while Hiku chanted the same words. They took a new cup, but failed.

Hiku commenced swinging the cup and threw. It glided and twisted around on the floor and struck the post. This counted five and won the first bet. Then he threw the cup numbered twenty, won all the property and gave it back to Kulioe.

At last he found Kewalu, but she was by the side of the high chief, Milu, who had seen the beautiful princess as she came into the underworld. More glorious was Kewalu than any other of all those of noble blood who had ever descended to Milu. The ghosts had welcomed the spirit of the princess with great rejoicing, and the king had called her at once to the highest place in his court.

She had not been long with the chiefs of Milu before

they asked her to sing or chant her mele. The mele was the family song by which any chief made known his rank, and the family with which he was connected, whenever he visited chiefs far away from his own home.

Hiku heard the chant and mingled with the multitude of ghosts gathered around the place where the high chiefs were welcoming the spirit of Kewalu.

While Hiku and Kewalu had been living together, one of their pleasures was composing and learning to intone a chant which no other among either mortals or spirits should know besides themselves.

While Kewalu was singing she introduced her part of this chant. Suddenly from among the throng of ghosts arose the sound of a clear voice chanting the response which was known by no other person but Hiku.

Kewalu was overcome by the thought that perhaps Hiku was dead and was now among the ghosts, but did not dare to incur the hatred of King Milu by making himself known; or perhaps Hiku had endured many dangers of the lower world by coming even in human form to find her and therefore must remain concealed.

The people around the king, seeing her grief, were not surprised when she threw a mantle around herself and left them to go away alone into the shadows.

She wandered from place to place among the groups of ghosts, looking for Hiku. Sometimes she softly chanted her part of the mele. At last she was again answered and was sure that Hiku was near, but the only one very close was a foul-smelling, dirt-covered ghost from whom she was turning away in despair.

Hiku in a low tone warned her to be very careful and not recognize him, but assured her that he had come in person to rescue her and take her back to her old home, where her body was then lying. He told her to wander around and yet to follow him until they came to the ieie vine which he had left hanging from the hole which opened to the upperworld.

When Hiku came to the place where the vine was

nanging, he took hold to see if Ku, his father, was still carefully guarding the other end to pull him up when the right signal should be given. Having made himself sure of the aid of the god, he tied the end of the vine into a strong loop and seated himself in it. Then he began to swing back and forth, back and forth, sometimes rising high and sometimes checking himself and resting with his feet on the ground.

Kewalu came near and begged to be allowed to swing, but Hiku would only consent on the condition that she would sit in his lap.

The ghosts thought that this would be an excellent arrangement and shouted their approval of the new sport. Then Hiku took the spirit of Kewalu in his strong arms and began to swing slowly back and forth, then more and more rapidly, higher and higher until the people marvelled at the wonderful skill. Meanwhile he gave the signal to Ku to pull them up. Almost imperceptibly the swing receded from the spirit world.

All this time Hiku had been gently and lovingly rubbing the spirit of Kewalu and softly uttering charm after charm so that while they were swaying in the air she was growing smaller and smaller. Even the chiefs of Milu had been attracted to this unusual sport, and had drawn near to watch the wonderful skill of the strange, foul-smelling ghost.

Suddenly it dawned upon some of the beholders that the vine was being drawn up to the upperworld. Then the cry arose: "He is stealing the woman!" "He is stealing the woman!"

The underworld was in a great uproar of noise. Some of the ghosts were leaping as high as they could, others were calling for Hiku to return, and others were uttering charms to cause his downfall.

No one could leap high enough to touch Hiku, and the power of all the charms was defeated by the god Ku, who rapidly drew the vine upward.

Hiku succeeded in charming the ghost of Kewalu into

the coconut shell which he still carried. Then stopping the opening tight with his fingers so that the spirit could not escape, he brought Kewalu back to the land of the mortals.

With the aid of Ku the steep precipices surrounding Waipio Valley were quickly scaled and the journey made to the temple by the kapu surf waters of Kona. Here the body of Kewalu had been lying in state. Here the auwe, or mourning chant, of the retinue of the dead princess could be heard from afar.

Hiku passed through the throngs of mourners, carefully guarding his precious coconut until he came to the feet, cold and stiff in death. Kneeling down, he placed the small hole in the end of the shell against the tender spot in the bottom of one of the cold feet.

The spirits of the dead must find their way back little by little through the body from the feet to the eyes, from which they must depart when they bid farewell to the world. To try to send the spirit back into the body by placing it in the lua-uhane, or "door of the soul," would be to have it where it had to depart from the body rather than enter it.

Hiku removed his finger from the hole in the coconut and uttered the incantations which would allure the ghost into the body. Little by little the soul of Kewalu came back, and the body grew warm from the feet upward, until at last the eyes opened and the soul looked out upon the blessed life restored to it by the skill and bravery of Hiku.

No more troubles arose to darken the lives of the children of Ku. Whether in the forest or by the sea, they made the days pleasant for each other, until at the appointed time together they entered the shades of Milu as chief and chiefess who could not be separated. It is said that the generations of their children gave many rulers to the Hawaiians, and that the present royal family, the "House of Kalakaua," is the last of the descendants.

MASS MARKET TITLES FROM
MUTUAL PUBLISHING

JACK LONDON

Stories of Hawaii by Jack London
Thirteen yarns drawn from the famous author's love affair with Hawai'i Nei.
$7.95   ISBN 0-935180-08-7

The Mutiny of the Elsinore by Jack London
Based on a voyage around Cape Horn in a windjammer from New York to Seattle in
1913, this romance between the lone passenger and the captain's daughter reveals London at his most fertile and fluent best. The lovers are forced to outrace a rioting band of
seagoing gangsters in the South Pacific.
$5.95   ISBN 0-935180-40-0

South Sea Tales by Jack London
Fiction from the violent days of the early century, set among the atolls of French Oceania
and the high islands of Samoa, Fiji, Pitcairn, and "the terrible Solomons."
$7.95   ISBN 0-935180-14-1

HAWAI'I

Ancient History of the Hawaiian People by Abraham Fornander
A reprint of this classic of precontact history tracing Hawaii's saga from legendary times
to the arrival of Captain Cook, including an account of his demise. Originally published
as volume II in An Account of the Polynesian Race: Its Origins and Migration, this historical work is an excellent reference for students and general readers alike. Written over a
hundred years ago, it still represents one of the few compendiums of precontact history
available in a single source.
$8.95   ISBN 1-56647-147-8

Hawaii: Fiftieth Star by A. Grove Day
Told for the junior reader, this brief history of America's fiftieth state should also beguile
the concerned adult. "Interesting, enlightening, and timely reading for high school American and World History groups."
$4.95   ISBN 0-935180-44-3

A Hawaiian Reader
Thirty-seven selections from the literature of the past hundred years, including such writers as Mark Twain, Robert Louis Stevenson and James Jones.
$6.95   ISBN 0-935180-07-9

Hawaii and Its People by A. Grove Day
An informal, one-volume narrative of the exotic and fascinating history of the peopling

of the archipelago. The periods range from the first arrivals of Polynesian canoe voy⋅
to attainment of American statehood. A "headline history" brings the story from 196(
1990.
$4.95   ISBN 0-935180-50-8

A Hawaiian Reader, Vol. II
A companion volume to A Hawaiian Reader. Twenty-four selections from the exotic liter-
ary heritage of the Islands.
$6.95   ISBN 1-56647-207-5

Kona by Marjorie Sinclair
The best woman novelist of post-war Hawai'i dramatizes the conflict between a daughter
of Old Hawai'i and her straitlaced Yankee husband.
$6.95   ISBN 0-935180-20-6

The Wild Wind, a novel by Marjorie Sinclair
On the Hana Coast of Maui, Lucia Gray, great-granddaughter of a New England mis-
sionary, seeks solitude but embarks on an interracial marriage with an Hawaiian cowboy.
Then she faces some of the mysteries of the Polynesia of old.
$6.95   ISBN 0-935180-30-3

Remember Pearl Harbor! by Blake Clark
An up-to-date edition of the first full-length account of the effect of the December 7,
1941 "blitz" that precipitated America's entrance into World War II and is still remembered vividly by military and civilian survivors of the airborne Japanese holocaust.
$4.95   ISBN 0-935180-49-4

Russian Flag Over Hawaii: The Mission of Jeffery Tolamy, a novel by Darwin Teilhet
A vigorous adventure novel in which a young American struggles to unshackle the grip
held by Russian filibusters on the Kingdom of Kauai. Kamehameha the Great and many
other historical figures play their roles in a colorful love story.
$5.95   ISBN 0-935180-28-1

Rape in Paradise by Theon Wright
The sensational "Massie Case" of the 1930's shattered the tranquil image that mainland
U.S.A. had of Hawaii. One woman shouted "Rape!" and the island erupted with such
turmoil that for 20 years it was deemed unprepared for statehood. A fascinating case
study of race relations and military-civilian relations.
$5.95   ISBN 0-935180-88-5

Mark Twain in Hawaii: Roughing It in the Sandwich Islands
The noted humorist's account of his 1866 trip to Hawai'i at a time when the Islands were
more for the native than the tourists. The writings first appeared in their present form in
Twain's important book, Roughing It. Includes an introductory essay from Mad About
Islands by A. Grove Day.
$4.95   ISBN 0-935180-93-1

The Trembling of a Leaf by W. Somerset Maugham
Stories of Hawai'i and the South Seas, including Red, the author's most successful story,

Rain, his most notorious one.
.95   ISBN 0-935180-21-4

Hawaii and Points South by A. Grove Day
Foreword by James A. Michener
A collection of the best of A. Grove Day's many shorter writings over a span of 40 years.
The author has appended personal headnotes, revealing his reasons for choosing each
particular subject.
$4.95   ISBN 0-935180-01-X

Pearl, a novel by Stirling Silliphant
In a world on the brink of war, the Hawaiian island of Oahu was still the perfect paradise.
And in this lush and tranquil Pacific haven everyone clung to the illusion that their spec-
tacular island could never be touched by the death and destruction of Hirohito's military
machine.
$5.95   ISBN 0-935180-91-5

Horror in Paradise: Grim and Uncanny Tales from Hawaii and the South Seas
edited by A. Grove Day and Bacil F. Kirtley
Thirty-four writers narrate "true" episodes of sorcery and the supernatural, as well as gory
events on sea and atoll.
$6.95   ISBN 0-935180-23-0

HAWAIIAN SOVEREIGNTY

Kalakaua: Renaissance King by Helena G. Allen
The third in a trilogy that also features Queen Liliuokalani and Sanford Ballard Dole, this
book brings King Kalakaua, Hawai'i's most controversial king, to the fore as a true renaissance man. The complex facts of Kalakaua's life and personality are presented clearly and
accurately along with his contributions to Hawaiian history.
$6.95   ISBN 1-56647-059-5

Nahi'ena'ena: Sacred Daughter of Hawai'i by Marjorie Sinclair
A unique biography of Kamehameha's sacred daughter who in legend was descended
from the gods. The growing feelings and actions of Hawaiians for their national identity
now place this story of Nahi'ena'ena in a wider perspective of the Hawaiian quest for
sovereignty.
$4.95   ISBN 1-56647-080-3

**Around the World With a King by William N. Armstrong, Introduction by Glen
Grant**
An account of King Kalakaua's circling of the globe. From Singapore to Cairo, Vienna to
the Spanish frontier, follow Kalakaua as he becomes the first monarch to travel around
the world.
$5.95   ISBN 1-56647-017-X

Hawaii's Story by Hawaii's Queen by Lydia Liliuokalani

The Hawaiian kingdom's last monarch wrote her biography in 1897, the year before the annexation of the Hawaiian Islands by the United States. Her story covers six decades of island history told from the viewpoint of a major historical figure.
$7.95   ISBN 0-935180-85-0

The Betrayal of Liliuokalani: Last Queen of Hawaii 1838-1917 by Helena G. Allen
A woman caught in the turbulent maelstrom of cultures in conflict. Treating Liliuokalani's life with authority, accuracy and details, Betrayal also is tremendously informative concerning the entire period of missionary activity and foreign encroachment in the Islands.
$7.95   ISBN 0-935180-89-3

HAWAIIAN LEGENDS

Myths and Legends of Hawaii by Dr. W.D. Westervelt
A broadly inclusive, one-volume collection of folklore by a leading authority. Completely edited and reset format for today's readers of the great prehistoric tales of Maui, Hina, Pele and her fiery family, and a dozen other heroic beings, human or ghostly.
$6.95   ISBN 0-935180-43-5

The Legends and Myths of Hawaii by David Kalakaua
Political and historical traditions and stories of the pre-Cook period capture the romance of old Polynesia. A rich collection of Hawaiian lore originally presented in 1888 by Hawai'i's "merrie monarch."
$7.95   ISBN 0-935180-86-9

Teller of Hawaiian Tales by Eric Knudsen
Son of a pioneer family of Kauai, the author spent most of his life on the Garden Island as a rancher, hunter of wild cattle, lawyer, and legislator. Here are 60 campfire yarns of gods and goddesses, ghosts and heroes, cowboy adventures and legendary feats among the valleys and peaks of the island.
$6.95   ISBN 0-935180-33-8

SOUTH SEAS

Best South Sea Stories
Fifteen writers capture all the romance and exotic adventure of the legendary South Pacific, including James A. Michener, James Norman Hall, W. Somerset Maugham, and Herman Melville.
$6.95   ISBN 0-935180-12-5

The Blue of Capricorn by Eugene Burdick
Stories and sketches from Polynesia, Micronesia, and Melanesia by the co-author of The Ugly American and The Ninth Wave. Burdick's last book explores an ocean world rich in paradox and drama, a modern world of polyglot islanders and primitive savages.
$5.95   ISBN 0-935180-36-2

In Search of Paradise by Paul L. Briand, Jr.
A joint biography of Charles Nordhoff and James Norman Hall, the celebrated collaborators of Mutiny on the "Bounty" and a dozen other classics of South Pacific literature. This book, going back to the time when both men flew combat missions on the Western Front in World War I, reveals that the lives of Nordhoff and Hall were almost as fascinating as their fiction.
$5.95   ISBN 0-935180-48-6

The Fatal Impact: Captain Cook in the South Pacific by Alan Moorehead
A superb narrative by an outstanding historian of the exploration of the world's greatest ocean—adventure, courage, endurance, and high purpose with unintended but inevitable results for the original inhabitants of the islands.
$4.95   ISBN 0-935180-77-X

The Forgotten One by James Norman Hall
Six "true tales of the South Seas," some of the best stories by the co-author of Mutiny on the "Bounty." Most of these selections portray "forgotten ones"—men who sought refuge on out-of-the-world islands of the Pacific.
$5.95   ISBN 0-935180-45-1

Home from the Sea: Robert Louis Stevenson in Samoa, by Richard Bermann
Impressions of the final years of R.L.S. in his mansion, Vailima, in Western Samoa, still writing books, caring for family and friends, and advising Polynesian chieftains in the local civil wars.
$5.95   ISBN 0-935180-29-X

A Dream of Islands: Voyages of Self-Discovery in the South Seas by A. Gavan Daws
The South Seas... the islands of Tahiti, Hawai'i, Samoa, the Marquesas... the most seductive places on earth, where physically beautiful brown-skinned men and women move through a living dream of great erotic power. A Dream of Islands tells the stories of five famous Westerners who found their fate in the islands: John Williams, Herman Melville, Walter Murray Gibson, Robert Louis Stevenson, Paul Gauguin.
$4.95

How to Order
For book rate (4-6 weeks; in Hawaii, 1-2 weeks) send check or money order with an additional $3.00 for the first book and $1.00 for each additional book. For first class (1-2 weeks) add $4.00 for the first book, $3.00 for each additional book.

Mutual Publishing
1215 Center Street, Suite 210
Honolulu, HI 96816
Tel (808) 732-1709 Fax (808) 734-4094
Email: mutual@mutualpublishing.com
www.mutualpublishing.com